FASCINATION

FASCINATION

TRANCE, ENCHANTMENT & AMERICAN MODERNITY

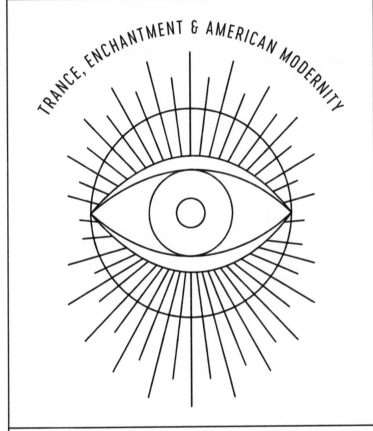

PATRICK KINDIG

LOUISIANA STATE UNIVERSITY PRESS ‖ BATON ROUGE

Published by Louisiana State University Press
lsupress.org

DESIGNER: Michelle A. Neustrom
TYPEFACE: Whitman

COVER IMAGES: Eye illustration courtesy iStock;
velvet background image courtesy Shutterstock.

Chapter 2 first appeared, in somewhat different form, as "Amuletic Aesthetics and the
Fascination of Decadent Style," *Arizona Quarterly,* 76.3 (Fall 2020): 55–79. Published by
Johns Hopkins University Press. Copyright © 2020 Arizona Board of Regents.

The conclusion first appeared, in somewhat different form, as "Perverse Attention(s):
Djuna Barnes, John Rechy, and the Queer Modernist Aesthetics of Entrancement,"
Twentieth-Century Literature, vol. 68, no. 3 (2022): 273–94.

CATALOGING-IN-PUBLICATION DATA ARE AVAILABLE
FROM THE LIBRARY OF CONGRESS.

ISBN 978-0-8071-7851-5 (cloth: alk. paper) — ISBN 978-0-8071-7911-6 (pdf) —
ISBN 978-0-8071-7910-9 (epub)

for Derek

CONTENTS

ACKNOWLEDGMENTS

THIS BOOK BEGAN AT Indiana University (IU); it was completed at Brandeis University during the COVID-19 pandemic. Much of it was thus written under conditions of extreme stress, conditions that were in part the product of a series of national and global crises and in part the result of my own position as a precariously employed junior scholar. If I had tried to write it on my own, I likely would not have finished it. I am thus extremely grateful to the various actors—both human and nonhuman—that helped to bring this project to fruition.

There are several institutions without whose support I could not have completed this book. First and foremost, I am grateful to the IU Department of English, which provided me with both the education and the financial resources necessary to embark on this research in the first place. I am also grateful to the IU College of Arts and Sciences for a year-long fellowship, during which I wrote most of the original version of this book. Thanks, too, go to the Brandeis University Writing Program (for providing me with a last-minute teaching position when I had all but given up on the pandemic job market) and to the various conferences—including the Modern Language Association's Annual Convention, the Midwestern Modern Language Association's Annual Convention, the Society for the Study of Midwestern Literature's Annual Symposium, and the Occulture's Tuning Speculation conference—that permitted me to share material from this book with new audiences. I would like to thank the (now closed) Pourhouse Café in Bloomington, Indiana, for providing me with coffee, windows, and the physical space necessary to write much of *Fascination*.

Even more important than these institutions were the individual people who helped to bring this book into the world. I am forever indebted—both personally and intellectually—to Jennifer Fleissner, whose influence is evident in everything from the conceptual framework of this book to its style. I am also grateful to Shane Vogel, Rebekah Sheldon, and Judith Brown for pushing me to clarify the scope and implications of my argument in various ways. Thanks go to Rae Greiner and Patty Ingham for helping me overcome several administrative hurdles during my time at IU and to Kristen Renzi for pointing me toward Bloomington in the first place. And thank you to Susan Gubar for being an indefatigable cheerleader over the years, writing multiple letters of recommendation (and hosting multiple parties) on my behalf.

I am also grateful to the various people whom I primarily know through email but who have nonetheless been vital to this book's development. This includes the librarians and library staff at both IU and Brandeis, who tracked down, reserved, and scanned countless sources for me. It also includes the wonderful team at Louisiana State University Press, who facilitated this book's actual publication. Thank you to James Long for seeing something of value in my initial manuscript and for helping me to navigate the review process; thank you to the rest of the press as well. I am also deeply appreciative of the two anonymous readers assigned to *Fascination*, as their generous and insightful feedback ultimately helped to produce a better book.

Several friends played an instrumental role in this book's development. To Julie Chamberlin and Rachel McCabe: thank you for providing the motivation necessary to write that first terrible chapter—I could not ask for a better pair of writing buddies (or regular buddies). Thanks also go to Sam Tett, who revealed after several years of friendship that her research agenda was virtually identical to my own. And thank you to Stephanie Kung, whose intellectual camaraderie has shaped my thinking in important ways and who has provided me with a futon on which to sleep during more than one Chicago conference.

I am, of course, also grateful to my family for supporting my work. To Barbara Hughes-Kindig: thank you for instilling in me my love of literature. To David Kindig: thank you for my interest in science and my fascination with the way things work. To Ted Kindig: thank you for pointing me in the direction of *Nanook of the North*; this book's fourth chapter would not exist without you. And to Gabby Kindig: thank you for reminding me that I am a person first, an academic laborer second.

Last but not least, thank you to my small, sweet dogs, Wilbur and Foxy. Wilbur slept in my lap as I wrote much of this book; Foxy supervised from a safe distance. And thank you most of all to Derek Granger, whose wooing and fascinating eye captured my attention years ago in an Indiana gay bar; I hope to remain forever in your thrall.

FASCINATION

INTRODUCTION

The Fascination of Modern Life

IN AN OFT-RECOUNTED scene in *The Education of Henry Adams*, Adams describes how, during his visit to the Gallery of Machines at the Great Exposition of 1900, he decides to see "the great hall of dynamos." Upon entering the hall, he finds himself filled with a kind of religious awe by the sheer power of the machines he encounters there. Unable to wrap his mind around the "occult mechanism" by which such technology works, he is both captivated and confounded by it, enthralled and overwhelmed. "Before the end," he goes so far as to write, "one began to pray to it" (380). This experience prompts his famous meditation on the totemic power of the dynamo: the source of a "mysterious energy" that, like the power exerted over early Christians by "the Cross," defies rational explanation, the machine exerts an almost supernatural influence over those around it, compelling both attention and devotion (383). Even as Adams tries to resist this influence, he ultimately gives in. Prostrated before the sheer power of the machine, he finds himself "lying in the Gallery of Machines at the Great Exposition of 1900, his historical neck broken" (382).

What is perhaps most surprising about this episode is that Adams frames the power of the dynamo not as a force of production or destruction but as one of attraction. If, he claims, the dynamo and the cross share a "common value," "this common value could have no measure but that of their attraction on his own mind." Indeed, the dynamo and the cross are *only* comparable in terms of their supernatural powers of captivation, representing "two kingdoms of force" that have "nothing in common but attraction" (383). Even, then, as the dynamo might most readily embody for today's readers the forces of modern production—those awesome powers unleashed by the discovery of electricity—this is not what strikes Adams during his visit to the Gallery of Machines. Instead, he is intrigued by a power that exceeds the dynamo's productive capacities, one that manifests as a force of irresistible attraction. Both caught and immobilized by this force, he posits the principal power of the machine as its allure.

But what, we might ask, is the precise nature of this allure? On the one hand, it seems too forceful to be reduced to something as everyday as interest.[1] On the other, it seems messier than something like the sublime, refusing, as it does, to be tamed by the rationalizing impulses of Adams's critical judgment.[2] Nor does it seem synonymous with the appeal of glamour, a phenomenon that most often conjures up images of fame and celebrity, not industrial machinery.[3] And there seems to be something a touch too sinister in its breaking of Adams's historical neck for it to be easily described as wonder.[4] How, then, are we to characterize the dynamo's attraction? What exactly are we to call it?

Adams himself offers us some useful clues. In the first place, the allure of the dynamo is linked to a sense of limitlessness, the revelation of a universe of forces that exceed human control and understanding. Indeed, the dynamo chiefly seems significant to Adams as a "symbol of infinity," the embodiment of absolute, inhuman power: "Among the thousand symbols of ultimate energy, the dynamo was not so human as some, but it was the most expressive" (380). Like the cross, it represents the unrepresentable, functioning as a conduit for the irrational and unrationalizable forces of the "supersensual world" (381).

The limitlessness of this force, moreover, shrouds the dynamo in an aura of unknowability. After all, the dynamo's most striking sensible characteristic is its silence, the way it covers its awesome power with an unsettling sonic reserve: "Scarcely humming an audible warning to stand a hair's-breadth further for respect of power . . . it would not wake the baby lying close against its frame." This is, for Adams, a key ingredient in its attraction, for it is both the machine's limitless power and the soundlessness of this power—the way the dynamo channels "silent and infinite force"—that compels his veneration (380). Indeed, even as it attracts Adams's attention, the machine's inaudibility thwarts his attempts to fit it into conventional historical narratives about technological innovation, producing a radical break between the dynamo and such relatively recent inventions as the steam engine: "Between the dynamo in the gallery of machines and the engine-house outside, the break of continuity amounted to abysmal fracture for a historian's objects. No more relation could he discover between the steam and the electric current than between the Cross and the cathedral." This historical and conceptual illegibility leaves Adams in what he calls a "Paradise of Ignorance," his desire to comprehend the workings of the dynamo both incited and refused in a single gesture (381). The attraction exerted by the dynamo is thus intimately linked to its occult nature, the way it promises a kind of knowledge of the supersensual world and then refuses to divulge this knowledge.

In some ways, this oscillation between the promise of supersensual knowledge and the foreclosure of this promise echoes another movement that, for Adams, contributes to the dynamo's allure: the movement of the machine between modern present and premodern past. The primary object of Adams's analysis, after all, is the dynamo's historical uncanniness, the way its power of attraction is both startlingly novel and strangely familiar. Even if the discovery of radiation and electricity signifies, for Adams, the "sudden irruption of forces totally new," these forces are, as he repeatedly insists, also supremely ancient, equivalent to the mystical power exerted by the cross (382). Simultaneously new and old, modern and premodern, the attraction of the dynamo bridges the historical gap between the nineteenth-century present and the ancient past.

For Adams, then, the attraction exerted by the dynamo is fundamentally "occult, supersensual," and "irrational," an inhuman force that compels human attention with its unfathomable power (383). On the one hand, this force is a product of the machine's epistemic impenetrability, the way its seemingly infinite power both solicits curiosity and refuses rational comprehension. On the other, it springs from a certain collapse of linear, historical time, folding the nineteenth-century present into the ancient past, the forces of modern science into those of premodern mysticism. The dynamo's attraction might thus be understood as a kind of magic that has somehow emerged from the rationalizing process of modernization: a remainder of the ineffable in a largely scientized world, it is what has become of the supernatural, Adams implies, in an age in which the forces of nature have been rationalized, technologized, and otherwise productively operationalized. Paradoxically, then, the attraction of the dynamo represents an essentially modern phenomenon. The byproduct of the historical process by which mystical belief becomes scientific empiricism, it designates a kind of occult excess that only appears as such in a thoroughly modern world.

Indeed, modern technology itself seems to have a magical quality for Adams, a supernatural power to attract and enchant. To put things simply, it has the power to *fascinate*, to simultaneously draw attention to itself and overwhelm one's faculties of rational comprehension in quasi-mystical ways. Captivated by the machine's aura of occult excess, Adams finds himself intellectually incapacitated by a force that, while equivalent to that of the ancient cross, nonetheless seems to be the unique property of a piece of modern technology. Attributing an occult allure to a hypermodern machine, he suggests that the scientific and technological innovations of the modern world are themselves imbued with mysterious powers of fascination.

In this book, I will argue that this belief in the modern world's potential to fascinate was at the heart of a much broader attempt in the late nineteenth and early twentieth centuries to grapple with the dramatic changes taking place in the United States. In fact, it is my primary contention that, in response to the unprecedented cultural and scientific innovations of this period, many thinkers and writers came to understand and describe modern life the same way Adams did: as fundamentally defined by its power to fascinate. In a historical moment seemingly characterized by its propensity for perpetual, productive motion, these thinkers and writers found themselves drawn to those moments in which movement—particularly the movement of the thinking and perceiving mind—ground to an inexplicable halt. According to them, the modern world was in fact marked, on the one hand, by the proliferation of objects and cultural practices that had a natural capacity for capturing attention, and, on the other, by the development of technologies and representational techniques overtly meant to enchant and entrance. Like Adams, they found themselves simultaneously intrigued by these cultural and technological phenomena and concerned about the effects such phenomena might have on the coherence and autonomy of the conscious mind. In framing modernity as fascinating, then, they were able to express a certain ambivalence about the conditions of modern life as well as about the process of historical progress that, for better or worse, had produced these conditions. Both drawn to and unnerved by the powerful forces that modernity had unleashed upon them, these thinkers and writers turned toward the concept of fascination in order to process, describe, and offer qualified critiques of the strange new world in which they found themselves.

Theorizing Fascination

In some ways, the concept of fascination should be quite familiar to us. After all, one need not dig too deeply through the *New York Times* archives to find a think piece bemoaning the power of smartphones and social media to compel our attention.[5] In everyday speech, too, we use the language of fascination to describe objects and ideas that we find unusually interesting, anything that, in and of itself, seems to force us to attend to it. When I suggest that Adams finds the dynamo fascinating, however, I do not simply mean that he finds it exceptionally interesting; rather, I intend to invoke a particular historical and theoretical discourse surrounding perception and attention that deals with the power of attention to overwhelm the rational mind.[6]

The term *fascination*, after all, has its etymological roots in the ancient Greek verb "*baskanos* ('bedeviling,' 'bewitching,' 'defaming,' 'envious')," a term that, according to Andreas Degen, was "closely linked with, but not limited to, belief in the potentially damaging power of gazing (the Evil Eye)" ("Concepts" 373, 374). For the ancient Greeks and Romans, this term designated a kind of malicious, supernatural "*actio in distans*" (action at a distance), a "'bewitchment' via eye-contact" (Weingart 77). This understanding of the concept carried over into early Christian thought: a useful metaphor for the pernicious allure of heretical ideas, it came to signify both the actions of envious demons and the "seductive power and acceptance of that which is opposite to [doctrinal] truth," a kind of heresy that caught the mind's eye and refused to let it go (Degen, "Concepts" 380). While some medieval Christians eventually distanced themselves from the language of heresy and demoniacal magic (offering instead "physiological explanation[s]" for the deleterious effects of envy and heresy), Reformation thinkers returned the phenomenon to its classical roots, solidly framing it as a form of witchcraft (Degen, "Concepts" 381). From antiquity through the Reformation, then, the verb *to fascinate* meant to practice a kind of oculocentric black magic, to use the power of sight to enchant and bewitch.

It was also around the Reformation, however, that the term *fascination* began to signify in more secular ways, coming to describe not a bewitching action but a quality of irresistible attractiveness (Degen, "Concepts" 386). While folk belief continued to associate it with witchcraft and the evil eye, intellectuals began to use the term to designate a quasi-supernatural "power of attraction" and "increasing of attention" (387, 392). By the late eighteenth century, this was the sense in which the word was most frequently used—to describe a state of passionate interest, one in which feeling, according to Immanuel Kant, posed a "problem [for] judgment" (392). While it may have been used by classical and medieval thinkers to denote black magic, fascination came, with the advent of Western modernity, to signify compulsive interest and attention.

This is, of course, how we largely use the term today. Yet even in its relatively benign, secular, metaphorical form, fascination remains haunted by a sense of the supernatural and the sinister. Indeed, the concept's most recent theorists frame it not only as a problem for judgment—a "loss or suspension," as one critic puts it, "of critical faculties"—but as a problem for the very autonomy and coherence of the human subject (Abbas 50). Jean Baudrillard, for example, describes it as a state in which there is "no active or passive . . . no subject or object, or even interior or exterior"; it is a state in which the fundamental difference between subject and object collapses, a mode of perception that "plays on both sides of the border with no border separating the sides" (160). This scrambling of subject and object is accompanied by an unnerving sense of temporal disruption: not only does it "rob . . . us of our power to give sense"; it also dilates time, "seiz[ing]" the very experience of seeing and, in the words of Maurice Blanchot, "render[ing] it interminable" (32). Even, then, as fascination involves what Jean-Paul Sartre calls a "pure negation" of the perceiving subject, a mode of perception that undoes the very conditions from which the perceptual relationship arises, it also entails a disruption of linear temporality, a "suspension of chronological time" (Sartre 177; Bennett, *Enchantment* 5). While thinkers such as Baudrillard, Blanchot, and Sartre may not use the language of witchcraft or black magic, they certainly do not see fascination as a harmless intensification of interest; instead, they see it as a force powerful enough to undo the subject, a mode of attention that stops time and negates the self.

When I say that thinkers such as Adams viewed the modern world as fascinating, then, I do not simply mean that they saw the modern world as interesting or attractive; I also mean to evoke certain anxieties—both modern and ancient—about the power of the senses to unsettle the self. Indeed, fascination designates a very particular phenomenon, one that cannot be separated from its long supernatural history. I would like to suggest that this phenomenon is defined by four fundamental characteristics. First, it involves a fixing of attention that is either voluntary (as in the casting of the evil eye) or involuntary (as in post-Enlightenment thought). Second, it relies upon a mode of perception whose purpose and effect extend well beyond the collection of sensory impressions (for example, to cursing, seducing, or immobilizing). Third, because this mode of perception troubles the interpersonal boundaries between bodies and minds (as well as the intrapersonal boundary between body and mind), it poses a threat to the autonomy and coherence of the modern subject. And, last but not least, fascination freezes or interrupts the movement of linear, progressive time, suspending its forward flow and collapsing the present into the past.

Historicizing Fascination

If fascination entails all of these things, it makes sense that Adams should be so taken with the phenomenon. After all, late-nineteenth-century

Americans were both intrigued by and anxious about the way modern life was reconfiguring consciousness, perception, and time. Thanks to a flurry of advances in medical science, physicians and philosophers of mind were becoming increasingly convinced that the rational mind was not the sole (or even the primary) force that governed human actions; rather, many "visible actions and behaviors" were "governed by non-rational processes unavailable to consciousness" (Dames 106). Indeed, the mind suddenly seemed to be shaped by both subconscious and superhuman forces. On the one hand, phenomena such as attention and perception were coming to be explained in physiological terms, their locus shifting from the im-material mind to what Jonathan Crary calls "the thickness of the body"; on the other, both the physical and the natural world were coming to be understood as "system[s] of force," the playthings of abstract, inhuman motivators such as entropy and natural selection (Crary 13; Martin xi). These epistemic shifts were accompanied by a proliferation of philoso-phies, pseudoscientific theories, and healing practices (such as mesmer-ism, hypnotism, and mind cure) that took the powers of unconsciousness seriously, treating the wellness of the mind as a mere epiphenomenon of the body's relative wellness. Altogether, the late nineteenth century over-saw a wholesale revision of scientific and philosophical ideas about the relationship between mind, body, and physical world.

This revision, of course, took place against a backdrop of widespread and dramatic cultural transformation.[7] As Nancy Bentley points out, this moment saw the "institutions of religion, art, and the state los[e] their effective monopoly over social imaginaries and personal imaginings," fa-cilitating the emergence and proliferation of such sensational forms of entertainment as the Wild West show and the World's Fair (8). American culture rapidly came to be synonymous with the flash of mass culture, the visceral pleasures of the amusement park and the vaudeville stage. Indeed, it was arguably in this moment that American society began to function as what Guy Debord has termed a "society of the spectacle," a society in which "all of life presents itself as an immense accumulation of *spectacles*," or visually seductive phenomena that "concentrate . . . all gazing" and "immobilize" "the spectator's consciousness" (para. 1, 3, 160). Cultural life, then, practiced what the period's scientists and philosophers preached: apparently capable of capturing, holding, and manipulating attention below the level of rational thought, mass cultural attractions called into question the primacy and autonomy of the rational self.

The emergence of mass culture and its attendant spectacles, of course, are often understood to be both a cause and a symptom of what Crary terms modernity's "ongoing crisis of attentiveness" (14). According to Crary, the cultural and technological developments of the mid-nineteenth century facilitated an unprecedented dispersal and fragmentation of attention. Suddenly overwhelmed by the incessant stream of sensory stimuli that characterized modern life, people gave themselves over to "reception in a state of distraction" (Benjamin 242). This led to a cultural struggle between distraction and attention, between the alluring visual pleasures of modern life and the capitalist-industrialist imperative to "pay attention" (Crary 1). For Crary, distraction and attention represented two sides of the same coin in this historical moment: distraction embodied the bad, irrational, unproductive way of being modern, and attention embodied its good, rational, productive alternative.

This fragmentation of attention was, per the wisdom of most twentieth-century cultural critics, accompanied by an equally significant shift in epistemology. If modernization in part involved the fragmentation and dispersal of attention, it also involved what Max Weber famously describes as a process of "disenchantment," one aimed at quashing irrational belief and consolidating the power of scientific rationalism.[8] Weber's so-called disenchantment narrative revolves around two central claims: that, as Jane Bennett sums it up, "our modern, highly rationalized world, characterized by calculation, stands in stark contrast to a magical or holistic cosmos, a cosmos toward which we have a double orientation of superiority and nostalgia"; and that, "although this world opens up a domain of freedom and mastery, we pay a psychic or emotional toll for demagification [that is, disenchantment] in the form of a lack of community and a deficit of meaning" (57). To be modern, according to this narrative, is to have conquered irrational belief with rational calculation, to have traded the capacity for wonder for the power to control. Framing a belief in magic as that which

must be overcome to become modern, it posits modernity and enchantment as antitheses of one another.

Crary's account of modernity as a state of distraction and Weber's account of it as a state of disenchantment, however, only tell half the story.
For, as we will see throughout this book, many thinkers, writers, scientists, and cultural critics actually viewed modernity in opposite terms: as
characterized by its capacity to fascinate, to capture and hold attention in
quasi-supernatural ways. This view, I suggest, invites us to reconceptualize
modernity in at least two important ways. In the first place, it calls into
question Crary's widely accepted assertion that modernity is structured
by a conflict between good, productive attention and bad, unproductive
distraction, as, for the thinkers and writers taken up in this book, compulsive attention posed just as much of a cultural problem as distraction did.
Whereas distraction designated a failure of attention, fascination represented its obverse—a perverse and excessive *intensification* of attention.
Rather than remedy distraction's problematic unproductiveness, fascination replicated it: focusing attention so intently that rational thought and
action became impossible, it proved just as problematic for capitalist pro-
ductivity as distraction did.

In the second place, this view resonates with and extends a growing
body of work that emphasizes the limits of Weber's disenchantment narrative. Bennett, for example, is highly critical of disenchantment narratives, arguing that, insofar as "the contemporary world" can still support
moments of awe and wonder, it "retains the power to enchant humans"
(*Enchantment* 4). Scholars such as Alex Owens, Catherine L. Albanese, and
Molly McGarry all locate modern enchantment in the persistent phenomena of religion and the occult, arguing that the nineteenth and twentieth
centuries actually saw a proliferation of practices of enchantment rather
than their suppression.[9] Such work engages in what might be called a critical project of re-enchantment, one aimed at identifying and analyzing
structures of irrational belief that, for one reason or another, have survived
(or emerged from) the process of modernization, persisting, despite rationalism's best efforts, into the modern world.

Yet this project of re-enchantment is somewhat paradoxical, as the very act of identifying specific institutions, practices, and moments in the modern world as "enchanted" ultimately functions to reinforce the idea that modernity itself is *not* enchanted, that the broader cultural background against which these phenomena appear to be enchanted is itself essentially rational. Indeed, as Emily Ogden puts it, "if we are talking about enchantment at all, we must be talking about a modernizing gesture," for, insofar as the very idea of enchantment is the product of a modern episteme that separates legitimate forms of rational knowledge (such as science) from illegitimate ones (such as superstition and religious belief), it "can *only* be modern" (*Credulity* 10, 9). The important question when it comes to modernity's relationship with enchantment, then, is not whether the modern world is enchanted or disenchanted, as the very notion of disenchantment is, in the words of Talal Asad, "a salient feature of the modern epoch"; it is *to what extent* these two categories have historically been used to describe (and thereby define the boundaries of) modernity (13).

This is precisely the line of questioning that scholars such as Ogden, Asad, and John Lardas Modern have pursued. Arguing that we should think of modernity as neither straightforwardly enchanted nor uncomplicatedly disenchanted, they suggest that we reconceptualize it as governed by an epistemic regime—the regime of secularism—that produces and relies upon both modes of existence. Rather than critique modernity's supposed rationalism or irrationalism, they contend that modernity shores up its cultural power by strategically constructing and deploying both discourses, setting up the categories of enchanted and disenchanted as the terms according to which "modern living is required to take place, and nonmodern peoples are invited to assess their adequacy" (Asad 14). This has allowed them to construct a surprisingly rational theory of modern irrationalism. For, if the very concept of enchantment functions as a kind of disciplinary mechanism—one that, when paired with the concept of disenchantment, provides the framework through which subjects are interpellated as either modern or premodern—its effects are more rationalizing than they are irrational.

According to these scholars, then, practices of enchantment may have proliferated in the nineteenth century, but they did so to distinctly rationalizing ends. Modern, for example, argues that if science's secular agenda promoted "cognitive control . . . as natural (and therefore neutral)," so, too, did industrious Protestants "idealize" "piety . . . as a mode of immediate cognition, intentionality, and self-mastery" (*Secularism* 16). In other words, the primary goals of science and religion were essentially the same: to imagine the modern subject as autonomous and self-disciplined, to shore up the boundaries of the self. Extending this line of analysis, Ogden suggests that "the skeptic of this period sought to manage enchantment, not to suppress it": "Mesmerists"—those archetypical agents of nineteenth-century enchantment—"did not believe in magic, but they did believe in the utility of others' belief. They were not enchanted themselves, but they were eager to use the enchantment of others" (*Credulity* 5, 3). For Modern and Ogden, enchantment may figure as shorthand for the irrational underside of modernity, but even this irrational underside served a distinctly rationalizing purpose in the nineteenth century: the biopolitical regulation of the self and others. In other words, nineteenth-century discourses of enchantment emerged and were deployed as a way to rationalize the irrational, to consolidate—however unsuccessfully or incompletely—the agential powers of the modern subject.

For writers and thinkers who conceived of the modern world as fascinating, however, enchantment represented something a bit more unruly. While the early nineteenth century—the period in which Modern and Ogden are most interested—may have mobilized enchantment as a force of social control and containment, this force grew, by the late nineteenth century, more or less untamable. This is in part because late-nineteenth-century thinkers and writers became increasingly convinced that even partial forms of conscious, rational agency did not exist, that the autonomous subject was merely a fiction covering over those nonrational and inhuman processes and forces that constituted the true core of the self. For these thinkers and writers, the supernatural was not a matter of credulity or belief; it was an objective reality. Indeed, an individual could be fascinated whether they believed in the efficacy of fascination or not. Rather than consolidate or rationalize the self, fascination called into question this self's coherence and autonomy.

In many ways, this position should seem familiar to contemporary cultural critics, as it resonates with much recent work on the limits of humanist subjectivity as an interpretive category. While this work has been produced by scholars in different fields with a range of disciplinary investments, it is generally driven by a disillusionment with the Enlightenment ideals of autonomy, rationality, and unencumbered volition. Such work takes for granted that consciousness represents only one small aspect of human experience, that much of what we attribute to our own rational choices is actually shaped by "visceral forces beneath, alongside, or generally *other than* conscious knowing" (Seigworth and Gregg 1). In other words, we are not in control of our own bodies and minds; instead, we are subject to the forces of affect. This line of thinking has, of course, been elaborated most explicitly by scholars who work in the field of affect theory (such as Brian Massumi), but it has also shaped the thinking of scholars who work in adjacent fields (such as posthumanist theory and feminist new materialisms). Figures as diverse as Elizabeth Grosz, Karen Barad, Mel Y. Chen, Tavia Nyong'o, Anne Anlin Cheng, and Bennett herself have thus, in one way or another, offered up affective accounts of the self, highlighting the important role played by nonrational (and sometimes irrational) forces in our experience of the world. Like nineteenth-century theorists of fascination, these scholars have drawn attention to the self's fundamental porousness and instability, the way it is radically open to the world around it.

Yet those nineteenth-century thinkers and writers who conceived of the modern world as fascinating did not simply anticipate the ideas of affect theorists in an uncomplicated way. For, as we shall see throughout this book, whereas affect theorists and posthumanist critics tend to celebrate the freedoms afforded by affect—emphasizing the agentive possibilities opened up by a self that is unconstrained by the shackles of subjectivity— nineteenth-century theorists of fascination were much more ambivalent about the self's openness. Indeed, even as many of them were intrigued by fascination's potential to expand the boundaries of human selfhood and agency, many were also concerned about the phenomenon's potential for domination and subjugation. Many of the texts examined in this book are thus animated by a profound ambivalence, and, while I do not go so far as to argue that they posit fascination as essentially harmful or destructive, I do suggest that, in the eyes of many turn-of-the-century thinkers and writers, fascination could be deployed to both liberatory and conservative ends. In foregrounding this ambivalence and then highlighting some of its implications for contemporary critical theory, I hope to gesture toward the shortcomings and limitations of affective, posthumanist, and new materialist accounts of the self, using the history of fascination to intervene in ongoing debates about subjectivity, rationality, and agency.

Improperly Modern Subjects

This will be one of the main thrusts of my argument in *Fascination*—that, in identifying an array of modern technologies and cultural phenomena as fascinating, people such as Adams theorized the modern world and the modern self in ways that should be simultaneously familiar and unfamiliar to us. The theories they constructed, moreover, have significant implications for the way we think about consciousness and agency today. Another important thrust, however, is that these theories were not socially or politically neutral; in fact, they were just as tangled up with the radical social changes of the late nineteenth century as they were with the period's scientific, technological, and cultural changes. After all, the late nineteenth century saw the emergence of a wide range of new social figures (such as the freed slave, the New Woman, and the effete degenerate) that called into question long-standing ideas about who qualified as a legitimate social and political subject. Troubling established racial and sexual hierarchies in American society, these figures often came to be seen as avatars for the disruptive power of fascination.

This was made possible by the fact that, despite the very different social positions each of these figures occupied, they were thought to be united by a certain intellectual paucity, a shared but "differential . . . irrational[ity]" (Fretwell 184). While they may have "*aim[ed]* at 'modernity,'" their supposed inability to regulate their own bodies and minds resulted in a "failure . . . to assume . . . full humanity" (Asad 13; Modern, *Secularism* 21). Guided, according to the period's medical science and cultural common sense, by intuition, superstition, and the nonconscious compulsions of their bodies, these figures were considered more impressionable and suggestible than their white male counterparts. For many, this not only made them seem out of place in the increasingly rationalized milieu of modern society (and therefore dubious candidates for recognition as full social and political subjects); it also made them seem unusually susceptible to fascination.

Of course, white people had been treating Black and Indigenous people as irrational for centuries, depicting them as savage and excitable, too evolutionarily underdeveloped to control their thoughts or their actions. This treatment was only exacerbated in the late nineteenth century by the work of early psychologists, who purported to show that people of color were less perceptually discerning and intellectually refined than white people.[10] Whereas white people, they suggested, had naturally malleable minds—minds that could change, learn, and grow in response to new sense impressions—Black and Indigenous people were "unimpressible," or perceptually uneducable, and therefore incapable of self-improvement, "unable to move forward through time" (Schuller 13). This intellectual backwardness supposedly extended to Black and Indigenous people's faculties of attention as well, making them too weak willed to discipline their wandering eyes or roving minds.

Not all white people, however, were capable of such discipline either. For while the period's science may have maintained that Black and Indigenous people had not achieved the same level of civilization as white people, it also suggested that a growing number of white people were overshooting the mark and sinking into a state of effete, impotent over-civilization. After all, anxieties swirled in the late nineteenth century about the deleterious effects of degeneration and neurasthenia, two conditions brought on by the overstimulating conditions of modern life itself. Much psychological research on mesmeric and hypnotic trance, moreover, maintained that women, being of an unusually refined and sensitive nature, were particularly vulnerable to hypnosis, hysteria, and nervous fits, psychic states in which the rational mind was overpowered by the reflexes of the body and the suggestions of others. This made them just as out of place in the modern world and just as susceptible to fascination as Black and Indigenous subjects, albeit by virtue of their excessive modernity, their over-civilization. Figures of both under-civilization and over-civilization, then—figures that, collectively, we might call *improperly modern subjects*— were often treated in the same way: as unusually vulnerable to entrance-ment and enchantment.

As the coming chapters will show, however, such depictions proved to be a double-edged sword. For even as physicians and psychologists main-tained that women and people of color were more likely to *be* fascinated than white men, the popular discourse that sprung up around them sug-gested that they also had an unusual talent for *fascinating*. As we will see in chapter 1, white people worried throughout the nineteenth century about the fascinating powers of Black and Indigenous subjects, attribut-ing to them certain gifts of enchantment and entrancement that, with the advent of modern psychology, eventually came to be explained in quasi-scientific terms. Superhuman powers of attraction and suggestion were also ascribed to such hypermodern figures as the sensuous degenerate (taken up in chapter 2) and the popular actress (dealt with in chapter 3), who transformed their supposed susceptibility to entrancement into an uncanny talent for capturing the attention of others. Dominant psycho-logical and medical discourses may have branded socially marginalized subjects as irrational, suggestible, and improperly modern, then, but, as we shall see, these qualities imbued such figures with a certain fascination all their own.

Fascination, Aesthetics, and Narrative Form

The line of argument that improperly modern subjects capitalized upon their own susceptibility to fascination, turning themselves into agents of entrancement and enchantment, dovetails with another that I pursue in this book. This second line of argument maintains that several of the aes-thetic movements of the late nineteenth and early twentieth centuries aimed to do precisely what improperly modern subjects did: harness the power of fascination in productive ways. This is not to say, of course, that either improperly modern subjects or the period's aesthetic artifacts were fully capable of taming the forces of fascination, for, as I have already suggested, these forces were thought to be in their essence untamable. I do, however, suggest that certain nineteenth- and early-twentieth-century cultural figures—including a range of writers, filmmakers, and performers—hitched their wagons to fascination, hoping that they might be pulled along to their own cultural prominence and success. After all, just as the late nineteenth century witnessed the emergence of new technologies, new sciences, new forms of popular entertainment, and new social hierarchies, so, too, did it witness the emergence of several distinctly modern literary movements. Insofar as these movements simultaneously reflected and commented upon the fascinating cultural circumstances from which they arose, they offer us a unique window into the way Americans both attempted to understand and worked to produce modernity in the moment of its emergence. Even, then, as this book's argument will draw at various points on a wide range of philosophical, scientific, and cultural critical texts, its primary object of analysis will be literary (and filmic) texts. For it is through these texts that we might most clearly see how modern science, technology, and philosophy shaped the American cultural imaginary around the turn of the century, producing new strategies and techniques for imagining, representing, and narrating the experience of modernity.

The best-known literary movement of the late nineteenth century, of course, was realism. As Amy Kaplan has persuasively argued, realist fiction aimed to "captur[e], wrestl[e], and control . . . a process of change"—namely, the modernization of American culture—that "seem[ed] to defy representation" (10). Its project was also a secularizing one, in part aimed at taming the irrational and the supernatural by consigning them "to the status of the detail, the ephemeral," the "minor," and the "eccentric" (Reckson 67). Simultaneously "imagining and managing" the period's social and cultural upheavals (as well as the inhuman forces they unleashed), it tried to defuse the threats these upheavals posed to the coherence and autonomy of the self by fitting them into the rational structure of literary narrative (Kaplan 10). This narrative form was typically linear and teleological in nature, and it traded in the assumption that, at least most of the time, human actors behaved in rational, autonomous ways. Indeed, "*realism*," as Jennifer Fleissner puts it, might be understood "as the term for a historicizing project . . . that does not overly threaten the aesthetic, moral, or political agency of human subjects" (*Women* 38). Attempting to tame the unruly process of modernization by narrativizing it, realism posited the modern subject as both self-contained and self-directed.

If fascination, in its essence, works to undo the coherence and autonomy of this kind of subject, it should come as no surprise that realism will not be the primary focus of this book. While realist writers such as William Dean Howells and Henry James will make occasional appearances, they will largely act as foils to authors and filmmakers whom, for the sake of my argument, I find much more interesting. Indeed, the primary focus of this book will be those turn-of-the-century literary movements that actively rejected the narrativizing conventions of realism, including decadentism and regionalism (addressed in chapter 2), naturalism (taken up in chapter 3), and modernism (examined in the conclusion), as well as certain kinds of early cinema (analyzed in chapter 4). The specific texts that this book will examine, moreover, simultaneously reflect and comment upon the aesthetic practices and concerns characteristic of the movements to which they belong. Rather than embrace the rationalizing techniques of realism, these movements employed such unusual representational practices as pointlessly elaborate description, nonteleological narrative movement, and psychological and aesthetic flatness. What is more, instead of attempting to contain the disruptive forces of modernity, these movements actively worked to cultivate and amplify them, producing fascinating creative works that captivated readers and viewers just as the dynamo captivated Adams and popular theater captivated the masses. Much of this book will thus be about the way writers and early filmmakers—particularly antirealist ones—adapted and transformed popular cultural ideas about fascination in their own work, making the most of those irrational forces to which they found themselves subjected.

These literary movements, of course, do not represent an aesthetic monolith. The sensuous, cosmopolitan aesthetic of decadentism, for example, is in many ways far removed from the rustic stylings of regionalist writing or the biologistic aesthetic of naturalism; early cinema differs from all three of these movements in both medium and narrative style. What unites them, however, is their shared investment in rejecting, complicating, and reimagining the narrative forms passed down by the realist tradition. For whereas realism aimed to rationalize the experience of modern life by fitting it into cohesive, coherent, and (most importantly) linear narrative structures, these antirealist modes of writing were more interested in the way modern life could cause narrative to fragment and fail. In fact, they actively aimed to slow, stop, and suspend the movement of narrative at every turn. On the one hand, they embraced literary strategies of exhibition and display, privileging the pleasures of lyrical description over the exigencies of plot. On the other, they cultivated a kind of formal circularity, offering up strangely plotless stories that treated narrative direction as more or less unimportant. Employing narrative forms that unexpectedly stopped, stalled, and looped back on themselves, these literary movements rejected the logic of narrative progress.

This would have seemed somewhat scandalous to these movements' contemporaries, as the late nineteenth century was in many ways *the age* of progress. As Dana Luciano puts it, "The advent of modernity constructed a new vision of time as linear, ordered, progressive, and teleological. Nineteenth-century developments in historiography supported this sense of time . . . devising accounts of humanity's movement through time that stressed the rise of civilizations and the growth of knowledge (*Arranging Grief* 2). Such an approach to time, of course, explains the popularity of realism in the period, as realism's linear form expressed and reflected popular beliefs about the power of historical progress. It also, however, explains several other aspects of nineteenth-century American culture, as everything from the period's most popular medical diagnoses (including neurasthenia and degeneration) to the spatial organization of the period's great fairs (which were arranged so as to depict the United States as the pinnacle of civilization) grew out of an ideological investment in historical progress.

Writers intrigued by the aesthetic possibilities of fascination, of course, were skeptical of this ideology. After all, if fascination disrupts the forward flow of time, diverting it into loops and stalling it in moments of suspension, it makes sense that these writers should reject the idea of progress in both its historical and its literary form. For these writers, the aesthetics of fascination opened up new and unexpected formal possibilities, new ways to imagine narrative beyond the bounds of linear, teleological temporality. To understand modernity the way these writers did, then, was to conceptualize narrative, time, and history in an unorthodox way. It was not to understand modernity as a discrete historical moment, the result of a decisive cultural or historical break from the past; it was to see it as a state of temporal precarity, one indebted to (and, in many ways, partially stuck in) the enchanted world of the premodern past. It was to approach the modern condition as a historically ambivalent one, a state of constant movement between the modern and the premodern. Reframing modernity as a state of temporal and epistemological indeterminacy, these writers depicted the modern world as a place where the mystical beliefs of the past entered into uneasy alliance with the scientific truths of the present.

On Structure and Methodology

Perhaps unsurprisingly, *Fascination* itself is not entirely linear. On the one hand, this is because there is a great deal of historical overlap between its chapters: while the book's argument proceeds in roughly chronological order (beginning, as it does, with the late-nineteenth century phenomena of decadentism and regionalism and ending with the early-twentieth-century experiments of modernism), its chapters often bump up against and build upon one another. On the other hand, each individual chapter includes some thoughts on how its analysis might intervene in ongoing critical debates about the relative autonomy and coherence of the human subject. This means that, like the thinkers and writers it discusses, *Fascination* sometimes sacrifices the coherence of its historical narrative in order to more usefully illuminate our current cultural moment, employing an antirealist mode of historicism that makes the ideas of the past do work in the present. Putting forward an argument that itself sometimes stops, stalls, and loops back on itself, this book is meant to be read as a piece of historicist cultural criticism, not a work of cultural history.

It does, however, begin by offering a broad overview of the historical role played by fascination in American culture. Chapter 1, "From Mesmerism to Mind Cure: A History of American Fascination," traces the development of fascination in popular and academic discourse over the course of the nineteenth and early twentieth centuries. Beginning with a brief summary of how colonial Americans approached fascination, it explores the way fascination was theorized and practiced by proponents of mesmerism; mesmerism's more widely respected ideological successor, hypnotism; and the popular-psychological doctrines of New Thought. This culminates in an extended examination of two vitalist philosophers, William James and Henri Bergson, and the surprisingly important role played by fascination in their theories of consciousness and attention. Foregrounding the similarities between their worldview and the worldview of earlier theorists of fascination (as well as between these worldviews and those of contemporary scholars of affect), chapter 1 ultimately suggests that the metaphysical models offered by these thinkers took fascination to be a fundamental element of modern existence, a kind of foundational mode of being in the world.

Chapter 2, "Amuletic Aesthetics and the Fascination of Decadent Style," turns from philosophy to literature, exploring the role of fascination in the undertheorized genre of American decadent fiction. Taking as its primary object of study Harriet Prescott Spofford's short story "The Amber Gods" (1860), this chapter reads Spofford into two seemingly unrelated contexts: the nineteenth-century discourse of decadence, which tied a predilection for ornamental style to a host of degenerative psychological traits; and the ancient system of beliefs surrounding *fascina*, or apotropaic amulets thought to defend against the evil eye. Highlighting decadent fiction's tendency to equate, along the axis of artifice, its own hypercivilized aesthetics with those of premodern cultures, chapter 2 argues that decadent fiction worked to collapse the epistemic boundaries between the modern and the premodern, intentionally developing and deploying an enchantingly ornamental style that itself might be called amuletic. The chapter concludes with a meditation on the contaminative power of amuletic aesthetics, arguing that these aesthetics have a tendency to pop up in unexpected places, including the nineteenth-century genre of southern regionalism (exemplified by Charles Chesnutt's short story "Dave's Neckliss" [1889]) and the work of contemporary critical race theorists.

Chapter 3, "Gesture, the Actress, and Naturalist Fiction," directs its attention toward a less ornamental genre of writing, examining the relationship between fascination, gesture, and the figure of the actress in naturalist fiction. Situating two naturalist novels, Theodore Dreiser's *Sister Carrie* (1900) and Paul Laurence Dunbar's *The Sport of the Gods* (1902), in the context of turn-of-the-century writings on trance and theater, chapter 3 suggests that even as the naturalist figure of the actress seems unusually susceptible to the forces of fascination, she is also capable of harnessing them through the power of theatrical gesture. The shape taken by her gestures, I go on to argue, is racially dictated, and while white actresses are encouraged to cultivate "grace" in their movements, Black actresses must embrace the caricaturally animated aesthetics of minstrelsy. These racially distinct brands of gesture ultimately affect the differential forms taken by naturalist novels themselves, as their peripatetic structures mirror the movements of their theatrical protagonists. I conclude by suggesting that this understanding of naturalist movement might help us to clarify what is at stake in recent theoretical accounts of movement, particularly those embraced by feminist new materialist theorists.

Chapter 4, "Primitive Flatness and Early Ethnographic Cinema," examines how the development of film technology transformed popular understandings of fascination. While naturalist writers such as Dreiser and Dunbar linked fascination to embodied movement, many Americans came, in the early decades of the twentieth century, to associate fascination with surface and the screen. This association, I contend, arose from the intersection of two seemingly unrelated discourses: that of early film and that of early academic anthropology. Though cinema's relationship with surface may be more immediately legible, early anthropologists deployed representational techniques strikingly similar to those of film, treating so-called primitive bodies as objects of display and curating museum exhibits that resembled filmic tableaux. Because of this, the chapter turns to the genre of ethnographic cinema—a genre that blended the practices of filmmaking with those of anthropology—and analyzes the relationship between fascination and surface in two of its earliest products, Robert J. Flaherty's *Nanook of the North* (1922) and Edward S. Curtis's *In the Land of the Head-Hunters* (1914). Both Flaherty and Curtis, I argue, cannily map the fascination of primitive surface onto the fascination of the early cinematic screen, rendering primitive culture according to the flat aesthetics of primitive film. I then use this line of analysis to examine recent critical accounts of virtuality, suggesting that such work often overlooks the phenomenon's historical entanglement with the colonial gaze of the ethnographic camera. I conclude by arguing that ethnographic film was instrumental in redefining fascination for the twentieth century, postulating it as, in the words of Maurice Blanchot, a "passion for the image" (32).

The book's conclusion, "From Modern Fascination to Modernist Fascination," both synthesizes the conceptual work done in the previous chapters and extends this work into a new historical moment (the moment of modernism) and a new discursive context (the context of sexology). Investigating what happened to fascination when, in the early twentieth century, vitalist accounts of mind began to give way to psychosexual ones, I show that this process was uneven and incomplete; in fact, twentieth-century ideas about sexual fixation and inversion (as well as the kind of modernist writing that thematized these phenomena) remained heavily indebted to the discourse of fascination. To demonstrate this, I offer a brief reading of Djuna Barnes's *Nightwood*, arguing that both its thematic treatment of sexual inversion and its stylistic engagement with modernist aesthetics represent the culmination of fascination's turn-of-the-century history. In the end, I suggest that even if fascination may seem to have lost its critical power by the 1920s and 1930s—eclipsed, as it was, by the unconscious forces of the psychosexual mind—its influence was widespread and long-lasting, shaping American culture well into the twentieth century.

1

From Mesmerism to Mind Cure

A History of American Fascination

IN 1841, Nathaniel Hawthorne wrote a letter to his fiancée, Sophia, warning her not to consult a mesmerist for help with her debilitating headaches:

> Belovedest, my spirit is moved to talk with thee today about these magnetic miracles, and to beseech thee to take no part in them. I am unwilling that a power should be exercised on thee, of which we know neither the origin nor consequence, and the phenomena of which seem rather calculated to bewilder us, than to teach us any truths about the present or future state of being. If I possessed such a power over thee, I should not dare to exercise it; nor can I consent to its being exercised by another. Supposing that this power arises from the transfusion of one spirit into another, it seems to me that the sacredness of an individual is violated by it; there would be an intrusion into thy holy of holies—and the intruder would not be thy husband! (588)

The "magnetic miracles" of which he wrote were, of course, those miraculous medical cures effected by animal magnetism, a relatively new fad that turned fascination toward therapeutic ends. Thought to treat everything from paralysis to gout, it represented for its proponents a kind of marvelous panacea, a revolutionary practice that would change modern medicine forever. It would not have seemed terribly strange, then, for Sophia to seek out the help of a mesmerist: thought by many to be working at the cutting edge of medical science, mesmerists were often called upon to treat both mental and physical disorders.

As Hawthorne's letter suggests, however, not everyone embraced this new practice, and some viewed animal magnetism less as a novel form of healing than as a violent incursion into the self. For Hawthorne and his compatriots, mesmerism seemed to foster a dangerous irruption of occult forces into the increasingly rational milieu of nineteenth-century life. While its practitioners were adamant that it was simply a benign medical procedure, its critics viewed things differently: resurrecting old anxieties about the pernicious potential of black magic, mesmerism appeared to many to involve a kind of violation, by supernatural means, of that "holy of holies," the human soul. For every Sophia intrigued by its therapeutic potential, there was a Nathaniel anxious about the threats it posed to the integrity of the self. Even, then, as its practitioners lauded its discovery as an important advance in medical science, animal magnetism retained for many Americans "a sense of the diabolical and sinister" that, in the words of Robert C. Fuller, mesmerists were "never able to fully expunge" (38).

In some ways, the disagreement between Nathaniel and Sophia about Sophia's mesmeric treatment is emblematic of the way fascination was generally treated throughout the nineteenth century. Understood alternately as a marvelous scientific discovery and a kind of atavistic revival of black magic, it arose from and embodied those cultural tensions that drove the process of American modernization. On the one hand, practices such as mesmerism and hypnotism appeared to be supremely modern phenomena: translating recent discoveries in the physical sciences concerning electricity and magnetism into the language of medicine, they marketed themselves as the pinnacle of rationality. On the other, they remained burdened by fascination's historical associations with witchcraft and the evil eye. Straddling the line between rational science and irrational superstition, fascination functioned as a site of conceptual crossover between the modern and the premodern.

It is the historical development of this position that I examine in this chapter. Looking at a collection of texts written by nineteenth- and early-twentieth-century practitioners of fascination (such as mesmerists, hypnotists, and New Thought enthusiasts), I explore these texts' ambivalent engagements with both rationalism and mysticism, tracing the conflicted relationship they exhibit between scientific optimism and antimodern pessimism.[1] I then turn to the work of two turn-of-the-twentieth-century vitalist thinkers, William James and Henri Bergson, in order to extend this genealogy, arguing that, by folding the ideas of earlier theorists of fascination into their exceedingly modern philosophies of mind, these thinkers transposed a phenomenon often treated as pseudoscience from the cultural margins to the very center of modern life.[2] I conclude by briefly examining the legacy of this transposition, arguing that vitalist theories of fascination still play a surprisingly important role in the way we think about the mind and the body today, though they often masquerade under the name of affect theory. Ultimately, I aim to shed light on the ambivalent place fascination occupied in nineteenth- and early-twentieth-century American culture as well as the way this phenomenon continues to shape contemporary theories of the self.

Early American Fascination and the Rise of Animal Magnetism

Even before the discovery of those "magnetic miracles" about which Hawthorne was so anxious, fascination played a prominent role in the fears of early American colonists. Much of the anxiety surrounding witchcraft in colonial America, for example, centered on the supposed ability of witches to enchant others with the evil eye, to fix their gaze on unsuspecting victims and to paralyze them, perhaps even control their actions. While active belief in witchcraft began to dwindle in the eighteenth century, the fear of the evil eye that accompanied this belief did not disappear; instead, it simply shifted its locus. Rattlesnakes, widely believed to be capable of controlling "birds, small animals, and even children" with their gaze, took the place of witches in the popular imagination, refiguring fascination not as a form of magic but as a natural (albeit dangerous) phenomenon. Because such beliefs were probably borrowed from the folklore of various American Indian cultures, the fascinating power of snakes also came to be metonymically associated with the figure of the Indian as well as with nonwhite people more generally (Hutchins 678, 679). Many, for example, believed that

Indians themselves "possessed the rattlesnake's power to fascinate"; some believed that Black slaves worshipped a snake god—a supposed holdover from the religious practices of their native Africa—that endowed them with "the power and allure attributed to rattlesnakes and other serpents" (688–89, 697). For early white Americans, then, there was a certain slippage between the entrancing powers of witches and serpents and the entrancing powers of so-called primitive cultures and bodies (about which we will hear more in chapter 4), one that fed anxieties about interracial social and sexual relations. Fascination thus signified not only a threat to the integrity of the individual body but a threat to the integrity of the race, the nation, and civilization itself.

As the nineteenth century progressed and American culture began to secularize, however, fascination came to be linked to a more civilized threat: that of modern rationalism. In fact, even though fascination was most frequently taken up as a metaphor for the destructive powers of miscegenation, it was also—and nearly as frequently—employed in antimodern critiques of "religious declension and the rise of reason," used to warn against the seductions of a modern way of life governed not by religion but by science (Hutchins 700). It thus occupied a strangely ambivalent place in public discourse: representing the threat of both the not-modern-enough (in the form of primitive cultures and bodies) and the too-modern (in the form of modern rationalism), fascination slowly came to combine the threat of an intrusive, racialized past with the threat of an increasingly intrusive, secular future.

Prior to the emergence of mesmerism, then, Americans conceived of fascination in largely negative terms. A highly malleable rhetorical figure, it played a prominent role in conservative critiques of everything from miscegenation to secularization. Even when it was viewed as a natural phenomenon, it was a natural phenomenon that was to be carefully avoided, the nineteenth-century equivalent of the witch's evil eye. For early-nineteenth-century Americans, fascination represented a kind of uncanny threat to both mind and body, one that, whether associated with primitive magic or modern rationalism, was most often approached with anxiety.

This all changed when animal magnetism reached the United States in the 1830s.[3] Part metaphysical doctrine and part collection of therapeutic practices, animal magnetism was based on the belief that the human body was filled with a quasi-mystical "magnetic fluid" that could be manipulated by the will of a magnetic operator. This fluid, according to magnetists, was the vital principle that endowed the human body with life, and the diversion of this fluid to the proper parts of the body could cure or alleviate the symptoms of a variety of maladies. Sometimes, however, the curing of disease was not all that happened when a person was magnetized; occasionally, patients would be thrown into a state of somnambulism, a condition that made them insensible to the world and placed them largely under the control of their magnetizer's will. For many, this phenomenon unnervingly recalled the symptoms of the evil eye that were so feared in colonial times, and, while most animal magnetists viewed their work as a carefully theorized, empirically rooted offshoot of mainstream medical science, others could not help but speak of it in supernatural terms. Even, then, as mesmerists aimed to scientize and operationalize fascination, their work remained haunted by many of the old anxieties concerning fascination's negative effects on the will.

While people were performing mesmeric experiments in Europe as early as the 1770s—beginning, of course, with the strange group healing rituals of Franz Anton Mesmer himself—Americans did not begin to take an interest in animal magnetism until it was imported from France by a man named Charles Poyen.[4] Poyen, the son of a Guadeloupean sugar plantation owner, was studying medicine in Paris in 1832 when he was struck by "a very complicated nervous disease" that halted his studies (*Progress* 39). Upon the recommendation of a friend, he consulted a mesmerist and his somnambulist, a woman who purportedly could, in the somnambulic state, diagnose and prescribe remedies for the sick. When she successfully described Poyen's symptoms to him (without, however, offering a cure for his condition), he was immediately converted to the gospel of animal magnetism, and, after a fourteen-month-long stay at his family's plantation in the West Indies, he relocated to Massachusetts, where he began to lecture on mesmerism. Though his early lectures garnered little attention from New Englanders, this changed when he encountered Cynthia Gleason—a textile worker unusually susceptible to his magnetic influence—and he began to offer practical demonstrations of the power he could exert over her. Public curiosity aroused, Poyen and Gleason proceeded to tour New England, making animal magnetism, in Poyen's own words, "the object of a lively interest throughout the country," "the most stirring topic of conversation among all classes of society!" (*Progress* 35).[5] Poyen published a detailed account of this tour in 1837, which he titled *Progress of Animal Magnetism in New England*, before moving back to France and spending the rest of his life in Paris.[6]

While the control Poyen demonstrated over his magnetized subjects may have resembled the power historically attributed to witches and snakes, animal magnetism differed from earlier forms of fascination in several key ways. First of all, animal magnetism was meant to be therapeutic rather than life-threatening. Direct manipulation of a sick person's magnetic fluid, a magnetist cited in *Progress of Animal Magnetism* claimed, could cure "inflammation, gout, rheumatism, inflammation of the throat and eyes, hemorrhage, epilepsy, hysterics, mania, headache, toothache, all kinds nervous pain, dyspepsia, cholic, pains in the stomach, vomiting, asthma, palpitations of the heart, cough, deafness, paralysis, tic doloreux, &c." (175). Animal magnetism also played a role in diagnosing and prescribing more conventional cures for various illnesses, as some accomplished somnambulists (including both Gleason and the woman Poyen consulted about his nervous disorder) were thought to be capable of "feeling" another person's disease "as though they were themselves affected with it," using the "unusually exalted state of the sympathies" that accompanied somnambulism to pinpoint the seat of a patient's malady (145). And before ether was discovered to be a reliable anesthetic in 1846, some doctors capitalized on the insensibility to pain that accompanied magnetic sleep to pull teeth and remove tumors.[7] Rather than see it as a threat to the integrity of the self, Poyen and his followers viewed mesmerism's deadening of sensation and consciousness as a potential force of medical innovation.

Another key difference between mesmerism and earlier forms of fascination involved the differential application of the senses. While the evil eye was a purely visual phenomenon, taking control of a person's body with nothing but a charged glance, Poyen's brand of animal magnetism involved multiples senses. As Poyen outlined in one of his lectures, sight was indeed an important part of mesmeric practice, and it was vital that an operator "bring all his attention" to his patient while magnetizing. Even more important than sight, however, was touch. According to Poyen, the most efficient method for magnetizing involved sitting in front of a person and holding his or her thumbs until "the same degree of heat is established" between operator and subject, then drawing one's hands "by a sort of friction very light . . . along the arms, down to the extremities of the fingers." This was to be followed by a series of passes over the subject's head and down his or her torso, sometimes maintaining contact with the subject's body (in the case of male subjects), sometimes not (in the case of female subjects) ("M. Poyen's" 9). If these passes caused the subject to slip into a state of somnambulism, this led to a modification of the subject's own sensory experience, deadening his or her corporeal senses while endowing him or her with the power of clairvoyance, "the faculty of seeing through various parts of the body, the eyes remaining closed" (*Progress* 63). While earlier forms of fascination were clearly rooted in the visual, then, magnetic fascination involved a crossing and reorganization of the senses, allying sight with touch and expanding the sensorium to include a sixth mode of perception.

Perhaps the greatest difference between mesmerism and other modes of fascination, however, lay in the fact that Poyen adamantly believed his practice was not a practice of enchantment but a highly modern science. Because mesmerism appeared against a backdrop of rapid technological development, Poyen and his admirers often justified their belief in the existence of magnetic fluid by comparing it to other modern, invisible forces, claiming, for example, that the properties governing this fluid bore "some analogy to certain laws already known of the electric and galvanic phenomena" (*Letter* 10).[8] Much of part 1 of *Progress of Animal Magnetism* is, in fact, devoted to proving the scientific status of animal magnetism. Very clearly distinguishing mesmerism from witchcraft, which Poyen dismisses as superstition because it relies on an "a priori" "belief in the existence of the devil," he insists that the wondrous effects of mesmerism are "*a matter of fact*," that the magnetic principles he embraces do not constitute some occult "*secret practice*" but an empirically verifiable "*natural science*" (28, 23, 46). Highlighting in the preface that, "in this advanced period of historical existence," "cool reasoning" is paramount to the investigation and evaluation of seemingly inexplicable phenomena, he makes the surprising claim that those who are wary of mesmerism are simply not rational or modern enough, scared off by "the novelty of this science" (vi, 13). For Poyen, animal magnetism represented a radical departure from outmoded superstition. Though its practical effects may have resembled those of black magic, he vehemently disavowed any association between the two phenomena, glorifying the discovery of mesmerism as a step toward a modern medical future.

Despite Poyen's enthusiasm, it is not difficult to see why his experiments made many of his contemporaries uneasy. As Hawthorne's concern for his fiancée suggests, the penetration of a generally female subject's mind by that of a generally male mesmerist often raised sexualized concerns about the moral and spiritual integrity of the subject, concerns exacerbated by the 1837 republication of the fifty-year-old *Report of Doctor Benjamin Franklin and the Other Commissioners Charged by the King of France with the Examination of the Animal Magnetism, as Now Practised at Paris*, which described Mesmer and his followers as moral degenerates who would magnetize women "to the point of insensibility," then carry them off to "elaborate bedrooms" to, it was ominously suggested, "recover" (Ayer 248–49). The report's implicit allegations of sexual misconduct, in fact, haunt much of Poyen's *Progress of Animal Magnetism*, as many of the experiments it describes involve the convulsing of female bodies before primarily male audiences, and two instances are even mentioned in which Gleason was, for the sake of "experiment," magnetized by strange men without her consent.[9] Sexual impropriety, however, was not the only disconcerting element of Poyen's experiments; bodily harm also played a central role. To prove that their subjects were not feigning magnetic sleep, Poyen and his associates would prick them with pins, pull their hair, make them inhale ammonia, and fire off pistols next to their ears.[10] These violences seem like mere discomforts when compared to the bloody tooth extractions and tumor removals some doctors performed, often before rapt audiences of other medical practitioners. Poyen, then, may have claimed that animal magnetism had nothing to do with earlier methods of overpowering the will, but his experiments in fact evoked many of the same fears that attached themselves to witches, snakes, and primitive bodies. While he hoped to frame mesmerism as a novel, scientific phenomenon, he largely just physiologized phenomena conventionally associated with witchcraft, prompting people to translate their old anxieties about pernicious supernatural forces into the language of modern medicine.

If Poyen's lectures were the most significant factor in the antebellum explosion of interest in animal magnetism, perhaps the second most significant factor was the 1837 publication of Thomas C. Hartshorn's English translation of *Practical Instruction in Animal Magnetism,* an instructional text by the French mesmerist Joseph Phillipe François Deleuze. What Fuller calls a kind of "do-it-yourself manual for inducting individuals into the mesmeric state," its primary purpose was to explain the mechanics and effects of mesmerism, a task it performed so effectively that it was widely cited as, in Poyen's words, "the best [text] on this subject" (R. Fuller 29; *Progress* 20).[11] Thus while Poyen's experiments were in many ways meant to excite curiosity with their novelty, Deleuze's approach offered interested parties a more measured primer on the theory and practice of mesmerism.

In fact, even as Poyen professed to be greatly influenced by Deleuze's work (and actually incorporated parts of *Practical Instruction* into his own lectures almost verbatim), it is the differences between Poyen and Deleuze that are perhaps most interesting.[12] Nowhere are such differences more evident than in the two men's approaches to experimentation. As we have already seen, experimentation was central to the work of Poyen, largely because he wanted to demonstrate that animal magnetism could and should be treated like a modern, empirical science. Deleuze, on the other hand, explicitly and repeatedly warned against practicing mesmerism to satisfy one's "curiosity" or to "exhibit" one's powers, instructing his readers to treat the practice as a "religious act" and to regard the idle use of it as a "profanation" (35, 38). He also cautioned against allowing somnambulic patients to enter the deepest and most spectacular form of magnetic sleep, "magnetic exultation," as it weakened patients' health, and he discouraged readers from testing somnambulists' clairvoyant abilities by asking them any questions that did not pertain to the somnambulist's physical well-being (103, 100). In stark contrast to Poyen, Deleuze was guided by a desire to *curtail* curiosity about animal magnetism. Fixated solely on the curative value of the practice and declaring its other "wonderful effects" distractions, Deleuze's writing was deeply infused with a religious, moralizing tone, proscribing any actions that did not accord with his own ethical code (58).

This moralizing was linked to Deleuze's more romantic approach to the past. Whereas Poyen's *Progress of Animal Magnetism* went to great lengths to discredit supposedly unscientific beliefs about somnambulism and to prove that mesmerism was, in fact, a modern phenomenon, Deleuze was more invested in highlighting the continuities between animal magnetism and premodern entrancement. Indeed, the purpose of animal magnetism for Deleuze was to return patients to a kind of Rousseauian state of nature: "simple" folk, after all—in whom the "course of nature" had not been interrupted by the luxuries of modern life—supposedly responded much more readily to mesmerism than "those who have lived in the world" and whose "nerves are irritated" (35). This purpose, moreover, was described in strikingly premodern terms, terms drawn not from modern medicine but from the ancients: a footnoted discussion of somnambulism, for example, opens with an extended quotation from Pliny the Elder, and the movement of magnetic fluid is described in the language of "action at a distance," that favorite philosophical problem of classical and patristic thinkers (325, 29).[13] While Poyen emphasized the supposed modernity of mesmerism, Deleuze foregrounded its connections to the premodern past, linking it both to the uncivilized "simple" life and to ancient mysticism.

Even though they were both published in the same year, then, *Progress of Animal Magnetism* and the Hartshorn translation of *Practical Instruction* offered readers two different approaches to the relationship between mesmerism and modernity. Poyen embraced animal magnetism as an empirical science, performing countless demonstrations and experiments meant to arouse the curiosity of the American public. Deleuze, on the other hand, treated it as a religiously inflected healing ritual, cautioning against the profane temptation to use it (as Poyen did) to induce somnambulism and clairvoyance. Consequently, while Poyen tried to dismiss the idea that mesmeric powers could be used to abuse rather than help subjects, Deleuze explicitly warned against the moral and medical perils of magnetizing for the wrong reasons. Taken together, the work of these two men demonstrates the way popular understandings of fascination became complicated in the 1830s: no longer did the phenomenon solely represent a threat to bodily or national integrity; now it began to function as a more ambivalent phenomenon, a concept that mediated between the scientific and the occult, between modern medicine and premodern philosophy, and even, for some, between good and evil.

Animal Magnetism's Legacy

As numerous historians have pointed out, public interest in animal magnetism peaked in the 1830s and 1840s, then experienced a gradual decline throughout the middle of the century.[14] This shift is generally attributed to, on the one hand, the growing use of ether as an anesthetic (which rendered the induction of magnetic sleep during surgical procedures unnecessary) and, on the other, the replacement of animal magnetism in the public eye with spiritualism, a phenomenon that borrowed mesmerism's trance states but stripped them of their therapeutic use.[15] The publication of tracts on animal magnetism, however, did not end with Poyen and Deleuze; in fact, texts on the subject continued to appear in the United States from the 1840s through the 1880s.

Though they sometimes tweaked or embellished the theories of Poyen and Deleuze, these texts largely represented extensions of their work. *The History and Philosophy of Animal Magnetism*, for example—published by a pseudonymous "Practical Magnetizer" in 1843, the heyday of mesmerism—discussed Poyen's experiments at length, and it described the techniques of magnetism in almost the same language as both Poyen and Deleuze (though it lent more importance to eye contact than to physical touch) (6–7, 11–12). The author, moreover, followed Deleuze in linking effective animal magnetism to natural good health, encouraging those with "nervous disability, bad humours, or chronic disease" to leave the practice to those with a "strong physical constitution full of vital fluid" (13, 11). He also devoted an entire chapter to an explanation of how the premodern arts of witches, Gypsies, and snake charmers—as well as snakes themselves—made use of mesmeric techniques (25–26). With the exception of an increased attention to the power of eye contact, then, *The History and Philosophy of Animal Magnetism* largely recapitulated the ideas of Deleuze five years after they first appeared in translated form.

Nearly forty years later, these ideas still maintained their hold on a certain segment of the American public, even though the scientific community was largely beginning to treat animal magnetism as a debunked pseudoscience. In fact, while *The History and Philosophy of Animal Magnetism* offered a rather sedate summary of Deleuze's work, John B. Newman's 1880 *Fascination, or the Philosophy of Charming* elaborated some of Deleuze's more intensely unmodern ideas. Pushing Deleuze's moralizing against the abuse of mesmerism one step further, Newman claimed that, while the techniques of mesmerism had indeed been known in the ancient West and continued to be used in the heathen East, these techniques were "imparted by Satan himself, either in a direct manner, or by prompting the mind to a series of experiments that led to the discovery" (28). He also explicitly connected the mesmeric powers of humans to the fascinating powers of serpents, using this connection to justify his preference for the term *fascination* (which was typically used to describe the entrancing power of snakes) over *animal magnetism* (14). Rather than attribute snakes' power to fascinate to their glare, however, he attributed it to "a vapor which they secrete" (and which humans were also "undoubtedly" capable of secreting), further troubling the relationship between fascination and the senses by introducing smell as an important mode of entrancement (19, 20).[16] Expanding on the ideas of Poyen and Deleuze about mesmerism's relationship with nature and history, Newman made quite explicit the connection between animal magnetism and premodern forms of enchantment that, forty years earlier, had been less taken for granted.

By the late nineteenth century, then, animal magnetism had begun to shift and mutate, often retaining many of its key theoretical and practical elements while being rebranded as a new (or at least newly rediscovered) phenomenon. Homing in on mesmerism's associations with premodernity and its tendency to employ multiple senses in the induction of somnambulism, those who followed in the footsteps of Poyen and Deleuze solidified the conceptual links between animal magnetism's supremely human operations and the naturally fascinating powers of animals. Thus as American culture at large began to modernize—and, simultaneously, to grow increasingly concerned about the cultural and epistemological changes wrought by modernization—those interested in fascination turned more and more to the past and to the natural world, precariously situating the phenomenon between the discourses of modern rationalism and premodern enchantment.

This, of course, brings us to the final few decades of the nineteenth century, a moment in which fascination, reflecting the state of American culture at large, became even more unstable and multivalent than it already was. For if, as we saw in the introduction, the late nineteenth century represented a period of rapid modernization, one characterized by unprecedented scientific and technological innovation, it was also a moment in which anxieties about modern life coalesced into a kind of countercultural sentiment, an antimodernist stance of resistance that was not to be ignored.[17] These cultural shifts led to a bifurcation of the discourse surrounding fascination. For some, fascination came to be understood in purely neurological terms, conceptualized as a phenomenon that was thoroughly explicable by modern science. For others, it came to represent a purely mystical experience, the resurgence in the modern world of ancient forces of enchantment. By the turn of the century, then, mesmerism had given birth to two new schools of thought concerning the nature of fascination: that of the hypnotists (who embraced the empirical methods of scientific investigation) and that of the New Thought enthusiasts (who approached fascination as a tool of mental magic). Taken up in different ways by both modern science and antimodern mysticism, fascination became one of the key terms through which the cultural conflicts of the late nineteenth century were worked out.

Hypnotism

Because of its dubious scientific grounding, animal magnetism was largely a popular rather than an academic phenomenon, and it remained that way until, in the 1880s, respected doctors across the West began to take notice of the very real (and very strange) behaviors mesmerists were capable of eliciting from their patients. In France, Jean-Martin Charcot (about whom we will hear more in chapter 3) began to induce somnambulism in his hysterical patients as early as 1878, and soon the French medical community was interested enough in the phenomenon for a lively scholarly debate to emerge concerning its precise nature and causes.[18] Charcot and his fellow investigators did not, however, speak in the language of animal magnetism; instead, they spoke of hypnotism, a purportedly more scientific phenomenon, one that had nothing to do with serpentine vapors or magnetic fluids.[19] This French work on hypnotism slowly made its way to the United States—thanks largely to the intellectual-ambassadorial work of Pierre Janet—and, by the end of the nineteenth century, it had usurped the cultural position occupied by animal magnetism.[20]

Although it did not gain much traction until the 1880s, the word *hypnotism* first appeared at the peak of the American mesmerism craze, coined in 1843 by the Scottish physician James Braid. In *Neurypnology, or the Rationale of Nervous Sleep Considered in Relation to Animal Magnetism or Mesmerism* . . ., Braid went to great lengths to "entirely separate . . . Hypnotism from Animal Magnetism," maintaining that hypnotism was no "universal remedy" for disease (as someone like Poyen believed animal magnetism to be) but, rather, "a peculiar condition of the nervous system . . . into which it can be thrown by artificial contrivance," a condition that just so happened to be useful in the cure of certain nervous disorders (86, 94). Hypnotism involved no manual passes over the body; it simply required the "fixed and abstracted attention of the mental and visual eye, on one object, not of an exciting nature," which could practically be achieved by having a patient stare at a bright object eight to fifteen inches in front of his or her face (94, 109). According to Braid, then, the primary difference between animal magnetism and hypnotism involved a consolidation of the senses. No longer did the induction of somnambulism require a multimodal assault on the body's sensorium, one that involved sight, smell, touch, and even an extrasensory engagement of the will; now the process was entirely visual.

As Braid's ideas were taken up later in the century (first in France, then in the United States), the distinction between the sensorial messiness of animal magnetism and the clean visuality of hypnotism solidified. This distinction resulted in a revision of practitioners' understanding of the agential relationship between hypnotizer and hypnotized. George Miller Beard, who, though best known for his work on neurasthenia, was also one of the few prominent American physicians to embrace the practice of hypnotism, firmly believed that, while trance could be triggered by things like shock and wonder, it was largely a phenomenon that originated in the entranced subject's own nervous system. Thus, while the effects that mesmerists were capable of producing were very real, they did not result from the manipulation of some vital force; instead, they resulted from the subject's "expectation" that he or she would be mesmerized, an unconscious "will to lose [one's] will" (Beard, *Scientific* 8, 7).[21] Subjects particularly adept at surrendering their wills in this way tended to be "mentally unbalanced through excessive and disproportionate endowment of imagination and emotion" and to have "ill-trained minds"; the most "typical subject" for mesmeric trance, according to Beard, was "the average shop-girl" because she was "delicate in body," "feeble in mind," and "half-matured" (23, 24). In Beard's writing, gone was the association between somnambulism and the natural world; now trance was aligned with the most modern of figures: the urban shopgirl. As supposedly more modern ideas about hypnotism and suggestion began to replace those put forward by animal magnetists, the locus of fascination shifted, moving from the eyes and hands of the mesmerist to the mind of the trance subject herself. No longer was trance a state to be induced by an expert magnetist; now the potential for entrancement was endemic to the human mind.

Beard did not merely write about trance states, though; he also offered, in the tradition of Poyen, hypnotic demonstrations, which were often met with mixed reactions from his audiences. Like Poyen, he would assemble a handful of medical practitioners and journalists, then perform experi-

ments on a number of trusted subjects, throwing them into fits of artificial catalepsy and alternately heightening and deadening their senses.[22]
He also employed the familiar tricks of pricking his subjects with pins
and making them inhale ammonia.[23] Beard's experiments differed from
Poyen's, however, in that they were largely performed on men rather than
women, and, taking Charcot's association of hypnotism with hysteria for
granted, he tended to choose subjects with "a trace of the neurotic disposition" ("Mesmeric Experiments" 8). Thus while Beard seemed simply to
mimic the work of animal magnetists in his demonstrations, he distinguished himself from Poyen in the way he framed them. On the one hand,
he eliminated the overt threat of sexual impropriety that haunted Poyen
and his followers by using male instead of female subjects; on the other,
he viewed the very state of hypnotic sleep as a disease, approaching those
susceptible to it as innately inclined toward neural pathology.[24]

Because of this alignment of hypnotism with mental illness, it retained
for its critics many of the dangers associated with mesmerism, often translating what was once seen as a moral threat into the language of psychic
pathology. While it is true that hypnotic demonstrations were a staple for
a while at fashionable parties, hypnotism did not enjoy quite the national
attention that mesmerism did, largely because the practice's critics were
more vocal and explicit about its dangers.[25] One critic of Beard, for example,
railed against his engagement with what he termed "a depraved state of the
brain and nervous system," claiming that only "hysterical girls, effeminate
youths, and credulous adults"—"certainly not the best of their race"—were
capable of being hypnotized; he also suggested that repeated subjection to
hypnosis resulted in "mental enfeeblement," "nervous degeneration," and
"disease" (J. Browne 379). This critic was not alone in viewing hypnosis
as pathological; in fact, the American medical community actually considered drafting legislation aimed at limiting the practice of hypnotism.[26]
And, of course, no matter how clearly its practitioners tried to distinguish
hypnotism from animal magnetism, many of the old anxieties about sexual impropriety lingered: writing in the *North American Review* in 1888,
Georges Gilles de la Tourette explicitly claimed that "the crime that may
fairly be charged upon hypnotism is rape . . . committed by the hypnotizer

upon the hypnotized," offhandedly remarking that "the detection of rapes committed upon lethargic subjects is comparatively frequent" (141, 140). Pointing to both the medical and the moral dangers of being hypnotized, many critics condemned Beard's experiments with induced trance, maligning Beard as a kind of scientific pervert and his patients as degenerates.

Thus even as antebellum ideas about animal magnetism were modified and academized in the 1880s and 1890s under the aegis of hypnotism, many remained skeptical about the legitimacy of this rediscovered science. While hypnotism differed in significant ways from its popular precursor, it remained dogged by the same old concerns about the mental, physical, and moral integrity of those on whom it was practiced. Perhaps the most significant effect of the transformation of mesmerism into hypnotism, then, was its acceptance by the American medical community—however ambivalent—as a valid subject of investigation. Even if its merits remained a topic of debate, the clinical study of fascination was now, for better or worse, ensconced in the academy, and respected psychologists and philosophers of mind had to reckon with the implications thereof.

New Thought

Before turning our attention to two philosophers of mind who tried to reckon with the implications of fascination's newfound legitimacy, however, we must make a brief detour through animal magnetism's other intellectual progeny, which, instead of taking up the scientific elements of earlier writings on mesmerism, embraced animal magnetism's more mystical side: New Thought. Based largely on the teachings of Phineas Parkhurst Quimby, a clockmaker–turned–mesmerist–turned–spiritual guru, the New Thought movement was built around the idea (borrowed from animal magnetism) that all disease could be overcome by an effort of the will, by simply changing one's erroneous views of the relationship between mind, body, and spirit. And even though Quimby repeatedly referred to this doctrine as a "science" in his writings, his followers tended not to be medical professionals but pseudoscientific and religious enthusiasts. While hypnotists adopted Poyen's earlier claims that the induction of trance was an empirical, highly modern enterprise, then, proponents of New Thought aligned themselves more with Deleuze's antimodernism, positioning their practice of willing oneself well as a cure not only for modern ailments like neurasthenia but for the affliction that was modern medicine itself. Consequently, while hypnotism may have hefted more institutional weight, New Thought drew to itself a sizable number of nonacademic followers dissatisfied with modernity, followers who remained loyal to the movement well into the twentieth century. If hypnotism represented mesmerism's most scientific offspring in the late nineteenth century, New Thought represented the most significant unscientific alternative.

The genealogical connection between New Thought and mesmerism is almost easier to trace than that between hypnotism and mesmerism, as many of Quimby's teachings were explicitly based on mesmeric ideas. In fact, it was a demonstration by Poyen himself that introduced Quimby to animal magnetism in 1838, and Quimby spent much of the 1840s working as a practicing mesmerist.[27] This work slowly gave rise to the collection of beliefs and practices that Quimby would come to call his science, a system of mental healing that, like Beard's hypnotism, borrowed liberally from mesmeric dogma, taking up and reframing the ideas of animal magnetists so that they fit into Quimby's Christian worldview. The idea that the body emits some sort of undetectable vapor, for example—an idea that harked back to mesmeric ideas about magnetic fluid and looked forward to Newman's claims about serpentine fascination—came to play a significant role in Quimby's writings, which asserted that people "throw from [themselves] an atmosphere or vapor" in which "all their ideas, right or wrong" (and even their "identity"), are contained (P. Quimby 247, 72).[28] Other extrasensory phenomena, such as telepathy and clairvoyance, were put to use as diagnostic tools by Quimby, who would enter trance states in order to divine what psychic traumas were at the root of his patients' medical complaints; this worked to decenter the element of visuality so important to hypnotism, expanding rather than consolidating the sensory experience of treatment.[29] Quimby's science thus appropriated and modified the basic tenets of animal magnetism, rebranding them as novel parts of his own mystical worldview.

While Quimby's science resembled animal magnetism in many technical ways, perhaps its most significant similarity to mesmerism— particularly the Deleuzean kind—was its fraught relationship with modernity. Quimby unreservedly rejected, for example, modern medical authority, claiming that most diseases were actually the result of "impressions produced by medical men," implanted rather than resolved by the work of conventional doctors (70). He even suggested that he could only "with the greatest difficulty keep [his] temper" around doctors, and his writings on mental healing repeatedly turned and returned to the Bible rather than modern medical science for their justification (231).[30] Quimby thus employed very few of the therapeutic techniques his more credentialed peers did in his healing sessions, combining elements of clairvoyance and telepathy with what we would now call the "talking cure" to produce a practice that, in the words of Fuller, "actually resembled those of a shaman" more than those of a psychologist or physician (123). Turning away from medical science and toward Christian mysticism, Quimby offered up his strange hybrid doctrine of the mind as an antidote both to modern diseases such as nervousness and to modern medicine itself.

As Quimby's ideas were taken up by others in the late nineteenth and early twentieth centuries, they slowly began to coalesce into a theory of mind and body that resembled that of the early hypnotists, albeit with more magical overtones. This theory recentered eyesight in the experience of entrancement, but it retained its decidedly mystical elements. William Walker Atkinson, one of the foremost advocates of New Thought around the turn of the century, in fact published an entire book in 1907—*Mental Fascination*—that was devoted to consolidating "Animal Magnetism, Psychological Influence, Hypnotism, Mesmerism, Charming, etc. etc." under the umbrella term *mental fascination* (8). According to Atkinson, all of these things (as well as the fascinating powers of snakes and "even the . . . attraction" "atoms manifest . . . for each other") were accomplished through the exertion of "Desire-Force" and "Will-Power," powers most effectively exerted through the "Magnetic Gaze" or the "Fascination of the Eye": "the eye is one of the most effective mediums for the passage of Mentative Currents from one person to another," largely because, according to "advanced occultists," the brain lights up during "strong emotional effort, or exercise of will," and the eyes emit "great beams of . . . incandescent energy" (12, 49, 224, 223). Atkinson's explanation of sight's role in fascination, then, inverted the hypnotic model: while hypnotists relied on the eye to passively receive and transmit entrancing sensations to the brain, Atkinson conceived of the eye as a projective organ, drawing more on colonial ideas about the evil eye (and on classical and medieval understandings of the eye as a kind of lantern) than on modern physiology.[31] While the eye played a privileged role in both the scientific experiments of hypnotists and the "mental magic" of Atkinson, hypnotism focused on the eye of the hypnotic subject (who passively absorbed sensations and threw herself into a trance), and New Thought focused on the eye of the fascinator, who, through Will-Power, overwhelmed the mind of his subject.

As this brief overview of Atkinson's work makes clear, the discourse surrounding fascination underwent a decisive split in the late nineteenth century. Whereas hypnotists approached it as a rational phenomenon explicable by rational means, Atkinson and his followers embraced its mystical potential, its usefulness as an occult technique of self-improvement. This ideological difference was emblematic of a more general cultural tension in the period, one that pitted scientific rationalism against antimodern mysticism. Caught between these two poles, fascination developed into a heuristic by which the relative merits of modern life were hashed out. Central to the thought of scientists and mystics alike, it played an important role in debates about what it meant to be modern.

Fascination and Vitalist Thought

The terms of this debate shifted radically when fascination was taken up at the turn of the century by vitalist philosophers of mind. While the phenomenon had designated for many nineteenth-century thinkers a kind of exceptional psychic state, one that could only be produced under particular circumstances and by particular techniques, it represented for vitalist thinkers something much more ubiquitous. More or less explicitly appropriating the language of animal magnetism (which posited magnetic fluid

as the "vital principle" that animated all bodies), well-respected philosophers of mind such as William James and Henri Bergson in fact came to locate fascination and its associated phenomena at the center of their metaphysical worldviews. Intrigued, like so many other turn-of-the-century
thinkers, by those "non-rational processes unavailable to consciousness"
that seemed to shape human behavior, they embraced the idea that the
mind was not as free as it appeared to be, that it was in fact directed and
constrained by forces beyond its control (Dames 106). Taking up those elements of fascination that had for so long seemed intensely problematic—
its inhibition of rational thought and its incapacitation of the will—they
reframed them as essential parts of normal psychic experience. Drawn to
the occult mechanism of the unconscious mind, both James and Bergson
came to understand fascination as an inescapable fact of psychic life, a
primordial way of relating to the world.

For many, of course, there seem to be two different William Jameses:
the mystical James and the analytical James.[32] It was the mystical James
who devoted two whole lectures in *The Varieties of Religious Experience* to
the topic of mysticism, and it was the mystical James who himself exper-
imented with drug-induced trance states.[33] This James was the one who
briefly presided over the Society for Psychical Research, and it was he who
believed in and investigated telepathy and mediumistic trance.[34] It was
also arguably the mystical James who was so taken with the idea of hypnotism that he met with Pierre Janet at the Salpêtrière in the late 1880s and
published a number of articles on the phenomenon in the *Proceedings of
the American Society for Psychical Research*.[35] The connections between this
James and the history of fascination seem almost too obvious to be worth
noting: drawn, as he was, to the parapsychological phenomena of trance
and mediumship, the mystical James was clearly invested in fascinated
experience.

But it was not just the mystical James whose work borrowed from
nineteenth-century theories of animal magnetism; the analytical James,
too, engaged with mesmeric ideas. His philosophy of pragmatism, after
all, privileged practical results over questions of origin, and he evaluated
ideas not against some objective standard of truth but according to their

"cash value."[36] This led him to offer an unusually positive evaluation of the "mind-cure movement" in *The Varieties of Religious Experience:* "The blind have been made to see, the halt to walk; lifelong invalids have had their health restored. The moral fruits have been no less remarkable" (94, 95). And even if his pragmatist leanings led him to care more about the results of mesmerism or mental magic than about the mechanism by which they actually worked, he was inclined to believe in the existence of a "spiritual force" that, while not identical to magnetic fluid, recalled the "vital principle" embraced by people like Deleuze (*Principles* 295).[37] The ideas of mesmerists and mind-curists echoed throughout both his mystical and his analytical work, influencing his understanding of both irrational experience and the rational mind.

This influence is perhaps nowhere more evident than in his massive *Principles of Psychology,* a text in which James is both at his most analytical and at his most invested in fascinated states of compulsive attention. In the chapters titled "Attention" and "The Will," he follows in the footsteps of the mesmerists and the hypnotists and suggests that the relationship between these two faculties is of an intimate, essential nature: "volition," in fact, "is nothing but attention"; "attention with effort is all that any case of volition implies. *The essential achievement of the will, in short, when it is most 'voluntary,' is to ATTEND to a difficult object and hold it fast before the mind*" (*Principles* 815, 291). For James, all of the intellectual and corporeal movements conventionally associated with acts of the will are secondary phenomena, simply the result of involuntary mental association and unconscious physiological processes. It is the exertion of attention on a particular object or idea that is "*the essential phenomenon of the will*" (816). Conversely, states of "distraction," in which "the attention is dispersed so that the whole body is felt, as it were, at once, and the foreground of consciousness is filled, if by anything, by a sort of solemn sense of surrender to the empty passing of time," are figured by James as thoroughly passive, states in which the will fails to be exercised. Such are the states into which "subjects of the hypnotic trance seem to lapse" (261). James thus associates focused attention with a strong, functioning will, and he links inattention to passivity, trance, and volitional incapacitation.

This binary, however, is more complicated than it might at first seem, for there are, James goes on to explain, actually two kinds of attention: derived attention, which can be either voluntary or involuntary; and immediate attention, which is always involuntary. The kind of voluntary attention James associates with the strong will "*is always derived*" (269). It is this kind of attention that actively selects and holds ideas before the mind's eye, employing the will and exerting effort. This kind of effort, however, can never be sustained "*for more than a few seconds at a time*," and the vast majority of our time is spent attending to things involuntarily (272). Involuntary attention can be of two types: involuntary derived attention or involuntary immediate attention. In involuntary derived attention, the mind passively watches as a series of ideas or sensations parades past it, swept along by a process of automatic association. Such associative chains, however, must always begin in moments of involuntary immediate attention, moments in which "we don't bestow" our attention on an object; rather, "the object draws it from us." In moments such as these, "the object," simply by virtue of being interesting, "has the initiative, not the mind"; it overpowers us, forcing us to attend to it whether we want to or not (292). This kind of attention, James notes, is "sensorial" in nature; it precedes apperception and intellection (270). Volition, then, is merely a secondary phenomenon for him: if the will constitutes the voluntary fixing of attention on an object or idea, it only arises from and is subtended by an involuntary fixing of attention, a passive state of sensory stimulation in which the will is overwhelmed by whatever seems most interesting at the moment.

Such a state, of course, might be called one of perpetual fascination—involving, as it does, purely passive, involuntary attention—and it seems striking that this state not only appears in James's work on mysticism but also lies at the heart of his more scientific work on perception. Influenced by the theories of nineteenth-century mesmerists and hypnotists, he constellates sense perception and fixed attention with the incapacitated will in a way that would also be very familiar to twentieth- and twenty-first-century theorists of fascination. Once considered the unique purview of occultists and pseudoscientists, fascination comes, in James, to designate our most primordial mode of being in the world, a perceptual relationship in which our wills are at the mercy of whatever sensory stimulus happens to catch our eye.

This primordial state of fascination receives an even more detailed treatment in the work of James's close friend and professional comrade Henri Bergson, whose "philosophy of *pure experience*" (James's words) elaborates on the metaphysical implications of James's psychology (*Correspondence* 10:203).[38] Even, however, as Bergson's writing elaborates on James's model of fascinated attention, it also reframes it in a significant way. For if James merely views fascination as inescapable, a kind of perceptual mode into which the mind often and inevitably slips, Bergson goes so far as to suggest that it might actually be a desirable state of (un)consciousness, one that we should strive to inhabit. Constructing perhaps the most positive theory of fascination to emerge from the turn of the century, he suggests that the reimmersion of the mind in states of pure experience (such as those produced by fascination) might actually be a project worth pursuing. In some ways, then, his work represents the culmination of that mystical line of thought most clearly developed by the mesmerists and the mind-curists: arguing that unconscious life might offer us something that the restrictive world of everyday rational consciousness cannot, he comes almost to valorize the psychic capacity to be fascinated.

According to Bergson, there are two possible approaches to the world, one spatial and one temporal. When we take the spatial approach, we overlay everything with a "mental diagram of infinite divisibility," "mark[ing] out divisions in the continuity of the extended" according to "the needs of practical life" and transforming a world of fundamentally indivisible matter into a world of discrete objects (*Matter* 202, 206). This process of division extends beyond the material realm, objectifying our own mental states as well and transforming what is actually a unified flux of experience into a series of discrete experiences. Because, according to Bergson, mental life is lived temporally, this objectification of our mental states causes us to spatialize time, to "substitut[e] for the true duration [*durée réelle*], lived by consciousness, an homogenous and independent time" that really resembles abstract space more than it does our primordial experience of time (203). Bergson calls this division of time according to the logic of space a "useful habit," as it is "much better adapted to social life in general," and it is according to this logic that we live our everyday lives (203; *Time* 128). Treating time, space, and mental life as divisible and quantifiable phenomena, he suggests, is what allows us to act in conscious, pragmatic ways.

This pragmatic kind of life, however, involves but a "ghost, a colourless shadow" of ourselves, and our true selves, Bergson claims, exist in the space of the "durée réelle" (*Time* 231).[39] In the *durée réelle*, states of consciousness cannot be transformed into discrete objects, as they bleed into one another. Consciousness does not divide itself into a series of sequential states but joins "both [its] past and [its] present states into an organic whole," constantly modifying its present nature by incorporating its past (100). Theorizing consciousness thusly, suggests Bergson, allows us to "conceive of succession without distinction, and think of it as mutual penetration, an interconnexion and organization of elements, each one of which represents the whole, and cannot be distinguished or isolated from it except by abstract thought" (101). The temporality of the *durée réelle*, then, is not the homogeneous time of everyday life; it is a mode of becoming, a process of experienced, qualitative change rather than an accumulation of individual moments. It is this approach to the world, Bergson says, that is metaphysically primordial, the state of immediate experience from which our everyday, rational consciousness arises.

This movement from the *durée réelle* to everyday consciousness is, according to Bergson, achieved through the act of perception, an act that is closely bound up with free will. In pure perception—the sort of perception that occurs in immediate experience, at the level of the *durée réelle*—there is no division between percept and perceiver; "subject and object" actually "coincide" (Bergson, *Matter* 218). This kind of perception, however, is merely a theoretical phenomenon, as perception involves a consciousness that is always already shot through with memory, and actual perception involves a separation of self from world and world from perceived object. "Such is the primary and the most apparent operation of the perceiving mind," claims Bergson: it throws a grid of homogeneous space and time beneath the world and thereby "marks out divisions in the continuity of the extended." While this kind of spatial division does produce the color-less, pragmatic shadow-self previously mentioned, it is also what allows consciousness to act on and in the world. While perception may involve a "solidification and . . . division" of the "moving continuity of the real," an action that pulls both perceiver and percept out of the *durée réelle*, it is precisely this action that gives us "a fulcrum for our action." Rather than submit mechanically to natural necessity, which involves the "reply, to an action received, by an immediate reaction" that "adopts the rhythm of the first," conscious perception allows us "to fix, at long intervals, that becom-ing to which [our] own becoming clings . . . to solidify it into distinct mo-ments" and to "free [our]selves from the particular rhythm which governs the flow of . . . matter." This removal of consciousness from the uncon-scious rhythms of matter, this interruption of the natural flow of time, is what allows "actions that are really *free*, or at least partly indeterminate," to be performed (206–7). In other words, the spatial and temporal divisions effected by actual perception are what allow consciousness to act freely. The *durée réelle* may be the space of the true self, but it is also a space in which natural necessity has free rein, and while everyday consciousness may not be as rich or vital as the immediate experience of the *durée réelle*, it is also the kind of consciousness that can exercise free will.[40]

Because the *durée réelle* constitutes an irrational mode of immediate experience in which free will plays no role, it would not, I think, be in-appropriate to identify it with that primordial mode of experience dom-inated, for James, by immediate attention. Nor would it be farfetched to suggest that it is this state into which nineteenth-century trance subjects were thrust by the techniques of mesmerism and hypnosis. This state is characterized by a few key tendencies. First, it enacts a dissolution of the distinction between subject and object, a return to that mode of true per-ception in which perceiver and percept coincide. Second, it involves a collapse (or at least a distortion) of linear temporality, pulling the fasci-nated subject out of the flow of everyday time and thrusting him or her back into the *durée réelle*, in which present bleeds into past and experience expands and contracts into durations of heterogeneous length. Finally, because the length of each duration in this state varies, the experience contained in these durations varies in intensity as well, potentially collapsing long stretches of homogeneous time into brief moments of "intenser life" (Bergson, *Matter* 204).

This model of pure experience, I would like to suggest, functions in the history of fascination as a point of intellectual transition from the nineteenth to the twentieth century, both retroactively explaining the phenomena associated with mesmerism and hypnotism and looking forward to the way fascination would come to be conceptualized by twentieth-century philosophers such as Jean Baudrillard and Maurice Blanchot. The amnesia commonly experienced by nineteenth-century trance subjects, for example, could be explained by the dissolution in the *durée réelle* of the discrete, remembering subject. And what should we call mesmeric clairvoyance and telepathy if not "intenser" modes of perception, ones that care nothing for the divisions effected by homogeneous time and space? The similarities between this model of experience and later theories of fascination are, of course, almost too obvious to be worth noting, united, as they are, by a shared interest in the collapse of subject-object relations and linear time. Centering fascination in their theories of pure experience, James and Bergson brought a phenomenon often associated with mysticism and pseudoscience into the philosophical mainstream of the twentieth century.

Affect Theory and the Afterlife of Fascination

This mainstreaming of fascination would come to have sweeping effects on the way Americans thought through, wrote about, and critiqued modernity throughout the twentieth century. Influencing the way everyone from psychologists and anthropologists to writers and filmmakers conceived of the modern self, fascination would be seen as an integral aspect of modern life. The chapters to come, of course, will show in greater detail how this understanding of modernity shaped turn-of-the-twentieth-century science, literature, and popular culture; for the remainder of this chapter, however, I would like to turn toward our present historical moment, as, I suggest, the worldview embraced by James and Bergson is still very much with us today, even if we do not express it in the terms of vitalist thought.

While I could examine any number of recent trends in critical theory to support this claim (and, in later chapters, I will look at some of these other trends in detail), I would like to focus for now on one intellectual movement that has been particularly influential in the humanities in recent decades: affect theory.[41] A catchall term for scholarly work on forces such as feeling and sensation that circulate "in excess of consciousness," the field in many ways represents a twenty-first-century revival of nineteenth-century ideas about the nonconscious basis of the self (Clough 2).[42] Both contemporary theories of affect and turn-of-the-century theories of fascination, after all, frame their respective subjects as nonrational phenomena that exceed human control, "affect" being, according to the *Affect Theory Reader*, "the name we give to those forces—visceral forces beneath, alongside, or generally *other than* conscious knowing, vital forces insisting beyond emotion—that can serve to drive us toward movement, toward thought and extension, that can likewise suspend us" (Seigworth and Gregg 1). Affect, like fascination, compels and suspends action without the intervention of rational thought. Like the magnetic fluid of mesmerism or the vitalists' vital principle, it affects the body below the level of consciousness.

It is perhaps unsurprising, then, that affect, like fascination, is often understood to trouble the boundaries of the discrete subject. Because affect theory theorizes the body as porous and relational, as "always aided and abetted by" a "field or context of its force-relations," it posits the self not as an autonomous entity but as a fleeting, unstable phenomenon: "emerg[ing] out of muddy, unmediated relatedness and not in some dialectical reconciliation of cleanly oppositional elements or primary units," affect dissolves the boundaries between self and world, between subject and object, making "easy compartmentalisms give way to thresholds and tensions, blends and blurs" (Seigworth and Gregg 3, 4). Like the subject of Bergson's *durée réelle*, the subject of affect theory is really no subject at all: it is simply a body engaged in "perpetual becoming (always becoming otherwise, however subtly, than what it already is), pulled beyond its seeming surface boundedness by way of its relation to, indeed its composition through, the forces of encounter" (3). Like fascination, affect collapses the distance between feeling and perceiving subject and felt and perceived world. It radically opens the self to external influences, calling into question the very possibility of maintaining a firmly bounded subjectivity.

In certain fundamental ways, then, fascination and affect designate very similar forces. Then again, this similarity is perhaps to be expected, as much affect-theoretical work draws on and reworks elements of vitalist thought in more or less explicit ways. For example, Brian Massumi—a thinker who has been called "one of the most influential affect theorists in the humanities and social sciences today" (and whose work we might take as representative of certain broader trends in the field)—often cites Bergson and James as major intellectual influences; indeed, in a direct nod to James, he calls his overarching philosophical method a form of "speculative pragmatism" (Leys 435; Massumi, *Politics* 6).[43] Moreover, most of the key concepts that populate his philosophy (such as "intensity" and the *durée réelle*–like state of "the event") are essentially vitalist in nature, often borrowed with only slight modification from the work of Bergson.[44] Even his theories of perception and attention are decidedly Jamesian, framed, as they are, in terms of fascination: "if you pay attention to paying attention, you quickly sense that rather than you directing your attention, your attention is directing you," drawing you into perceptual moments that suspend the "linear progress of the narrative present from past to future . . . like a temporal sink, a hole in time" (Massumi, "Perception" 26). In many ways, Massumi's brand of affect theory represents an intentional reworking of vitalist thought, an attempt to translate the ideas of James and Bergson into the idiom of the twenty-first century.

Vitalist philosophy, however, is not the only turn-of-the-century discourse that has left its mark on Massumi's writing. This is to say that Massumi's work, like that of the mind-curists and New Thought enthusiasts, could easily be called pseudoscientific, exhibiting, as it does, a self-conscious tendency to "cherry-pick" ideas from the sciences in a "relatively shameless way" (Wetherell 10). What starts in his work as a "specific point about bodies, brains and minds"—one rooted in empirical data produced by experimental psychologists—quickly "metamorphose[s]," in the words of Margaret Wetherell, "into an entire, programmatic world-view" (60). Indeed, Massumi himself says that he likes to take "a scientific concept and use . . . it in such a way that it ceases to be systematically scientific" (*Parables* 20). Even, then, as the key concepts that structure his understanding of affect may be borrowed from James and Bergson, his chosen methodology more closely resembles that of turn-of-the-century mysticism and pseudoscience.

It is thus no surprise that affect is imbued for Massumi with an almost supernatural power, that his work exhibits an intense interest in techniques of enchantment that "could," he admits, be called "mystical" (*Semblance* 85). His influential essay "Arts of Experience, Politics of Expression: In Four Movements" (in *Semblance and Event*), for example, is largely about the bewitching power of premodern ritual and the way avantgarde artists have learned to harness this power. Celebrating the fact that "figural drawing returns a quasi-magical power of gesture to representational art," he offers up both primitive ritual and experimental art as exemplary techniques for channeling the transformative powers of affect (124). Like Henry Adams, he posits irrational force as the through line that connects the (post)modern world to the world of premodern magic. Conceptualizing affect as a mystical force that animates both ritual gesture and postmodern aesthetic experience, he locates it in that same epistemically and temporally liminal place that turn-of-the-century thinkers located fascination.

If, as I have been suggesting, Massumi is in many ways a turn-of-the-century philosopher at heart, it makes sense that he, like Bergson, should invest nonrational experience with a certain radical potential. For, according to Massumi, affect is a fundamentally revolutionary force, one defined by its relationship to a world to come: by nature "promissory," it is, he goes so far as to suggest, "the word [he] use[s] for 'hope'" (*Politics* 209, 3).[45] This is because affect represents for him a force of constant and unqualified change, the embodiment of that pure potential for becoming that characterizes the monadic moment of the event (or, for that matter, the metaphysically undifferentiated state of the *durée réelle*). Such an understanding of affect, moreover, is not idiosyncratic to Massumi; it is a central tenet of affect theory as a field. The *Affect Theory Reader*, after all, celebrates the way affect embodies matter's potential for "infinitely connectable, impersonal, and contagious belongings," the way it figures "the 'not yet' of a body's doing, casting a line along the hopeful (though also fearful) cusp of an emergent futurity" (Seigworth and Gregg 4). Tweaking Massumi's language only slightly, it conceives of "affect as promise" (12). As a field, then, affect theory largely frames affect (as well as itself) as, in the words of Clare Hemmings, "the way forward," the harbingers of an "ontological future" that will be "bright, many-faceted," and "surprising" (550, 557). Carrying on Bergson's legacy of optimism regarding the transformative potential of nonrational experience, affect theory posits affect as a force of radical futurity.

If we think back to the beginning of this chapter, however, such optimism should perhaps give us pause. For if affect represents a kind of postmodern reincarnation of fascination, I think it is important that we attend not only to its potential for innovation and change but also to its potential for more conservative action. After all, this is how fascination was conceptualized around the turn of the century: as both the avatar of an emergent, modern future and a force of stasis, suspension, and even atavism. It seems prudent, then, to approach affect not as an unqualified force of futurity but as a more temporally and conceptually ambivalent phenomenon, one that is capable of reaching out to the future, the past, both, or neither. Indeed, many of affect theory's critics point out that it can even produce a kind of suspended present, as "some bodies"—particularly the bodies of marginalized subjects—are more often "captured and held by affect" than they are liberated by it, overwhelmed, like mesmeric subjects or victims of the evil eye, by forces beyond their control (Hemmings 562).[46] In pointing this out, such critics rehearse Hawthorne's concerns about the "sacredness of [the] individual," resurrecting those anxieties that were so widespread in the nineteenth century about the autonomy of the subject.

To put things more simply, the hopes and fears that surrounded fascination in the nineteenth and early twentieth centuries are still very much with us today; the critical popularity of affect theory is proof of this. Indeed, many of the conversations we still have in the humanities about the instability of the (post)modern subject rely upon a set of assumptions and conceptual tools that, as we have seen, were first taken up in the United States by mesmerists and mind-curists. While fascination, then, may have begun its life as an intellectually disreputable form of faith healing or folk magic, its influence on American psychology and philosophy has proven wide-ranging and long-lasting, shaping everything from turn-of-the-century pseudoscience to contemporary scholarly work on affect. As we shall soon see, its cultural influence has been no less important, molding, as it did, a wide array of quintessentially modern aesthetic practices, phenomena, discourses, and movements around the turn of the twentieth century. It is these cultural phenomena that will be the focus of the rest of this book; let us turn to them now.

2

Amuletic Aesthetics and the Fascination
of Decadent Style

"I KNOW THE PASSIONATE lover of fine style exposes himself to the
hatred of the masses," Charles Baudelaire once wrote in a preface to his
poetry collection *Les Fleurs du mal*, "but no respect for humanity, no false
modesty, no conspiracy, no universal suffrage will ever force me to speak
the unspeakable jargon of the age" ("Three Drafts" xxvi). "If there is any
glory in not being understood, or in being only very slightly so," he went
on, "I may without boasting say that with this little book I have at a single
stroke both won and deserved that glory" (xxviii–xxix). Incensed at the
censorship of portions of *Les Fleurs*'s first edition and "at certain attacks on
him in the press," Baudelaire, rather than counter the claims of his critics,
embraced them, perversely celebrating his own supposed illegibility with
irony and "fine style" (Matheus xi). Doubling down on the unhealthily
florid aesthetic of his poetry, he expressed a kind of antisocial pleasure in
the accumulation of delicious words, embracing ornament and obscurity
at the expense of his contemporary readers' pleasure.

In many ways, then, these remarks represent an early manifesto for
decadent style. Born, like mesmerism, in France, decadentism arose in
the second half of the nineteenth century as a response to the cultural
upheavals of modernization, developing and leveraging a critique against
what its proponents viewed as the shortcomings of mainstream modern
aesthetics, particularly realism.[1] This critique took various forms, but its
primary ideological underpinning was an antimodern belief (and perverse
tendency to luxuriate) in the decline of Western civilization, a conviction
that the modern subject was, through overrefinement, reverting to a state

of barbarism. For its critics, the decadent worldview seemed pathological, the aesthetic manifestation of a broader tendency toward degeneracy and hysteria. For its proponents, it represented a powerful mode of cultural critique. Disillusioned with the idea of historical progress, decadent writers embraced what they viewed as their own historical out-of-placeness, rejecting mainstream aesthetics in favor of the sensuous pleasures of ornamental style.

Perhaps unsurprisingly, decadentism was never particularly popular in the United States. Even if, as David Weir points out, a small cult of aestheticism arose in the 1870s and 1880s as an expression of discontent with "the martial ideals of the [Civil] war," it never flourished into a broader decadent movement the way it did across the Atlantic (*Decadent Culture* xvi). This was largely because the morbid subject matter and florid style of decadent literature were at odds with the values of vigor and progress that Americans held so dear, and it seemed to many that to embrace decadence was, in the words of Weir, "to somehow cease to be American" (xii). Those few Americans who did experiment with decadent style, then— whether in conversation with or independently of Europe's various decadent movements—were in some ways even more perverse than their European counterparts: not only were they out of historical place, refusing, like Baudelaire, to speak the "jargon of the age"; they were also out of cultural place, writing a kind of fiction that, for the rest of the United States, smacked unpleasantly of European degeneracy. Even though literary tastes began to move, after the Civil War, in the direction of social realism, American decadents, such as they were, doubled down on the perverse pleasures of lush description, rejecting the period's widespread obsession with narrative progress.

It is this peculiar turn away from narrative and toward ornament—as well, of course, as the relationship between this turn toward ornament and fascination—that I explore in this chapter. Put simply, I would like to suggest that those few Americans who did embrace decadence in the late nineteenth century did so in an attempt to mitigate the effects of modernization, turning toward the fascinating anachronisms of decadent style in order to resist and critique the logic of historical progress. Both employing ornamental style and incorporating the imagery of personal ornament in their fiction, these writers structured their stories around the aesthetics of the ancient amulet, a type of magical jewelry historically meant to protect against the evil eye. To demonstrate this, I turn to Harriet Prescott Spofford's decadent short story "The Amber Gods" (1860), exploring the role of ornamental aesthetics in the story's content and style and unpacking the vexed relationship between these aesthetics and the future-oriented time of modernity. I then examine the way decadent aesthetics shift and change when taken up in contexts traditionally considered undecadent, including the nineteenth-century genre of southern regionalism (exemplified by Charles Chesnutt's short story "Dave's Neckliss" [1889]) and the work of contemporary critical race theorists. In the end, I hope to show that decadent ornament can be (and has been) employed in strikingly different cultural contexts to surprisingly similar ends, troubling, in each of these contexts, modern notions of historical progress.

Decadence, Ornament, Amulets

Though most literary scholars would agree that the writing of someone like Baudelaire or Spofford should be called decadent, there is less critical consensus as to why. At first glance, the tendency of such writing toward florid and stylized description may seem like its defining characteristic; Paul Bourget, after all, famously decried decadence in 1883 for the way it privileged the sensual independence of the page, the sentence, and the individual word over the imperatives of narrative cohesion (25). At second glance, this kind of writing might seem to be defined by its parodic style, as the term *decadence,* in its etymologically purest form, designates "a *falling away* from some established norm," a tendency not to "boldly assert a new form" but to "elaborate . . . an existing tradition to the point of apparent dissolution" (Reed 10). While both of these definitions are, in their own ways, apt descriptions of decadent writing's formal strategies, they perhaps too easily gloss over the historical context of the style's emergence. Because decadentism arose in response to the changes wrought by modernization, it might be most useful to approach the phenomenon as Weir does: as the result of an attempt to grapple, in a moment of historical transition, with emergent and conflicting aesthetic ideologies, the ambivalent product of a general "*interference* of ideas and literary tendencies" (*Decadence* 13). Thus while its formal techniques may have involved both parody and lush ornamentation, the cultural effect achieved by these techniques—a muddying of aesthetic and epistemic waters, a collapse of conventional cultural binarisms—was also a vital part of its aesthetic project. In fact, paying attention to the genre's relationship with nineteenth-century culture at large usefully illuminates what, for generations of literary scholars, have appeared to be the genre's most glaring internal ideological contradictions: even, for example, as decadent writing seems to privilege the artificial over the natural, it reveals "the natural" itself to be an artificial construct; even as its cosmopolitan aesthetic seems a far cry from the primitive aesthetics of the ancient world, it draws a more or less overt equivalence between hypermodern and premodern style, espousing the idea that "the state of culture decays" and naturally reverts to "the state of nature represented by barbarism" (12). Rather than approach these collapsed binaries as a failure of ideological cohesion, then, we might, like Barbara Spackman, understand them as the result of decadence's powers of epistemological "contamination," its ability to undo the "logic of absolute difference" that structures oppositions between such things as nature and culture, civilization and barbarism (41). Approaching decadent style in this way foregrounds its sometimes overlooked potential for cultural critique, highlighting, as it does, that even if the decadent writing of the nineteenth century did have an essential relationship with artifice and parody, it also had an essentially deconstructive relationship with mainstream cultural values, a tendency to blur traditional aesthetic and epistemic boundaries.

For those who experienced this blurring of boundaries firsthand, decadent style caused quite a bit of anxiety. As I have already noted, decadentism was seen by its critics as symptomatic of a broader moral disorder, the aesthetic manifestation of a generalized physical and psychological atavism. In Europe, decadent style was aligned with degeneration, or evolutionary decline; influenced by Max Nordau's 1892 study of the phenomenon, the popular theory held that a predilection for decadence was the product of hereditary enfeeblement, the result of an overcivilized race reaching its inevitable conclusion. In the United States, it was linked less to heredity and more to the widespread phenomenon of neurasthenia, which had its roots in the overstimulating living conditions of modern life itself (Weir, *Decadent Culture* 9). Regardless of its root cause, however, decadent taste was treated in both Europe and the United States as the symptom of a disease. After all, while the hallmark of decadence was, for Nordau, a love of outmoded and decorative aesthetics, an inability or refusal to "abid[e] by one definite historic style," it was also linked to a host of other degenerate traits, including "unbounded egoism," "impulsiveness," "emotionalism," "a disinclination to action of any kind," and a propensity for "mysticism" (11, 18, 19, 20, 22). Uniting historically inappropriate aesthetic tastes with a broad range of hysterical personality traits, decadence represented for its critics a mixture of historical and psychological abnormality, a perverse embrace of antiquated style and antisocial behavior.

Rather than deny these charges of aesthetic and psychological perversion, decadents leaned into them, asserting that what their critics viewed as faults were, in fact, virtues. While Nordau, for example, decried decadence as an atavistic reversion to barbarism, Baudelaire celebrated this very historical movement as an important recuperation of primitive aesthetic values. In "The Painter of Modern Life," he argued that the popular convention of aligning the primitive with nature and civilization with artifice was wrongheaded, as "external finery" is actually "one of the signs of the primitive nobility of the human soul." "Those races which our confused and perverted civilization is pleased to treat as savage," he claimed, share striking similarities with nineteenth-century dandies, as they "understand . . . the lofty spiritual significance of the toilet" and have a natural "adoration of what is brilliant—many-coloured feathers, iridescent fabrics, the incomparable majesty of artificial forms" (32). In other words, Baudelaire suggested, a love of beautiful ornament was the aesthetic hallmark of both hyper-civilization *and* under-civilization; "like an ace that can be played high or low," ornament represented a point of commonality between the dandy and the barbarian (Theo Davis 14). Enacting a slippage between the modern and the premodern, decadent style collapsed the space between civilization and primitive culture, producing a kind of temporal short circuit.

Interestingly enough, this short circuit was linked for detractors and proponents alike to the ability to fascinate. Baudelaire, after all, famously celebrated the enchanting effects of decadent feminine artifice in "Painter," claiming that "woman is quite within her rights, indeed she is even accomplishing a kind of duty, when she devotes herself to appearing magical and supernatural," employing makeup and ornament to "astonish and charm us": "She is obliged to adorn herself in order to be adored . . . lay[ing] all the arts under contribution for the means of lifting herself above nature, the better to conquer hearts and *rivet attention*" (33, my emphasis). Nordau, too, noted the captivating power of elaborate style, complaining that, nowadays, "every single figure strives visibly by some singularity in outline, set, cut, or colour, to startle attention violently, and imperiously to detain it" (9). Even Friedrich Nietzsche, who understood decadence less as an aesthetic phenomenon and more as a rhetorical one, claimed that Socrates—for him the archetypical "decadent"—used decadent logic to "fascinate" his rhetorical opponents, "*paralys[ing]*" their "intellect[s]" by elaborating their arguments to the point of dissolution (*Twilight* 108, 112).[2] Not only, then, did decadent style collapse the boundary between past and present; it did so by deploying fascinating ornament. Capitalizing on the almost supernatural allure of stylized artifice, decadent style commanded a kind of irresistible, compulsive attention.

Fittingly, the very idea that fascination was bound up with ornament was itself a kind of perverse anachronism, a resurrection of premodern beliefs about decoration and enchantment. Fascination, after all, was a significant preoccupation of the ancient Greeks and Romans, designating, as it did, a very real kind of malicious magic practiced upon a person without his or her knowledge.[3] Most frequently associated with the evil eye, the practice of cursing something (usually a person or a person's possessions) with an envious glance, its results were thought to be catastrophic, resulting in, according to one encyclopedia of classical culture, the destruction of "everything [one] holds dear."[4] Perhaps the most unsettling aspect of ancient fascination, however, was that it could be practiced by virtually anyone—a neighbor, a family member, even a god—as long as that person was jealous enough.[5] Because the evil eye posed such a ubiquitous threat, the ancients carried around apotropaic amulets called *fascina*—a term that, strangely enough, was used to signify both the evil eye and the countercharm that protected against it—which were often carved from precious stones such as coral and amber (as these substances were thought to have innate apotropaic powers) and engraved with apotropaic images.[6] Explicitly produced and used as prophylactics against the evil eye, these amulets, like decadent style, connected the powers of fascination to personal ornament. To revive this connection in the nineteenth century, then—even implicitly, even in a metaphorical register—was in some ways to collapse, once again, the dividing line between present and past, to foster an irruption of premodern magic into the modern world.

If decadent style worked according to the same logic as ancient ornament, it is perhaps no surprise that, for many, decadence was also bound up with the affective force that the ancients most associated with fascination: envy. For just as classical fascination required the casting of a jealous glance, so, too, did critics of decadent style draw an essential connection between ornamental taste and an envious disposition. Nordau, for example, compared what he saw as the impotent nihilism of decadents to "the envy of a rich, hoary voluptuary, who sees a pair of young lovers making for a sequestered forest nook" (3). Nietzsche attributed the power of Socrates's decadent rhetoric to his intense feelings of *ressentiment,* his desire to "*revenge* himself on the upper classes whom he fascinates" (*Twilight* 112). In both its ancient and its decadent incarnations, then, fascination was thought to draw its power from feelings of envy. Tangibly realizing the socially destructive power of *ressentiment,* "that most dangerous blasting-stuff and explosive," fascination put the immaterial affect of jealousy to work effecting material harm (Nietzsche, *Genealogy* 163).

There are, of course, significant differences between the way the Greeks and Romans used ornament and the way nineteenth-century decadents did. The ancients, after all, used it to repel fascination, to deflect the envious gaze and its harmful effects. Decadents, on the other hand, used it precisely because it solicited the attention of others, employing ornament not to defend against fascination but to fascinate. But even as the purposes of ancient ornament and decadent ornament were inverses of one another, the mechanisms by which they worked were strikingly similar, for one of the reasons apotropaic amulets were thought to be effective was that they drew the gaze of envious rivals away from the body and toward themselves.[7] In working this way, they exhibited a kind of functional perversity worthy of the nineteenth century: while their avowed purpose was to deflect the evil eye, they did so by flaunting their own opulence, seducing the gaze with glimpses of precious stones. They thus embodied a paradox: even as they were meant to defuse the pernicious power of *ressentiment*, they themselves were clearly legible as signs of high social status, crafted, as they often were, from valuable materials. Both soliciting the envious gaze and protecting against its damaging effects, one might even go so far as to suggest that *fascina* deployed the techniques of modern fascination in order to counteract the effects of premodern fascination.

Decadent style and ancient amulets, then, worked in uncannily similar ways—such uncannily similar ways, in fact, that we might even call decadent style a kind of "amuletic aesthetic." If it is no secret that decadent writers often and explicitly made amuletic jewelry a motif in their writing—"endless lists of gemstones" making up, in the words of Spackman, a significant part of the "bric-a-brac" that "we have come to consider a fingerprint of decadence"—it does not seem inappropriate to offer such jewelry up as a useful figure for decadent style itself (39). Embodying the central tenets of decadent philosophy—its historical uncanniness, its ornamentality, its propensity to fascinate—the figure of the amulet offers us a useful way to think through the aesthetics of American decadence.

To Be in a Dream: Harriet Prescott Spofford's Fascinating Ornament

Perhaps no decadent writer (and certainly no decadent American writer) made better use of such amuletic aesthetics than Harriet Prescott Spofford, an unassuming young woman from New England who shocked readers with her highly wrought style. Though Spofford may seem like an unlikely decadent—long seen, in the words of Judith Fetterly, as nothing more than a "romanticist who began to write at a time when the literary establishment was moving in the direction of realism"—she was actually a contemporary of Baudelaire, and she was arguably at the vanguard of Western literary decadence (263).[8] This fact, however, is often overlooked, as, being an American woman instead of a European man, she largely proved illegible to contemporary readers (as well as to subsequent generations of critics) as a decadent author in her own right. In fact, when she submitted her first short story to the *Atlantic* in 1858—a story titled "In a Cellar," "a vivid tale of mystery and political intrigue" filled with "picturesque descriptions of Parisian society, brilliant flashes of dialogue, and a wickedly cosmopolitan tone"—James Russell Lowell was so taken aback by the story's worldly content and style that "he seriously doubted her authorship of the piece" (Bendixen ix). This incredible historical out-of-placeness, however, in some ways marks Spofford as the quintessential decadent. For if the project of decadent writing was to trouble conventional historical and aesthetic categories, Spofford, herself a disruptive presence in the canon, pushed this project to its limit: perversely flaunting not only her improper relation to history and aesthetics but her improper relation to gender and geography as well, she virtually embodied the decadent worldview. Writing, to borrow a phrase from Weir, "against the American grain," she luxuriated in a kind of ornamental style that was all the more decadent for being at odds with her gender, her class, and her nationality.

Arguably, the most decadent of Spofford's stories (and the story that makes the clearest use of amuletic aesthetics) is "The Amber Gods." The story is told from the perspective of Yone Willoughby, a sensuous young decadent who luxuriates in her own physical beauty and the beauty of the things she uses to adorn herself. When Vaughn Rose, the childhood sweetheart of her cousin, Lu, reappears in the family home after an extended period of study in Europe, Yone determines to win his affections. She is aided in her mission by the seemingly enchanted and enchanting amber rosary-cum-necklace that her father gives to her, each bead of which depicts a different pagan deity—the story's eponymous amber gods—and which seems to cast a spell over the story's various characters, alternately attracting and repelling them. Yone ultimately wins Rose over and the two are married, but their conjugal bliss is marred by the revival of Rose's feelings for Lu, and the story concludes with Yone's premature death.

Strangely enough, when critics write about "The Amber Gods," they tend to pay little attention to the amber beads for which the story is named.[9] When they do discuss the rosary at length, they focus on its connections to the prehistoric, the way it embodies for Yone a kind of amoral prehuman utopia, that "pristine world . . . of accentuated crises," as Yone puts it, that produced the amber from which it was fashioned (55).[10] I, however, am more interested in the cultural significance that has historically been attached to amber, the way Spofford, by conspicuously writing about a substance used by the ancients to make magical amulets, draws on and modifies premodern beliefs about apotropaic ornament. It is, in fact, amber's very human history, I suggest, that endows the beads with such fascinating power in the story and that enables them to enchant the story's various characters.

Amber, after all, has long been associated with the supernatural. While some ancient Greeks thought it was coagulated sunlight (produced when the sun's rays touched the ocean), others claimed that it was made of the solidified tears of the sisters of Phaethon, a demigod killed by Zeus.[11] Regardless of how it was produced, the Greeks and Romans frequently used it to fashion magical amulets, for, as we have already seen, it was thought to be a prophylactic against the evil eye. This was, in part, because it exhibited a number of strange properties, including the exudation, when heated, of a perfume-like scent and a "remarkable negative-electric property" that gave it the ability to attract and repel small objects (Burnham 346).[12] The latter property seemed so fantastical to the ancients that, according to one nineteenth-century writer, they believed "some intelligence of another world, some sprite or fairy, had selected [amber] for a dwelling-place" (Converse 599). Amber, the ancients thought, had an essential connection to the supernatural world, making it an ideal material from which to fashion amulets.

This connection to the supernatural was closely related to amber's status as a luxury good, one particularly associated with femininity. In fact, despite a brief discursus on amber's medicinal value, Pliny's *Natural History* denigrated it as a largely useless, ornamental substance, claiming that "not even luxury has yet succeeded in inventing a justification for using amber." Because it was too fragile to be used in the manufacture of practical things such as drinking vessels, it was primarily incorporated into ornamental objects "fancied only by women" (187).[13] Despite this uselessness (or perhaps because of it), it was extremely valuable, a substance whose possession was to be envied, and Pliny went so far as to suggest sardonically that a piece of high-quality amber was "more expensive than a number of human beings [that is, slaves], alive and in good health" (201). For the ancients, amber's magical properties were linked to its status as an expensive, feminized ornament, and even as amber amulets were meant to defend against envious enchantment, they themselves were hotly desired objects of envy. Alternately attracting and repelling desire, amber was both prized for its beauty and denigrated for its uselessness, seen as a physically fragile luxury good and a supernaturally powerful prophylactic.

Because of its connotations of both ancient enchantment and ancient luxury, the figure of amber offered Spofford an efficient method for injecting her fiction with a bit of premodern magic. After all, she was well educated, and she was certainly aware of at least some of amber's ancient uses, even mentioning Pliny's account of amber in "The Amber Gods" (66).[14] She was also aware of more modern accounts of amber's magical properties, as evidenced by her references to Wilhelm Meinhold's gothic novel *The Amber Witch* and Thomas Moore's epic oriental romance *Lalla-Rookh* (56).[15] Amber offered Spofford an image steeped in both ancient myth and nineteenth-century romance, a figure intimately bound up with both premodern enchantment and modern luxury. It worked, in the words of one nineteenth-century writer, to "bind . . . the dim poetic past with the changing, fleeting present," to bridge the historical gap between Pliny, Moore, and herself (Converse 601).

When the amber rosary–turned–necklace first appears in "The Amber Gods," it is, after all, explicitly described as a magical artifact. Lingering over it as she prepares herself for her wedding day, Yone implores the reader to "count the beads,—long, oval, like some seaweed bulbs, each an amulet." The beads, she says, are "very old" and "sculptured into hideous, tiny, heathen gods," gods she will later call "all those very Gnostic deities that assisted at creation" (40, 54). It is soon revealed that the necklace originally belonged to a slave of Yone's great-grandfather named simply "Little Asian," who used it to say "demoniacal prayers" while in captivity and who, according to family legend, used it to shipwreck a vessel meant to transport her to New Holland, "enchanting all her spirits from the beads about her, and calling and singing and whistling up the winds with them till storm rolled round the ship, and fierce fog and foam and drowning fell upon her capturers" (43, 44). After escaping the Willoughbys, Yone says, Little Asian fell into the service of a young Fiesolan woman—Yone's mother—to whom she gave her beads and who converted them, with the blessing of the pope, into a rosary. When this woman met Yone's father, one of the hated Willoughbys, and decided to marry him, Little Asian cursed the beads, claiming that if they ever "crossed the water" back to New England, "all their blessing would be changed to banning, and that bane would burn the bearer" (45). The beads, of course, did make their way back to New England, and that is how they have ended up in Yone's possession. Imbued with both Christian and pagan magic, the necklace is explicitly described from the beginning as amuletic.

In some ways, this description is strikingly apt. After all, the beads are made of amber, a naturally apotropaic substance, and they are engraved with "Gnostic deities," those foreign, syncretic deities that the ancients—who considered "magic that came from a distance" to be "especially powerful, particularly when it seemed to spring from a primitive way of life"—so often used to adorn *fascina* (Bonner 1).[16] The necklace, moreover, is itself a kind of palimpsestic, syncretic object, invested with supernatural power by both the heathen rituals of Little Asian and the Catholic blessing bestowed upon it by the pope. Rather than avert the evil eye, however, the beads cast their own sinister spell on those around them, attracting instead of repelling, inciting envy without quelling it. Thanks ostensibly to Little Asian's curse, their apotropaic function is inverted, enchanting rather than defending against enchantment. The necklace seems to be a kind of charm that, like the overripe fruits and flowers of which Yone is so fond, has gone bad.

Consequently, it exerts a magical power over those with whom it comes into contact, particularly Rose. When Yone first shows Rose her beads, they become tangled in her hair and he must help her untangle them, an intimate encounter that prompts Rose to call her "Circe" and "the Witch of Atlas," names, Yone says, Rose continues to call her as they grow more intimate (49). Later, once the beads have had some time to work their spell on Rose, Lu asks Yone if Rose seems somehow different since returning from Europe, something she has noticed "ever since [Yone] showed him [her] beads that day," and Yone replies: "Oh! It's the amber . . . They are amulets, and have bound him in a thrall . . . He's in a dream" (65). Like Homer's Circe or Percy Bysshe Shelley's Witch of Atlas, Yone uses the beads to enchant Rose, acting on him like a premodern sorceress.

The amber's ancient magic is compounded by a much more modern power: that of (animal) magnetism. Yone, who normally has a "luxurious calm" about her, mentions that she is, on occasion, overwhelmed by "a perfect whirlpool" of feeling, and it is on just one such occasion that, after Rose has been visiting the family for some weeks, she looks at Rose and leaps inexplicably to her feet, exclaiming: "There! it is insupportable! I've been in the magnetic storm long enough," attributing her emotional turmoil to a kind of magnetic influence on the part of Rose. When she leaves the room, Rose, too, becomes magnetized, following her "as if unwillingly drawn by a loadstone" (62). This magnetic mode of relating to one another is expanded upon by Yone's description of her particular intimacy with Rose, an intimacy she frames in the language of mesmeric rapport: like a magnetic somnambulist, Rose is affected by "change[s] in the atmosphere" around him, and "so sensitive is he, that, when connected with you by an intimate *rapport*, even if but momentary, he almost divines your thoughts" (69). The amber, it seems, facilitates a kind of magnetic resonance between Yone and Rose, bestowing on Yone a measure of its own "remarkable negative-electric" power. Thus while the beads are charged with the forces of ancient gods and premodern witchcraft, they are also aligned with mesmerism, a brand of fascination whose popularity peaked less than twenty years before the publication of "The Amber Gods." Fascinating those around it by both modern and premodern means, the necklace unites the supernatural beliefs of the past with those of the nineteenth-century present.

While ancient enchantment involved a malicious glance and animal magnetism was largely haptic, Yone's beads primarily affect through the sense of smell. As Yone mentions at the beginning of the story, she has a particular affinity for perfumes, "heavy fragrances, faint with sweetness, ravishing juices of odor, heliotropes, violets, water-lilies,—powerful attars and extracts that snatch your soul off your lips." "Couldn't you live on rich scents," she asks, "if they tried to starve you? I could, or die on them: I don't know which would be best" (40). This meditation on the life-giving and life-extinguishing power of scent tellingly precedes her introduction of the amber necklace, whose most powerful sensory property is its earthy smell. Rose calls this smell "acrid" and associates it with the grotesque "lower jaw of St. Basil the Great . . . being hard, heavy, shining like gold, the teeth yet in it" (55). But it is also the smell of amber that dominates his first meeting with Yone, the scene in which she first enchants him. When her beads become tangled in her hair and Rose leans in to help her untangle them, "at the friction of [their] hands, the beads gave out slightly their pungent smell that breathes all through the Arabian Nights . . . and the perfumed curls were brushing softly over his fingers . . . why, it was all a pretty scene" (48–49). In much the same way that snakes, according to some nineteenth-century writers, fascinate not with their glare but with the vapors they secrete, Yone and her beads catch and hold Rose with their "rich scents," entrancing him olfactorily.

Though the practices of enchanting through smell and magnetic attraction may seem peculiarly modern, all of the amber beads' methods of enchantment are intimately linked to the most ancient component of fascination: envy. Even as the story's practical techniques of fascination become less rooted in sight than in smell, their social and affective components remain unchanged, for jealousy and material inequality play a central role in the narrative. After all, the story begins when Yone is given the amber beads originally meant for Lu, and much of the story's action is driven by Yone's attempts to steal Rose from Lu "merely for the sake of conquering" (49). Such acquisitiveness seems particularly significant in light of the different socioeconomic positions of Yone and Lu, Yone being the legitimate heir to the Willoughby fortune and Lu an adopted cousin with few financial prospects.[17] The circulation in the story of both goods (such as the amber necklace) and bodies (particularly Rose) relies on a certain relation of inequality between Yone and Lu, an inequality that Yone, in her "splendid selfishness," continually and perversely works to exacerbate (39).

The role of envy in the story's relations of attraction and repulsion is nowhere more evident than at the Willoughbys' midsummer party, where Rose decisively shifts his attentions from Lu to Yone. When Yone goes for a stroll in the garden, she catches "a yellow gleam of amber" in one of the arbors—"Lu, of course," as she has borrowed Yone's beads for the evening—and realizes that Mr. Dudley, her unwanted suitor, is there with her, "bending low to catch her words, holding her hand in an irresistible pressure" (66). "Lu's kindness" being "too great to allow her to repel him angrily," she cannot escape the compromising situation, which Rose inevitably sees and misinterprets as a consensual lovers' rendezvous, a variation on Nordau's scene of "young lovers making for a sequestered forest nook": "Had Rose seen the pantomime? Without doubt. He had been seeking her, and he found her, he thought, in Mr. Dudley's arms." This is followed by a charged moment between Yone and Rose on the balcony, in which Yone, "swathed" in "clouds of delicious fragrance" and made "free and royal" by the "magnetic effect" of the moon, loses herself in Rose's gaze: "How long did my eyes swim on his? I cannot tell. He never stirred; still leaned there against the pillar, still looked down on me like a marble god . . . and still I knelt fascinated by that smile" (67). It is in this moment that the romantic link between Rose and Lu is severed and the one between Rose and Yone is forged.

This scene, of course, incorporates many familiar elements of both ancient and decadent fascination. The moon is described as "magnetic," and those heavy fragrances of which Yone is so fond again make an appearance. What is significant here, however, is the seemingly causal relationship between Rose's jealousy of Mr. Dudley and his connection with Yone; indeed, it is only when he sees Lu with another man that he turns his attention fully to Yone. Yone, usually the seductress, is then seduced by

Rose, who "fascinates" her, bewitching her as if with the evil eye. Jealousy is what drives both Yone's desire for Rose and Rose's desire for Yone, what enables each of them, in turn, to fascinate the other. Like the apotropaics of old, the amber beads both elicit and redirect envious attention, maintaining the material inequality between Yone and Lu while restructuring the affective relationships between Yone, Lu, and Rose.

In making the amber necklace central to the story's material and affective economies, Spofford thus draws on and modifies amber's historical association with fascination. Considered by the ancients to be an apotropaic substance, amber becomes for Spofford an agent of fascination itself, influencing those around it with its magnetic powers of attraction and its overwhelming scent. What appears to be an amulet meant to ward off the evil eye casts its own kind of malicious spell, attracting and repelling characters as if by magic. Perversely inverting the function of premodern amber, the necklace ornaments but also bewitches, figuring not as a protection against fascination but, like decadent ornament, a thing that itself fascinates.

This transformation of ornament from apotropaic to agent of fascination plays an important role in Spofford's particular brand of decadent style. When, as Dorri Beam points out, Spofford included "The Amber Gods" in her first collection of short stories, reviewers were largely critical of the book, accusing her of indulging her taste for ornate, stylized description at the expense of narrative (151–54). One reviewer in *Littel's Living Age* lauded a "certain splendor" in Spofford's descriptive language, marveling that "she writes, as it were, in oil colors," but claimed that "there is but little range in her command of character" (201). A reviewer for the *North American Review*—apocryphally a young Henry James—praised the "strength and brilliancy of her descriptions" but lamented that the "conception and evolution of her plots" were lacking (568–69). Her writing, claimed James in another review (this time of Spofford's 1864 novel *Azarian: An Episode*), epitomized "the ideal descriptive style" of Tennyson, a florid mode of writing that involved lush description and the "projection of one's fancy" onto the world (269). For Spofford's contemporary critics, the form of her stories overwhelmed their content in an unsettling way.

This decadent ornamentality unsettled critics precisely because of the way it seemed, like the amber gods themselves, capable of fascinating, of arresting both the reader's attention and the natural forward movement of narrative. For just as Yone perversely embraces her own beauty and the accessories with which she adorns it, so, too, did Spofford embrace a kind of lush style that, to borrow a phrase from Baudelaire, exposed her to "the hatred of the masses." In his review of *Azarian,* James pitted Spofford's "incoherent and meaningless" "word-pictures" against the measured descriptions of realistic fiction (270). She was, he claimed, largely a literary failure, as, instead of describing things (per the conventions of realism) "*only in so far as they bear upon the action,* and not in the least for themselves," she described "simply for the sake of describing" (273). Her descriptions, strung together like "beads on a leash," did nothing to further her stories' plots, and her elaborate style, uncannily like that of an amuletic necklace, halted her narratives' forward motion (270). And while the violence of his condemnation may have been idiosyncratic to James, he was not the only one to note a connection between Spofford's style and her ability to arrest motion, one reviewer writing that the "splendor of fancy . . . in the imaginative diction . . . of Miss Prescott's tales" gave them "a kind of fascination" ("Miss Prescott's Amber Gods" 201). For her contemporary audience, Spofford's perversely stylized writing resembled Yone's beads in that it was both ornamentally lovely and capable of fascinating, of halting the movement of the reader's mental eye.

It is the arresting nature of Spofford's style that, in the end, clarifies what is at stake in her particular engagement with amuletic aesthetics, what it means to Spofford for a person to be fascinated by ornament. At the end of the Willoughbys' May Day celebration, when Lu asks Yone, "Don't you think Rose a little altered . . . since he came home?" and Yone replies that "it's the amber . . . He's in a dream," Lu then asks, "What is it to be in a dream?" and Yone answers, "To lose thought of past or future" (65). In much the same way Spofford's descriptions disrupt the forward movement of her narratives, the amber, Yone suggests, has removed Rose from the proper flow of time, detaching him from both past and future, thrusting him into an eternal present. Like Spofford's readers, Rose loses his ability to orient himself temporally, overwhelmed by the amber's magical powers of attraction. This, in the end, is what it means to Spofford to fascinate: to freeze the flow of everyday time, to transport into the space of a dream. Reaching into the ancient past for the amuletic figure of amber and overlaying this figure with contemporary beliefs about animal magnetism, she erases "thought of past or future," suspending the reader's relationship with history. Much like Bergson's *durée réelle* or James's realm of immediate experience, Spofford's dream space allows for no intentional movement, no rational thought—only pure, sensual absorption in stylized ornament.

Charles Chesnutt's Black Magic: Toward a Decadent Regionalism

If Spofford, "a demure little Yankee girl," seems like an unlikely decadent, it would be almost absurd to suggest that Charles Chesnutt, a well-canonized Black regionalist, exhibits any affinity for the style (Bendixen ix). For if James Russel Lowell had a hard time believing Spofford was the author of her own works because, as Weir suggests, the artificiality of decadent writing was thought to be at odds with woman's natural affinity for the natural—her ability "to engender and sustain life"—decadence was thought to be even more incompatible with Blackness (*Decadence* 19). George Miller Beard, for example, believed that the overcivilized disease of neurasthenia appeared only in "the most 'advanced' races"; the nervous diseases of which decadent style was symptomatic, he claimed, "do not exist, or exist but very rarely among savages or semi-savages, or even among barbarians" (Weir, *Decadent Culture* 7; Beard, *American Nervousness* 188). This meant that while white people were extremely susceptible to the seductive perversities of decadence, there was "almost no insanity" among freed slaves, "no functional nervous disease or symptoms among them of any name or phase" (Beard, *American Nervousness* 189). To be Black and decadent was, for Beard, a contradiction in terms. Thus, while a writer like Chesnutt would have seemed at home to him in the genre of regionalism—a healthily rural, ostensibly unmodern genre—the overcivilized sensibility of decadence would have been beyond his grasp.

To abide by this logic, however, would be, on the one hand, to take the troublingly racist psychology of the nineteenth century at face value and, on the other, to ignore the contaminative power of decadence, its tendency to dissolve epistemic boundaries. It would be more productive, I think, to treat decadence, as Liz Constable, Matthew Potolsky, and Dennis Denisoff do, not as the static property of a particular historical moment or social class but as something more mobile, a kind of stylized, ironic, oppositional relation to mainstream aesthetics (12). Approaching decadence this way, we can detect its traces in a far broader array of texts than literary historians would typically have us believe, infiltrating, as it tends to do, genres with no overt investment in ornament or artifice. Regionalism, for example, might seem like the antithesis of decadent fiction: largely concerned with the quaint ordinariness of regional culture, its aura of rusticity is worlds away from the cosmopolitan perversities of "The Amber Gods." It does, however, lend itself surprisingly easily to decadent stylization. After all, it is a highly conventionalized genre, one ripe for the parodic contortions of decadent style. It also collapses the modern into the premodern in much the same way decadent writing does, offering an intensely civilized fantasy of the uncivilized, an artificially constructed image of the supposedly simple life. Keeping this in mind, I suggest that Chesnutt capitalized on regionalism's innate tendencies toward decadence, pushing the conventions of the genre to the point of dissolution in order to produce a kind of *decadent regionalism*. Perversely leaning into received regionalist tropes, he nurtured the genre's subversive potential for decadent stylization.

Being a Black writer concerned with issues of race, however, he turned not to the amuletic tradition of *fascina* but to the Black tradition of conjure, a set of beliefs and practices with roots in African animism. A kind of folk magic popular with slaves, conjure, Chesnutt believed, "grew, in the first place, out of African fetishism which was brought over from the dark continent along with the dark people"; it then mingled with elements of "Voodooism, or snake worship, a cult which seems to have been indigenous to tropical America," and "the witchcraft and ghost lore of the white man" as well as "the tricks and delusions of the Indian conjurer" ("Superstitions" 155). Much like the Gnostic amulets of the Greeks and Romans, conjure drew its power from religious and cultural syncretism, combining imported African beliefs with elements of Indian religion and European superstition—as well as "snake worship," that fascinating practice of which early American slave owners were so afraid—to create a new, uniquely African *American* brand of magic. By nature both fetishistic and syncretic, it figured, in the words of Richard Brodhead, as "a form of power available to the powerless in mortally intolerable situations," situations typically involving white violence and racial injustice (9).[18]

Because of its syncretic nature, conjure used practices commonly found in numerous folk traditions to achieve its ends. Like the ancients, believers in conjure thought that a malicious "look . . . could cast a spell" on an unwitting victim, and Old Aunt Harriet, the woman Chesnutt interviewed for his own expository writing on the subject, described how a conjure man once looked at her "wid' his evil eye," then sprained her ankle (Sundquist 366; Chesnutt, "Superstitions" 158). Another method of enchantment involved the administration of a "potion or poison." But the most common type of conjure involved assembling a bag or a ball "filled with secret ingredients" (variously called a "trick," a "mojo," a "toby," or a "hand"), then having a person do something particular with it, such as wear it on a specific part of the body (Sundquist 366). Chesnutt himself once bought a "hand" from a conjure man meant to "insure [him] good luck and 'keep [him] from losing [his] job,'" the practical instructions for which required it "to be wet with spirits nine mornings in succession, to be carried on the person, in a pocket on the right hand side, care being taken that it does not come in contact with any tobacco" ("Superstitions" 159). Such charms functioned as an economical class of amulet, and, while they may not have been cut from amber or coral, they largely served the same purpose as other forms of apotropaic jewelry.

These amulets were, of course, the subject of Chesnutt's conjure tales, a series of dialect stories written in an ironized version of the plantation tradition that thematized the power of magical objects.[19] These tales are filled with totemic charms and countercharms, talismans typically purchased from a "conjure woman" named Aunt Peggy that in many ways resemble Chesnutt's own good luck "hand."[20] Though several of the conjure tales involve actual magic, the one that makes the most striking use of an enchanting amulet does not; a story Eric Sundquist calls "one of Chesnutt's most disturbing and remarkable," "Dave's Neckliss" focuses, instead, on a kind of metaphorical conjure that has very literal consequences (378). It tells the story of Dave, a literate slave who falls in love with a woman named Dilsey. They start courting, and all seems to be going well until Wiley, a slave who "had be'n pesterin' Dilsey" before she took up with Dave, frames Dave for stealing a ham (127). As punishment, Dave's master and overseer, Mars Dugal' and Mars Walker, sentence Dave to wear a ham on a chain around his neck for six months. This causes Dilsey to leave Dave, driving him mad and instilling in him a belief that he himself is "turnin' ter a ham" (132). Even after the ham is removed, he ties a "lighterd-knot to a string" and wears it when no one else is around (131). In the end, Wiley is shot while stealing chickens from a neighboring plantation and confesses to framing Dave, but it is too late for anything to be done: Dave has already hanged himself in the smokehouse, joining all the other hams in the rafters "fer ter kyo" (134).

The most obvious achievement of "Dave's Neckliss," of course, is that it manages to literalize the figurative discourse of chattelism—a system that treats slaves as so much meat—and illustrate what happens when, in the words of Brodhead, a man "fiercely embraces the subhumanity an official degradation system assigns to him" (18).[21] I would like to argue, however, that the *way* the story makes this point—by taking up the image of an enchanted necklace, a ham that, at least figuratively, has amuletic powers—is just as important as the story's point itself. Indeed, I suggest that Chesnutt critically deploys fascinating ornament much like Spofford, using it to trouble and interrupt the flow of linear time, drawing his readers' attention toward the slaveholding past. In doing this, he is able to highlight the persistence of slavery's racial traumas in the present, the way the violence of the past continues to haunt the modern world.

As in "The Amber Gods," envy is perhaps the most conspicuous affect in "Dave's Neckliss." It is, after all, what binds the story's three main Black characters together. Wiley, "one er dese yer shiny-eyed, double-headed little niggers, sha'p ez a steel trap, en sly ez de fox w'at keep out'n it," "pester[s]"

Dilsey so much that, at one point, "she ha' ter th'eaten ter tell her marster fer ter make Wiley let her 'lone," and when "Wiley seed dat Dilsey had got ter thinkin' a heap 'bout Dave," he begins to plot against his rival: "W'ile he wuz laffin' en jokin' wid de yuther han's 'bout Dave en Dilsey, he wuz settin' a trap fer ter ketch Dave en git Dilsey back fer hisse'f" (127). In addition to giving Wiley the motive for "ketch[ing] Dave," envy gives him the means, too, as it is his theft of Mars Dugal's bacon and ham—luxuries inaccessible to enslaved people in everyday life—that he pins on Dave, provoking retribution on the part of their master. If envy in Spofford may seem perverse and unnecessary (perhaps even ornamental), envy in Chesnutt is a vital element of the social landscape. Faced with both a paucity of basic necessities (such as food) and their own commodification, Chesnutt's characters must treat each other as rivals in competition for limited resources or as objects of desire in themselves. Envy thus figures not only as an impetus for action in "Dave's Neckliss" but as a fundamental reality of slave life, a racially charged form of Nietzschean *ressentiment*.

The pernicious effect of this envy between slaves is compounded by the envy of the story's most conspicuous poor white: Mars Walker, the plantation's overseer. When the stolen ham turns up under Dave's floorboards, Mars Walker says "it wuz des ez he 'spected: he didn' b'lieve in dese yer readin' en prayin' niggers; it wuz all 'pocrisy, en sarve' Mars Dugal' right fer 'lowin' Dave ter be readin' books w'en it wuz 'g'in de law." It is then Mars Walker who, given permission by Mars Dugal' to "do des ez he wuz a mineter wid Dave," whips Dave and hangs the ham around his neck (128). As Brodhead points out, this sadistic punishment is rooted in Mars Walker's jealousy of Dave, a moral, literate Black man, and the story frames Walker as nothing more than "a lower-class white overseer envious of the slave's manifest superiority" (18). Even as Wiley's envy sets the story in motion, then, it is Mars Walker who, out of racist jealousy, devises and implements Dave's punishment. Like Nietzsche's fascinating Socrates, Wiley and Mars Walker transform their envy into a weapon, perversely forcing Dave to wear what would normally be considered a coveted luxury item—a ham—around his neck as punishment.

Strangely enough, the ham that Dave is forced to wear (and, later, the "lighterd knot" with which Dave replaces it) seems itself to take on magical properties, appearing in the story—much like Yone's necklace—as a kind of spoiled amulet. When Dilsey first encounters Dave after he has begun to wear the ham, she mockingly asks him if it is "a cha'm fer ter keep off witches," then shuns him (130). This is the beginning of the end for Dave, for, just like a "hand," the ham begins to affect all aspects of his life, giving him "fum dat time . . . nuffin but trouble" (128). He loses everything he holds dear: his lover, his social status, his permission to read and preach, and eventually his sanity and life. The ham, working like one of Aunt Peggy's conjured artifacts, bewitches Dave. It turns him from a person into a thing, figuratively transforming him into a ham and literally transforming him into a corpse.

These transformations may simply seem to function according to the logic of conjure, but it is significant that the particular kind of conjure presented in this story is linked, as in Spofford, to a necklace, an enchanted piece of ornament. The story's title, after all, highlights the ham's status as a kind of jewelry, and Dilsey, in addition to likening the ham to a "cha'm," asks Dave if it's "a noo kine er neckliss [he] got." The other slaves also mock Dave by asking him, "W'at yer take fer yo' neckliss, Dave?" (130). Even Dave's method of suicide involves the donning of a kind of necklace—a noose—and, while the image of his body hanging from the smokehouse rafters invokes the specter of lynching, it also transforms Dave's body into a kind of pendant, perversely equating, as one critics points out, "a black man hanging from a noose to a type of adornment" (Harding 241).[22] Not only do Wiley and Mars Walker conjure Dave, then, but they conjure Dave *with jewelry:* in a parody of white decadence, he is forced to ornament himself. But rather than enhance his social status, this ornamentation prompts and signifies his abjection, relegating him, like the rotting ham at his throat, to the world of objects.

Just as in "The Amber Gods," then, ornament, when combined with envy, becomes an agent of malicious enchantment. Dave's transformation into an object is spurred by the jealousy of Wiley and Mars Walker, and it is effected through compulsory contact with an amuletic necklace. In "Dave's Neckliss," however, both the motive behind and the means of enchantment are rooted in the institution of chattel slavery, a system that, in the first place, treats certain human beings like objects; in the second, fosters relations of envy; and, in the third, restricts the practice of personal adornment—which requires a certain amount of social and financial capital—to the white ruling class. While both Spofford and Chesnutt align the power to enchant with a position of socioeconomic power, then, the key difference is that Spofford's characters adorn themselves and Dave is adorned by his white masters, his body both ornamented and treated as a kind of ornament.

But while whites may seem to have a monopoly on magical ornament in the conjure tale proper, the story's frame narrative opens up space for a more subversive kind of enchantment. For critics tend to read the storytelling practice of Julius, the former slave who narrates the conjure tales, as itself a kind of conjure, a performance that entrances his white listeners, John and Annie, in order to achieve some ulterior objective (such as, in "Dave's Neckliss," securing a Sunday ham).[23] The magic of Julius's stories is more than mere sleight of hand; indeed, it exerts a kind of power over John and Annie—as well as the largely white readership of Chesnutt's stories— that rivals that of Yone's amber beads or Spofford's lush style. Absorbing the attention of John and Annie, who, according to one critic, are meant to be "proxies for [the conjure tales'] readers," the stories produce "a sense of being transported into the tale and disconnected from the world." This is at least in part due to the fact that they are written in dialect, which forces readers to abandon their usual reading practices and "slow down as they sound out the words," perhaps even causing them to "feel arrested as the story unfolds" (Harding 232). Much like Spofford, then, Chesnutt imbues his stories with the power to trouble narrative temporality, slowing his readers down by forcing them to engage with the orality of his diction. If enchantment is the property of whites in the conjure tale portion of "Dave's Neckliss," the story's frame bestows this power on Julius as well, as his highly stylized mode of speaking has the ability to fascinate white auditors, to transport and arrest those who hear him speak.

The fascinating power of Julius's dialect is emblematic of the conjure tales' power more generally, as they are, in the end, largely significant not for their content but for their style. After all, the genre of plantation fiction is highly conventionalized, and what makes each iteration of southern regionalism unique is not so much the content of the story it tells but the way in which this story is told. Even as, in the frame tale to "Sis' Becky's Pickaninny," Annie tells John that the fantastical elements of the story "are mere ornamental details and not at all essential" to the emotional realism of the tale, it was precisely these ornamental details that so appealed to Chesnutt's contemporary readers (92). For, as a number of critics point out, it was "an arm's length fascination with the exoticism of magic" that drew many whites to the "world of black folklore," making Chesnutt's conjure tales "palatable to members of a white reading public who might otherwise have responded with hostility to literature that was openly critical of slavery or of continuing racial inequality" (Murray 48; Minnick 85).

Chesnutt's writing, then, poses a problem for Beard's position that Blackness and decadence are incompatible, as its decadence actually arises from its embrace of those fantastical elements thought to be uniquely Black. In fact, while Spofford was criticized for her perverse love of ornament, Chesnutt's dialect stories were enthusiastically championed by such literary tastemakers as William Dean Howells, who, in a 1900 review of Chesnutt's first two collections, *The Wife of His Youth* and *The Conjure Woman*, praised them as "the creation of sincere and original imagination," "full of wild, indigenous poetry": "Whether Mr. Chesnutt invented their motives, or found them, as he feigns, among his distant cousins of the Southern cabins . . . the wonder of their beauty is the same; and whatever is primitive and sylvan or campestral in the reader's heart is touched by the spells thrown on the simple black lives in these enchanting tales" ("Mr. Charles"). This was in part due to the fact that, while the turn to mysticism by white authors such as Spofford was seen as decadent, the use of magic in stories by and about Black people was seen as natural, the result of an innate predisposition toward superstition. After all, superstition was a central element of Reconstruction ideologies of Black inferiority, for, as David Murray puts it, white people needed to "believe that African Americans believed"—that Black people were by nature irrational and credulous—in order to justify a pervasive system of racial exclusion and subjugation (50). In truly decadent fashion, then, Chesnutt embraced this ideology in his conjure tales, perversely working and reworking the trope of Black credulity to the point of dissolution, turning a racist construction of Blackness toward antiracist ends. Chesnutt's style is thus in some ways even more decadent than Spofford's, for while readers were able to identify and inoculate themselves against the decadent elements of Spofford's writing, Chesnutt infiltrated the mainstream literary establishment, contaminating the seemingly innocuous genre of regionalism with a critique of its racialized representational practices. More parodic, more subversive, and more effective at destabilizing aesthetic convention than Spofford, Chesnutt transformed the very thing meant to exclude him from the world of decadent style—his Blackness—into the driving force behind his brand of decadent regionalism.

Decadence, Racialized Objecthood, and the Posthuman Turn

Such a reading of Chesnutt is, I know, unconventional, as its central thesis—that Chesnutt's writing posits and relies upon a link between Blackness and decadence—runs contrary to conventional understandings of both Chesnutt's corpus and the literary history of decadence. It is, however, in surprising consonance with recent work in critical race studies, particularly critiques of liberal humanism that turn, as "Dave's Neckliss" does, on the historical construction of white people as rational subjects and Black people as "irrational/subrational Human Other[s]" (Wynter 264). For an increasing number of critical race theorists have embraced posthumanism, arguing that, insofar as the framework of humanism relies upon a "disavow[al]" of "the very possibility of black subjectivity," a fundamental belief that any "movement toward blackness" is also a "movement toward the nonhuman," it has outlived its philosophical usefulness (Reid-Pharr 8; Jackson 217). Indeed, they might be said to follow Chesnutt's critique of racism to its logical conclusion: if humanist thought has, throughout Western history, consistently treated Black people as objects rather than human subjects, its illusory promises of freedom and equality have little to offer people of color.

For many of these scholars, it is thus the historical exclusion of Black people from the category of the human that actually equips them to critique humanist thought and "imagin[e] humanity otherwise" (Nyong'o 25). Rejecting humanism's fixation on subjectivity, these thinkers have worked to theorize humanity and agency not by reclaiming the language of subjectivity but by celebrating the sensate body and its social, cultural, and ecological imbrications.[24] Like Chesnutt, these scholars lean into the historical elision of Blackness with inhumanity, transforming it from a technique of oppression into a critical resource, a tool of philosophical innovation. In other words, they decadently stylize humanism's racist foreclosure of Black subjectivity into a tool of antiracist critique, extending agency and value to bodies that have historically been treated as objects.

This kind of decadent, racialized posthumanism animates the work of non-Black critical race theorists as well. It is, for example, integral to the work of Anne Anlin Cheng, whose tellingly titled *Ornamentalism* deals not with Blackness but with the figure of "the yellow woman." For Cheng, the essence of the yellow woman lies in her status as an inorganic, aesthetic thing: more art object than human, she is "so suffused with representation that she is invisible, so encrusted by aesthetic expectations that she need not be present to generate affect." Because her vulnerability to "denigration and violence . . . peculiarly and insistently speaks through the language of aesthetic privilege," her "objectification is often the very hope for any claims she might have to value or personhood" (xi). This means that, in order simply to survive, the yellow woman must perversely embrace a kind of "ornamental personhood," engaging in "a defiance of objectification that results in more objectness" (3, 24). Cheng thus attributes a certain critical power to the yellow woman's status as a thing: valued not for her humanity but for her inhuman loveliness, she "troubles some of our deeply held, politically cherished notions of agency, racial embodiment, subjecthood, and ontology" (1).

Such an approach to personhood is, of course, deeply decadent, offering, as it does, an aestheticized account of value and agency that moves beyond the subject-object binary. Indeed, such an account would have appealed to both Chesnutt and Spofford, as Chesnutt explicitly depicts Dave as an ornamental person and "The Amber Gods" contains its own example of yellow womanhood: Little Asian, the original owner of Yone's amber necklace. As we have already thoroughly examined the ornamentality of Dave, I would like us to turn for a moment to Little Asian. Variously described as "exotic," "untamable," and "wilder than the wind," Little Asian is often treated by critics as a figure of primitivist fantasy, the embodiment of nineteenth-century beliefs about the savagery of nonwhite peoples (Logan 38; Ellis 261; Spofford, "Amber Gods" 43). This understanding, however, glosses over the fact that Little Asian, like everything else in "The Amber Gods," is highly aestheticized: when she escapes from Captain Willoughby and washes ashore in Fiesole, for example, it is her picturesqueness that allows her to make a living. Working for Yone's mother as a "mysterious tame servant," "she never grew; at ninety she was of the height of a yardstick,—and nothing could have been finer than to have a dwarf in those old palaces, you know" (44). While she may be seen by white readers as exotic and savage, it is precisely this exoticism and savagery that make her aesthetically desirable in the story, a "fine" ornament for "those old palaces." This condition, of course, is more or less that of Cheng's yellow woman: valued not for her humanity but for her potential as a decoration, Little Asian transforms her illegibility as a human subject into a tool of self-preservation.

While many critics draw analogical connections between Yone and the amber beads, then, it might make more sense to foreground the beads' similarities to Little Asian, an ornamental person if there ever was one. For much like amber, Little Asian is presented as a functionally useless (but nonetheless valuable) aesthetic object: unwilling or unable to perform the slave labor demanded of her by the Willoughby family, she finds a place for herself as a decorative fixture in an old palace. This functional uselessness, moreover, seems to be linked to her capacity for enchantment: though she may be an ineffective housekeeper, she is more than capable of magically "drowning . . . her capturers" en route to New Holland, and, "if there could have been such a thing as a witch," she seems to fit the bill (44). Indeed, the story depicts Little Asian herself as a kind of "hideous, tiny, heathen god," a thoroughly inhuman figure with supernatural powers of enchantment (40). Both grotesquely ornamental and magically gifted, she embodies not only the ornamental personhood of the yellow woman but also the amuletic agency of decadent style.

Race, Decadence, Fascination, Time

It would seem, then, that race has more to do with the aesthetics of decadence than many literary critics would have us believe. In light of this revelation, I suggest that we revise the way we think about decadent style in two significant ways. The first concerns the definitional parameters of decadentism. For, contrary to conventional critical wisdom (which posits decadent style as a distinctly white, male aesthetic), Spofford and Chesnutt show us that American decadentism is, in large part, rooted in the historical abjection and objectification of nonwhite bodies. Chesnutt, we have seen, decadently stylizes his own Blackness (and its attendant connotations of irrationality and credulity) in order to critique postwar American race relations. Bringing the hypercivilized techniques of decadent style to bear on the seemingly less-than-modern genre of southern regionalism, he uses irony and ornament to push back against the degrading depictions of Blackness that animate the genre. And though Spofford is perhaps more interested in "min[ing] the possibilities of gorgeous or ornamental style for a woman writer," "perversely developing its potential as a feminist aesthetic," she also attributes a disruptive, decadent potential to the racialized body, investing Little Asian with a certain enchanting, aestheticized agency (Beam 134). Indeed, if decadent fiction takes primitive magic and artifice as two of its privileged themes, it seems almost inevitable that it should end up thematizing the objectification of people of color.

My second proposed revision has to do with the temporality of decadence. As we have seen, both Spofford and Chesnutt use the amuletic aesthetics of decadent style to disrupt the flow of linear time, blurring the boundaries between the modern present and premodern past. They approach this project, however, in racially distinct ways. Spofford, after all, aims to pluck readers out of the flow of modern time and thrust them into a dream space: disrupting time almost for the sake of disrupting it, she seeks to return her readers to an atemporal state of immediate experience. Chesnutt, on the other hand, highlights the artificiality of plantation fiction in order to shake his readership free of its soporific hold: challenging the genre's easy elision of whiteness with civilization and Blackness with barbarism, he draws his readers' attention to the slaveholding past in order to "excavate," as Kara Keeling might put it, a more equitable "future" (41). Using fascinating ornament to disrupt the temporality of everyday life, Spofford and Chesnutt lead their readers into and out of dreamlike trances, alternately inducing and dissolving experiential states that resist the logic of linear time.

We might understand this, in the end, as the essential power of decadent writing: to disrupt, however temporarily, the forward flow of time, to gum up the machinery of narrative and historical progress. It is the power to captivate and immobilize, to entrance readers in the same way the spoiled amulets of Spofford and Chesnutt entrance the characters with whom they come into contact. Put simply: it is the power to fascinate and, in so doing, to trouble the boundary between the present and the past, the civilized and the barbarian. It is to show how these categories meet, commingle, and melt into one another, how they are always in danger of renegotiation and collapse.

3

Gesture, the Actress, and Naturalist Fiction

"PEOPLE IN GENERAL ATTACH too much importance to words," writes
Theodore Dreiser in *Sister Carrie* (1900): "They are under the illusion that
talking effects great results. As a matter of fact, words are, as a rule, the
shallowest portion of all the argument . . . When the distraction of the
tongue is removed, the heart listens" (109). Language, he suggests, is woe-
fully unexpressive. It is not what a person says that has the power to move
the heart; it is, rather, what one does—the manner in which one says what
one says, the gestures, both literal and figurative, that accompany this say-
ing. Indeed, for Dreiser, gesture—particularly theatrical gesture—holds a
power to charm audiences that words do not, an ability to touch the heart
and make it listen.

This is perhaps because, as some performance studies scholars suggest, "the power of gestures like music and dance . . . can overwhelm
audiences with the rhythms and emotions of enchantment": when engaged by gesture in a theatrical space, "we tap our feet and clap our hands,
and we become complicit in the rhetoric of the event" (Symonds and Taylor, "Performativity" 163). Gesture moves us in an intimate, physical way,
transgressing the boundary between performer and audience, "bleeding
across/through embodied identities": "the audience is affected physically
by the encounter," transformed from a collection of "objective observers"
into active participants in the show (Symonds and Taylor, "Singing" 6).
Such a transformation is made possible by the unique position gesture
occupies between expressive and mechanistic movement. If, on the one
hand, gesture can be understood as an index of "the presence and inten-

tionality of an individual human subject," it is also, on the other, the product of a careful coordination of biological and physiological processes, the
result of "humans act[ing] like machines" (Noland xi, xxiv). Gesture is
thus both produced and experienced at the point where mind and matter
meet, arising from a performer's kinetic sense of embodiment and affecting spectators through their own bodies, their tapping feet and clapping
hands. Moving between bodies like an electrical charge, it collapses the
space between performer and audience, enacting, to borrow a phrase from
classical and patristic thought, a kind of "action at a distance."

It is this kind of action that lies at the heart of much naturalist writing,
for, whereas decadent fiction located fascination in the amuletic powers
of ornament, naturalist fiction locates it in the power of movement, particularly the entrancing movement of actresses whose bodies "hide . . .
nothing and yet never show . . . —or 'say . . .'—everything" (McCarren,
Dance 11). We might, of course, turn to any number of naturalist texts to
explore this phenomenon. In Frank Norris's *The Pit* (1903), for example,
Curtis Jadwin finds himself "carried away" by the theatrical performances
of his wife, Laura, who, if Jadwin "hadn't made [her] love [him] enough
to be [his] wife . . . would have been a great actress"; in Stephen Crane's
Maggie: A Girl of the Streets (1893), the eponymous Maggie finds herself
"lost" in the music hall performances to which her lover Pete takes her,
the glamour of the stage blotting out all "thoughts of the atmosphere of
the collar and cuff factory" where she spends most of her days (Norris
272; Crane 60, 63). In this chapter, however, I would like to focus on two
novels that engage with the fascinating movement of actresses in particularly explicit and extensive ways. Reading Theodore Dreiser's *Sister Carrie*
and Paul Laurence Dunbar's *The Sport of the Gods* (1902) alongside turn-
of-the-century writings on hypnotism, New Thought, and theater, I argue
that, on the one hand, the superhuman "forces" of naturalist fiction are
often rendered as forces of fascination, and, on the other, the naturalist
actress is capable of using theatrical gesture to harness these forces for
her own survival and social advancement. The shape taken by the actress's
gestures, however, is racially dictated, and while Carrie (in *Sister Carrie*) is
encouraged to cultivate "grace" in her movements, Kitty (in *The Sport of the*

Gods) must come to embrace a very different gestural aesthetic. Not only, I suggest, do these racially distinct brands of gesture help us to understand the form of the naturalist novel itself (as its peripatetic structure mirrors the movements of its theatrical protagonists); they also illuminate the implicitly racializing logic of much recent feminist new materialist work on the power of movement. Ultimately, I show that, while the figure of the actress may seem, in the words of *Sister Carrie*, to be a "waif amid forces," she is actually capable of channeling these forces, using them to influence lovers, audiences, readers, and even contemporary critical theorists (3).

Fascination's Theatricality

When it first landed on American shores in the 1830s, practical fascination was already associated with theatricality. Charles Poyen, after all, only managed to gain a following by performing public "experiments," those dramatic demonstrations of induced somnambulism for which he was best known (*Progress* 44–45). These experiments were largely so popular because, as Robert C. Fuller points out, they were "great theater," appealing more to audiences' appetites for sensation and novelty than to any real sense of intellectual curiosity (18).[1] This was, in fact, the root of the most common criticism of animal magnetism: if, in order to reach larger audiences, even earnest mesmerists theatricalized their work, how was one to tell the difference between scientific demonstrations and shows put on by greedy charlatans? How was one to differentiate actual somnambulism from excellent acting, to identify what was reality and what was performance? These were concerns of which mesmerists were acutely aware. Poyen, for example, went to great lengths in *Progress of Animal Magnetism* to prove that the subjects with whom he worked were not fakers, including at least one eyewitness account of a demonstration that "was too well done to have been counterfeited, unless, indeed, [the subject] is a most accomplished actress" (87). He also devoted an entire chapter (and several testimonials) to the honesty and virtue of Cynthia Gleason, his favorite somnambulist, in hopes of debunking the idea that her abilities were part of some "concerted plan" (116). Faced with concerns about the artificiality of their public mesmeric experiments, Poyen and his followers explicitly tried to separate their work from that of entertainers, painting their subjects as either too moral or too unskilled to be actors. Simultaneously appealing to their audiences' tastes for dramatic spectacle and disavowing their own subjects' theatrical abilities, mesmerists relied on the language and conventions of performance to secure their standing in antebellum society.

This proclivity for theatrics played an important role in the work of hypnotists as well. Indeed, Jean-Martin Charcot—hypnotism's most internationally famous popularizer—was perhaps best known for the biweekly demonstrations he held at the Salpêtrière, spectacular lectures during which he exhibited hysterically hypnotized patients to a curious public.[2] These performances were in many ways even more dramatic than those of his mesmeric predecessors.[3] In the first place, they took place in a medical theater built to accommodate up to "five hundred spectators," and the performances' natural drama was heightened by "stage lighting" and "the use of photographic slides" (M. Evans xii; Gauld 307). In the second place, Charcot's subjects themselves behaved or were made to behave in decidedly theatrical ways. Hysterics had long been thought to be naturally theatrical, prone to deception and imitation; Charcot found no reason to contradict this medical common sense.[4] His demonstrations thus often entailed the manipulation of (generally attractive and female) patients' bodies into "exceedingly realistic"—"not to say dramatic"—poses of passionate emotional expression, "the erotics of display permeat[ing] and finally trump[ing]" his "positivist principles of observation" (Gauld 312; M. Evans xii). This practice of display ultimately spoke to and attracted more theater-minded audiences than medically minded ones, and Charcot found himself lecturing to the likes of Henri de Toulouse-Lautrec and Sarah Bernhardt.[5] While Poyen's itinerant life required that he hold demonstrations in lecture halls and private parlors, Charcot's institutional security offered him a highly public space to perform. Blurring the distinction between the medical theater and the popular stage, he and his somnambulists entertained just as much as they educated.

Charcot's work was internationally influential; indeed, at the same time that he was performing before rapt French audiences, George Miller

Beard (the preeminent American investigator of hypnotism) was following his lead and putting on his own hypnotic shows.[6] As we saw in chapter
1, Beard regularly held demonstrations that replicated the classic feats of
mesmerists, paralyzing and anaesthetizing subjects, pricking them with
pins and making them inhale ammonia—in short, offering what one reviewer called a series of "ludicrous and amusing episodes" ("Science of
Trance" 2). Perhaps unsurprisingly, then, he also faced many of the old
accusations leveled against mesmerists regarding fakery and collusion.[7]
(In fact, he even took a page out of Poyen's book in his 1882 tract on hypnosis, *The Study of Trance, Muscle-Reading, and Allied Nervous Phenomena
in Europe and America*, in which he shared a letter on "the moral character
of trance subjects" [36–40]). What differentiated Beard's performances
from those of Poyen, however, was their marked fashionableness: whereas
accounts of Poyen's demonstrations generally appeared in periodicals such
as the *Providence Daily Journal* and the *Pawtucket Chronicle*, write-ups of
Beard's were to be found in the society pages of the *New York Times*. This
resulted in hypnotism becoming a favorite practice at high-class parties,
where "dignified old men and ladies" were made to act out scenes from
their childhood, the "entertainment" of which stemmed from the fact that
"the action [was] as incongruous as possible with the age and position"
of the hypnotized subjects. This practice was for a time so popular that it
actually afforded certain members of the lower class—people who made
a living as professional hypnotic subjects—access to elite social events,
receiving for their appearance "a trifling compensation for their services"
and, more importantly, "the satisfaction of appearing in full evening dress
in circles of society ordinarily closed to them" ("Mesmerism in Society"
2). While Beard's hypnotic performances may not have been as drama-
turgical as Charcot's, Americans, like the French, often sought them out
not for their scientific value but for their value as a form of spectacular
entertainment.

Unsurprisingly, then, it was with open arms that, in 1907, Pierre Janet,
one of Charcot's former students, was greeted at Harvard, where he had
been invited to deliver a series of lectures on hysteria. Like Beard, Janet
believed that the hypnotic state was not fundamentally different from

states of spontaneous somnambulism; it was simply a manifestation of natural trance "obtained artificially" (115).[8] And like Charcot, he largely attributed both natural somnambulism and the ability to be hypnotized to a hysterical disposition (114–16). Both, he suggested, were precipitated by a "contraction" or "retraction of the field of consciousness," a pathological absentmindedness that was "not inattention" but "a suppression of all that is not looked at directly," a fixing of attention on one idea or image to the exclusion of all others (298).[9] In making this claim, he revised Charcot's theory of trance in a small but significant way: rather than treat hysteria as an underlying cause and hypnotizability as a symptom, he treated both hysteria and hypnotic trance as products of a more primordial disorder of attention, a primary tendency to be fascinated. When, then, he imported Charcot's ideas about hysteria to the United States, he foregrounded not the disease's ability to manifest spontaneously but its connection to forms of transitively induced trance.

Though Janet may have placed more emphasis than Charcot did on the role of fascination in hysteria, he retained Charcot's conviction that there was an intimate relationship between the disease and dramatic performance. For his first illustrative example of somnambulism, he turned not to the medical literature but to Shakespeare, quoting the famous scene in *Macbeth* in which Lady Macbeth's guilt causes her to sleepwalk (24–26). This example was followed by a series of case studies that Janet inflected with the language of performance. In one particular study, he described how a girl, upon witnessing the "very moving and dramatic"—one might even say "melodramatic"—death of her mother, began to have regular hysterical fits (29). During these fits, she "acted again all the events that took place at her mother's death": "The crises last for hours, and they show a splendid dramatic performance, for no actress could rehearse those lugubrious scenes with such perfection" (30). The girl "poses, and wears on her face expressions really worthy of admiration," and "when, in her drama, death has taken place, she carries on the same idea, and makes everything ready for her own suicide" (31, 30). Upon finishing, "she soon gets up and begins acting over again one of the preceding scenes" (31). For Janet, such behavior resembled a rehearsed performance: "The development of the somnambulic delirium is not only intense, it is also perfectly regular. The patient repeats the same words at the same moments, makes the same gestures at the same place, every time [she] begins [her] performance over again" (33). He thus explicitly theorized hysteria as a kind of theater, one complete with melodramatic narratives, expressive gestures, and regular rehearsals. Combining Charcot's understanding of hysterical theatrics with his own novel theory of contracted consciousness, Janet blurred the boundaries between trance and performance.

Such a tendency to equate somnambulism with acting was not the unique property of the Harvard lecture hall or the fashionable New York party, of course; it also permeated the realm of popular psychology. William Walker Atkinson (whom we will remember from chapter 1) built his entire system of "mental magic" around this idea, basing his various regimens of auto-suggestive self-improvement on the idea that miming the external expressions of a desired mental state—"acting" or "throwing yourself into the part"—could actually cause this state to manifest internally (*Secret* 102–3, 219).[10] According to his book *The Secret of Mental Magic* (which was equal parts self-help manual and treatise on parapsychology), "Physical Action produces Mental States": "I defy anyone to manifest the physical actions of any particular emotion or feeling, earnestly and actively, for a short time, without the corresponding mental state actually manifesting itself" (219–20). This assertion was, on the one hand, made possible by the work of Charcot, who found that, if you "put the limbs or hands or fingers of . . . a [cataleptic] patient into an attitude suggestive of such and such an emotion or state of mind," "she will at once assume the whole posture and expression of someone in that state of mind" (Gauld 312).[11] On the other hand, it was deeply influenced by William James's writings on movement and emotion; indeed, Atkinson often incorporated these writings into his own work verbatim, quoting, for example, the claim made in *The Principles of Psychology* that "if we wish to conquer undesirable emotional tendencies in ourselves we must assiduously, and in the first instance cold-bloodedly, go through the outward movements of those contrary dispositions which we wish to cultivate" (qtd. in *Secret* 223).[12] Drawing on the scientific work of Charcot and James, Atkinson refashioned it into a system of self-improvement for lay audiences, selectively using psychological research on trance, suggestion, movement, and emotion to offer practical methods for, say, improving one's confidence in business meetings. Capitalizing on the conventional association of entrancement with dramatic gesture, he offered up playacting as a powerful form of auto-suggestion that could reshape and regulate one's psychic life.

If acting indeed represented a kind of autohypnosis, professional ac-tors, Atkinson reasoned, should be particularly skilled at entrancing both themselves and others. In *Mental Fascination,* his "side-light" to *The Secret of Mental Magic,* he claimed that those with an "artistic temperament" were particularly susceptible to fascination, and talented actors and orators with strong wills could make themselves "become very 'impressionable' by rea-son of their active imaginations," "allow[ing] themselves to be so carried away with the idea of being impressed that they would 'throw themselves into the part' of the mesmerized subject, and *actually mesmerize themselves*" (62). This also allowed them to exert a certain fascinating power over their audiences, for "'play-acting' is all a form of suggestion," and the actor "who possesses the faculty of throwing 'expression' and 'feeling' into his words, actions and manner" could "charm" his audiences by "inducing a sympa-thetic rhythm of feeling and emotion" in them (*Secret* 77). Consequently, Atkinson claimed, there was a certain amount of overlap between "horses," or those who worked as professional trance subjects, and professional ac-tors, as some horses eventually "graduate into the cheaper grade of variety actors, and a few mount even higher up and develop genuine talent as ac-tors" (*Mental Fascination* 139). For Atkinson, playacting had the power to fascinate both the self and others, and the ability to be fascinated actually improved a person's acting abilities. He thus reframed the conventional association between trance and theatricality: not only was it the case that trance subjects behaved, as Charcot and Janet asserted, in theatrical ways, but theatrical subjects also behaved in entrancing ways, using the power of performance to hypnotize themselves and their audiences.

This figural slippage informed Atkinson's more general understanding of aesthetic experience, the power of which he equated with the power of suggestion. Music and literature, he claimed, might "lift you out of yourself on the wings of Fancy," but "more marked than any of the abovementioned cases, is the effect of a perfect stage performance, in which the world and characters of the play take such a hold upon you as to seem reality itself, and you laugh and cry with the characters in the play" (*Mental Fascination* 129). This was the result of what Atkinson called "induced imagination," a phenomenon in which an actor used his own creative powers (or his "Positive Imagination") to activate his audience's faculty of fancy (or "Negative Imagination"), contagiously inducing in them a desired mental state (129–30). Such a manipulation of imagination was particularly effective when it came to "hyper-impressionables," people in whom "a highly developed faculty of Fancy" combined with a propensity for imitation and a "decidedly hysterical tendency" (131–33). These traits made hyper-impressionables both excellent audience members—more easily affected, as they were, by theatrical performance than their less impressionable counterparts—and excellent trance subjects. Theater and fascination, then, worked for Atkinson in precisely the same way and affected precisely the same kind of person: both theatrical performances and public demonstrations of hypnotism moved their audiences through the power of suggestion, using carefully choreographed gestures to induce particular mental states.

By the turn of the twentieth century, the popular belief that fascination was innately theatrical had morphed into a belief that theater was innately fascinating. Though the public demonstrations of Poyen, Charcot, and Beard may have been spectacular in their own ways, it was Atkinson who pushed the equation of somnambulism with theatrical gesture to its logical conclusion. If the hypnotic subject was by nature dramatic, he suggested, the dramatic subject might also be by nature hypnotic, for, if she was talented, she could use the suggestive power of "'acting out' the part" to fascinate both herself and her audience (63). What was once conceived as an uncontrollable symptom of hysterical trance, then, became, for Atkinson, an agential behavior, an artistic technique that actors could employ to heighten the reality of their performances.

Fascinating Theatrics

Atkinson was not alone in identifying a connection between fascination and actual theatrical performance; in fact, much of the popular and professional discourse surrounding theater at the turn of the century explicitly linked performance to entrancement. In France, where Charcot's work was most influential, a number of female performers made names for themselves as "artiste[s] inconsciente[s]," or "trance dancers," marketing the strange gestures they produced under the influence of hypnosis as a form of theatrical art (Carroy 95; J. Marshall 6, 164). The French, however, were not the only ones to transpose the techniques of fascination from the medical theater to the popular one; indeed, as Joseph Roach notes, the language of auto-suggestion and hypnotism appeared in theoretical and critical accounts of performance across Europe.[13] In the United States, where trance had always been more closely associated with entertainment and spectacle than with institutional science, hypnotism and performance were linked in a particularly intimate way. Loie Fuller, for example—the American pioneer of modern dance—stumbled across the movements of her signature "serpentine dance" while playing the part of a hypnotized subject in an 1890 music hall production, and, by the 1910s, hypnotism had firmly become "associated in the minds of many" not with experimental psychology but with "the vaudeville stage" ("Hypnotism" 332).[14] Scientific and pseudoscientific assertions that trance had an essential relationship with theatricality were more than mere instances of figurative language: they represented a very literal approach to the psychology of performance that both described and influenced the work of turn-of-the-century entertainers.

While some performers overtly borrowed from the language and techniques of hypnotism, even those who did not were often described in the language of fascination. This was particularly true of actresses, for, as we have already seen, it was women who were most often associated with theatrical trance states. Amy Leslie's 1906 guide to the world of popular actresses, *Some Players: Personal Sketches,* for example, described the famous

Mrs. Fiske as a "small eerie priestess" with "witch-like eyes," whose "charm of the most intangible quality" was her "greatest weapon of attack . . . in her capture of an audience" (114, 115, 106). Helena Modjeska was described, too, as a kind of "Druid priestess" "ris[ing] out of the hurry and turmoil of modernity"; her portrayal of Shakespeare's Juliet was praised by another critic for the "delightful and fascinating qualities" with which her person infused it (Leslie 1; Strang 1:217). The actress most frequently described as supernaturally bewitching, however, was Sarah Bernhardt, who completed several American tours around the turn of the century. Endowed, according to one critic, with a "great personal magnetism" with which "she mesmerized her audiences," she was regularly described in terms of enchantment, Leslie, for example, calling everything from her face to "the bend in the instep of her foot" "fascinating" (B. Hewitt 44; Leslie 150, 153, 156). While some performers intentionally incorporated elements of trance into their artistic practice, others were perceived as entrancing whether they aimed to be or not. For many, actresses seemed to exert an inexplicable power over their audiences, charming like witches, "inscrutable and fascinating" (Leslie 150).

This fascination was intimately connected to the power of theatrical gesture. After all, many of the most popular actresses in the late nineteenth century did not speak English as a first language or even at all. Modjeska, for example, delivered her lines with a thick Polish accent; Bernhardt always performed in French. What they said onstage, however, was significantly less important to audiences than how they said it, for, as Felicia Hardison Londré and Daniel J. Watermeier point out, "their frequently emotionally charged performance styles, rich in expressive gesture and movement, generally transcended the language barrier" (212). Leslie, in fact, claimed that Modjeska, traveling abroad, was once asked by a group of "Brittany shepherds" to recite something in "American" for them, and, having no monologue at the ready, she astounded her audience by dramatically counting to one hundred: "She had solved the problem of gesture and punctuation completely. It was these the peasants applauded and enjoyed, rather than the eloquent words and phrases, or even sentiment" (160). Bernhardt had a similar effect on her American audiences, for, though she never performed in English, she was, in the words of Leslie, "a creature of utterance. Every sensitive nerve, every vein, every muscle in her composition speaks. Her foot, her hand, her lips, neck and back, all express" (166). She was "magnificently theatrical," captivating her fans with a "skillfully controlled voice" and "artfully designed movement," not with the content of the lines she delivered (B. Hewitt 44). Indeed, Modjeska and Bernhardt fascinated their audiences not despite their limited English but because of it: rather than reduce their appeal, it invested their gestures with an almost hypnotic power, a power that evoked desires and emotions in their audiences through purely kinetic means.

This understanding of theatrical gesture was, of course, connected to contemporaneous work on the science of aesthetic experience, particularly the relationship between movement and emotion. In France, Charles Henry's 1885 *Introduction à une esthétique scientifique* had already attempted to offer a physiological explanation of aesthetic pleasure, suggesting that we innately prefer certain movements (such as movements from left to right and from low to high) because of the way they mirror the movement of the sun (30). Even our experiences of music and color, he claimed, are directional, as we perceive colors as locations on a spectrum and tones as locations on a scale (16–28). In the United States, this line of thinking was taken up by William James, who, as Atkinson was fond of pointing out, believed bodily movement preceded the experience of emotion. In *The Principles of Psychology*, he claimed that "our natural way of thinking," which holds that "the mental perception of some fact excites the mental affection called the emotion, and that this latter state of mind gives rise to the bodily expression," is completely wrong; instead, "*bodily changes follow directly the perception of the exciting fact, and . . . our feeling of the same changes as they occur is* the emotion" (743). Emotion, suggested James, is primarily a sensation of bodily movement: we feel fear, for example, only after our bodies have begun to pull away from some fearful stimulus.[15] If, as Henry argued, the pleasure and pain we take in aesthetic experience is rooted in physiologically hardwired responses to movement, so, too, James suggested, are our emotions. Theatrical gesture, then, represented a vitally powerful phenomenon: working directly on the body's biological structures of feeling, it affected theatergoers in tangible, physiological ways.

If this was the case, we might say that the fascination exerted by popular actresses in the late nineteenth and early twentieth centuries was rooted in these actresses' corporeal mobility, in the fact that they were, first and foremost, bodies that moved. And not only did they move while onstage; they moved between stages and cities as well. It was the end of the nineteenth century, after all, that saw the rise of the traveling "combination" troupe, and, by 1905, "theater in America" had become "virtually synonymous with touring" (Londré and Watermeier 185).[16] Bernhardt herself could only be glimpsed by her American fans on one of her many international tours, and much of her appeal, as Sharon Marcus points out, came not only from her magnetic stage presence but also from the "circulat[ion]" of "her person on an almost superhuman scale"; she was, in every sense, "a body in perpetual motion" (1004).[17] In the eyes of the American public, actresses drew their allure from both theatrical and geographic movement, enchanting audiences with the gestures their bodies traced on- and offstage.

By the turn of the twentieth century, then, the relationship between fascination and theatricality had been inverted: if fascination had been conceived throughout the nineteenth century as theatrical, theatrics were now understood to be fascinating. This was particularly true when it came to the theatrics of actresses, as they both readily evoked the feminized discourse of hysteria and received more popular attention than their male counterparts.[18] These women captivated fans not with masterfully delivered dialogue but with dramatic gesture, the entrancing motions of their bodies. Charged with a kind of alluring kineticism, they used the power of theatrical movement to fascinate audiences.

The Magnet Attracts: Carrie and the Urban Theater

It is the power of fascinating movement, of course, to which I would like to draw our attention in *Sister Carrie*. For even before Dreiser began to write the novel, he was clearly intrigued by the creative possibilities of fascination. In an 1896 column for the women's magazine *Ev'ry Month,* for example, he commented on how easy it is "to be hypnotized by the beauty of a scene" like Niagara Falls, its "grandeur" "fascinat[ing]" us, "driv[ing] out other thoughts and fix[ing] attention upon itself," the "mind . . . too weak before its influence to resist" (55). This kind of hypnotic power was also at the center of his theory of magnetic "personality"—a lifelong interest of his—which he defined not as exceptional knowledge or ability but as "the hypnotic power of attracting attention" to one's knowledge or ability, the ability to exude "a sort of energy wave" akin to magnetic fluid or Atkinson's mystical "mentative energy" (*Hey Rub-a-Dub-Dub* 113; "Transmutation" 167).[19] Indeed, Dreiser's understanding of the human psyche resembled that of the animal magnetists in a more general way, for, even as he believed in the "chemic" determinisms of biology and physiology—two themes in his corpus about which critics have endlessly written—he also believed in the existence of "some all-important force" that "gives life its wonder and terror and meaning," a force that might usefully be compared to the vital principle of mesmeric thought (Walcutt 486).[20] Even, then, as critics typically highlight the central role played by evolutionary and economic forces in naturalist fiction, Dreiser likely borrowed some of his own forces from the discourse of fascination. (Indeed, the word *fascination* appears everywhere in both *Sister Carrie* and scholarship on *Sister Carrie.*)[21] Interested his whole life in the power of magnetic people and things, Dreiser was well versed in the phenomenology of fascination.

This knowledge was put to good use in *Sister Carrie,* a novel obsessed with the fascinating powers of the modern city. The very first chapter, after all, is titled "THE MAGNET ATTRACTING—A WAIF AMID FORCES," and the novel's famous meditation on what happens to a girl when she "leaves her home at eighteen"—"either she falls into saving hands and becomes better, or she rapidly assumes the cosmopolitan standard of virtue and becomes worse"—attributes this "becoming worse" to the "superhuman" power of the city itself: "The city has its cunning wiles, no less than the infinitely smaller and more human tempter . . . The gleam of a thousand lights is often as effective as the persuasive light in a wooing and fascinating eye" (3). Indeed, the city's perpetual novelty "is invariably fascinating. Next to love, it is the one thing which solaces and delights. Things new are too important to be neglected, and mind, which is a mere reflection of sensory impressions, succumbs to the flood of objects" (252). For Dreiser, the city itself exerts a kind of hypnotic influence over the minds of visitors, inexorably attracting them and influencing their behavior.

It seems important to note, however, that the magnetic city as a whole is not, as some critics suggest, "the main force at work in the novel"; indeed, it is the city's theaters—as well as its theatricalized urban spaces—that exert the greatest influence over the novel's characters (Lehan 67). It is Carrie's first trip to the theater, for example, that kindles her fancy, instilling in her a taste for luxury and causing her to become "the victim of the city's hypnotic influence" (75). This is because there seems to be something innately entrancing about the space of the theater, and, when she again goes with her sometimes-lovers Drouet and Hurstwood to the theater to see the famed actor Joe Jefferson perform, she is "really hypnotised by the environment, the trappings of the box, the elegance of her companion" (102). This connection between the theater and entrancement is so significant that even the novel's nontheatrical sites of fascination come to be figured in theatrical ways, the department stores that so attract Carrie taking on a dramatic quality and leaving the luxury goods they sell—commodities that have figured for generations of Marxist critics as the novel's primary locus of attraction—"theatricalized," in the words of Bill Brown, "within display cases and shop windows" ("Matter" 90).[22] If the city as a whole exerts a diffuse influence over its inhabitants, this power becomes unusually concentrated in the space of the theater.

No one, of course, is more defenseless before this power than Carrie, whose emotional, artistic temperament makes her unusually susceptible to theatrical fascination. As we have already seen, Atkinson suggested it was this temperament that characterized "impressionables," and Beard claimed that the "average shop-girl" made for the best trance subject (*Scientific* 24). Both of these theories seem to find justification in the figure of Carrie, who, "unwise" but "strong in feeling," has "emotional greatness," and for whom, according to her sister, the life of a shopgirl is "the destiny prefigured" (*Sister* 61, 335, 15). "An illustration of the devious ways by which one who feels, rather than reasons, may be led in the pursuit of beauty," Carrie's mind is like a "harp . . . in the wind," "respond[ing] to every breath of fancy" (454, 452). Both emotional and impressionable, she is, in many ways, the victim of her own artistic temperament.

This temperament is linked in the novel to Carrie's natural imitativeness, for, as Jennifer Fleissner points out, it was popularly believed in the late nineteenth century that imitativeness was an innate mark of both "the female temperament" and "the artistic impulse" (*Women* 174). Imitativeness was, of course, also a personality trait of Atkinson's "hyper-impressionable" as well as a widely described symptom of hysteria.[23] Despite (or perhaps because of) its connotations of feminized mental weakness, Carrie's imitativeness is precisely what makes her a successful actress, allowing her to transform herself from a fascinated spectator into a fascinating performer. This transformation begins when Drouet calls a woman on the street a "fine stepper" and Carrie thinks: "If that was so fine, she must look at it more closely. Instinctively, she felt a desire to imitate it" (95). This leads her to practice "those little modish ways which women adopt when they would presume to be something," "look[ing] in the mirror and purs[ing] up her lips," for example, "accompanying it with a little toss of the head, as she had seen the railroad treasurer's daughter do" (98). Because she is so often at the theater, she naturally begins to imitate not only the well-to-do women she sees on the street but also the actresses she sees on the stage, and, "seeing the airy grace of the *ingenue* in several well-constructed plays," she begins to be "moved to secretly imitate it, and many were the little movements and expressions of the body in which she indulged from time to time in the privacy of her chamber" (144). It is by this process that Carrie "double[s]" her "knowledge of grace," "'acting out' the part," to borrow a phrase from Atkinson, of the wealthy socialite and the actress (98). Her natural imitativeness, her emotionality, and her artistic temperament—in short, all the qualities that make her especially susceptible to fascination— are, in fact, the qualities that make her a good actress, that allow her to transcend her destiny as a shopgirl and become a popular performer.

This transformation from fascinated subject into fascinating subject is literally dramatized in Carrie's debut performance at Avery Hall. Playing the part of Laura in Augustin Daly's *Under the Gaslight*, she behaves in her first scene like an unimaginative somnambulist, delivering her lines as if she were "talking in her sleep." Her performance is, in fact, so bad that Hurstwood "fixe[s] his eye on Carrie, as if to hypnotise her into doing better" (163). Before her next scene, however, Drouet "buoy[s] Carrie up" in the wings, and she begins to throw herself into her part (165). Like a contagiously suggestible hysteric, she catches "the infection of something," and she starts to "feel the bitterness of [Laura's] situation," the "feelings of the outcast descend[ing] upon her." It is at this moment that Carrie begins to exert an influence over the audience, Hurstwood "blink[ing] his eyes and ca[tching] the infection," Drouet becoming "more fascinated, if anything, than Hurstwood" (166, 167). Carrie's acting suddenly enacts "a drawing . . . of attention, a riveting of feeling, heretofore wandering" in the audience, and her lovers, who, until now, have been consistently figured as themselves magnetic—Drouet "captivat[ing]," Hurstwood "fix[ing]" her with "the power of his eyes," "their magnetism"—succumb to *her* hypnotic power (166, 57, 126, 109). If, when Carrie first moved to Chicago, "she was as yet more drawn than drew," she now begins to develop her own drawing power, and, in the words of Ellen Moers, "her lovers, instead of turning their hypnotic glance or directing their electrical sparks toward Carrie, now begin themselves to absorb rays of force that emanate from her" (*Sister* 71; *Two* 108). In other words, she inverts the fascinated relationship between herself and her suitors, becoming hypnotist instead of somnambulist, magnetizer instead of magnetized.

Paradoxically, this inversion is made possible by Carrie's very susceptibility to entrancement, as she only becomes an effective performer by, in keeping with Atkinson's advice, mesmerizing herself. She is, after all, at her best when she slips into states of unconsciousness onstage. When, during the private performance she gives Drouet in their apartment, she manages to infuse her part with "considerable feeling," she only does so by "forgetting, as she g[ets] deeper in the scene, all about Drouet," and she is only able to impress the director of the Avery Hall show by "forg[etting] all about the company present" during rehearsal and moving across the stage "with a grace which was fascinating to look upon" (147, 154). During her triumphant performance, she becomes oblivious to the other actors and "hardly hear[s] anything more, save her own rumbling blood" (166). It is Carrie's trancelike unconsciousness of her surroundings that allows her to entrance others, her seeming mental powerlessness that gives her the power to fascinate. Her propensity to be fascinated, then—a propensity denigrated as the sign of a weak will by men like Beard—becomes, in the space of the theater, her primary source of agency.

The unselfconsciousness that this self-entrancement produces in Carrie is, interestingly enough, read by her audiences as a kind of naturalness and simplicity. When, in her first Broadway role as a chorus girl, she catches the attention of the show's manager, she does so because she "unconsciously move[s] about with an air pleasing and somewhat distinctive . . . due wholly to her natural manner and total lack of self-consciousness" (354). She gets her first promotion because the manager likes that she has a "chic way of tossing her head to one side," a mannerism that, as Fleissner points out, strangely knits together the idioms of naturalness and performance: "neither her naturalness nor her chic, but her natural ability to pick up on chic," is what lends her performances their charm (*Sister* 357; Fleissner, *Women* 174). Carrie thus captivates her audiences by, in the words of Priscilla Wald, "performing naturalness," by so effectively immersing herself in the "fascinating make-believe of the moment" that she collapses the distinction between performance and reality (Wald 189; *Sister* 170).[24] Conflating, through a kind of autohypnosis, her own identity with the roles she plays, she entrances her audiences with her apparent genuineness, the naturalness of her onstage movements.

For, of course, it is Carrie's movements, her graceful carriage and her gestures, that ultimately propel her to stardom. As Dreiser notes, Carrie is "no talker," onstage or off; she can "never arrange her thoughts in fluent order" (109). Consequently, it is not her dialogue that entrances during the Avery Hall performance but her movements. In fact, during her final monologue, Drouet and Hurstwood "scarcely hear . . . the few remaining words with which the scene conclude[s]"; they see only "their idol, moving about with appealing grace, continuing a power which to them [is] a revelation" (172). This kind of graceful movement is what propels Carrie's acting career forward, for, as we have already seen, she receives her first theatrical promotion courtesy of her chic head tosses, and her breakout role as a little quakeress is a virtually silent role. On her first night playing the part, the audience becomes "wearied by a dull conversation" onstage and shifts its attention to Carrie comically frowning: "As she went on frowning, looking now at one principal and now at the other, the audience began to smile. The portly gentlemen in the front rows began to feel that she was a delicious little morsel. It was the kind of frown they would have loved to force away with kisses. All the gentlemen yearned toward her" (401). Carrie's silent grimace causes her to become "the chief feature of the play," "every other feature pal[ing] beside the quaint, teasing, delightful atmosphere which Carrie contributed while on the stage" (402). Carrie thus goes from an amateur actress with numerous lines (as Laura in *Under the Gaslight*) to a professional actress whose chief attraction is her gestural expressivity (as the silent quakeress). Her social and professional status, in fact, seems to be inversely proportional to the number of lines she is given, and the more famous she becomes, the less she finds herself speaking. What garners her newspaper coverage and marriage proposals and the rapt attention of audiences is ultimately her capacity for expressive gesture, the grace of her movements.

This fascinating movement may seem at first glance to be confined to the space of the theater, for, unlike most turn-of-the-century actresses, Carrie declines to move about the country as part of a touring troupe. She is tempted to follow her first show on the road for the sake of job security, but Lola, her friend in the chorus, convinces her that she can "always get in another show" as long as she stays in New York (353). Carrie's decision to stay in the city thus enables a different kind of movement: an intracity circulation between stages and productions. After all, Carrie has already covered quite a bit of geographic ground, moving from Columbia City to Chicago to Montreal to New York, not to mention the movements she has made between apartments and lovers within these cities. It is the opportunity to move from theater to theater, playing different roles in the same city, that facilitates Carrie's social rise. Dreiser thus seems to posit the small but frequent movements enabled by the city—that "swirl of life" that so enchanted at the beginning of the novel—as a comparable (if not even more productive) strategy for generating celebrity (75).

In the end, then, the city maintains its magnetic influence over Carrie, and her continued residence in New York contributes to—rather than inhibits—her ability to fascinate audiences, Sarah Bernhardt's practice of touring be damned. Though she does spend much of her young adulthood moving within and between cities, the novel concludes with a tentative settling in New York. This apparent halting of movement, however, is just that: apparent. For, as Fleissner notes, what often appears in naturalist narratives of "the modern young woman" as a "stuckness in place" is, in fact, a kind of "ongoing, nonlinear, repetitive motion," a motion symbolized for generations of critics by the rocking chair in which Carrie is left at the end of the novel (*Women* 9). Carrie may have stopped circulating her person on a large geographic scale, but it is precisely her settling in a New York hotel—that most transitory of residences—that enables her to remain in constant (if limited) motion, enchanting and reenchanting audiences with each new show in which she appears. The magnetic city and the moving actress thus come in *Sister Carrie* to function symbiotically, to work together to fascinate impressionable theatergoers.

Kitty and the Coon Show[25]

I would now like to turn to another novel that, though similar to *Sister Carrie* in certain structural ways, represents a noticeable departure from the conspicuously white world of Dreiserian naturalism: *The Sport of the Gods*.[26] Largely focused on the trials and tribulations of a single Black family, the novel follows Fannie Hamilton and her two children, Joe and Kitty, as they are forced to migrate from the rural South to New York City; once there, Joe falls into drunkenness and criminality, Fannie marries an abusive man, and Kitty, like Carrie, becomes an actress. Critics, of course, have made much of Joe's narrative of decline, pinpointing it as the novel's most explicit example of naturalist troping. Much less has been said, however, about Kitty's equally naturalist narrative of theatrical ascent, a plotline that, though perhaps "not as carefully monitored by the narrator," is strikingly similar to the one followed by Carrie (Thomas 171).[27] After all, Kitty, like Carrie, is transformed by the city from fascinated theatergoer into fascinating actress, using her affinity for performance to secure a certain amount of financial security for herself as the rest of her family falls apart. Indeed, even if Dunbar's somewhat moralizing depiction of Kitty at the end of the novel plays on popular associations of acting with prostitution, she is ultimately the only member of the Hamilton family to find any kind of personal satisfaction, perhaps even happiness.[28] This is all possible, I would like to suggest, for the same reason it is possible in *Sister Carrie:* Kitty is able to operationalize her impressionability, to transform her susceptibility to fascination into a quality of entrancing allure all her own.

Kitty, after all, lives in much the same New York as Carrie, a city fundamentally characterized by its ability to fascinate. Like Dreiser, Dunbar introduces the city with a warning: when one visits it, "a something will take possession of him that will grip him again every time he returns to the scene and will make him long and hunger for the place when he is away from it." The longer he stays, the more "the lights in the busy streets will bewilder and entice him," and the "subtle, insidious wind of New York will begin to intoxicate him," working its magic until "the town becomes all in all to him . . . and to live elsewhere would be death" (36). This is precisely what happens to Joe, who in many ways follows the same plot of decline as Dreiser's Hurstwood. After all, his will, like Hurstwood's, is "as flabby as his conscience," and, when he is forced to look for work, he gives up his search after a single rebuff, not having "the heart to seek another shop" (80, 31). He consequently falls prey to the city's fascination and descends, like Hurstwood, into criminality, murdering his girlfriend and being sentenced to death. The city, both Dreiser and Dunbar suggest, exerts a peculiar influence over men, especially those, like Joe and Hurstwood, with weak wills and a taste for luxury. It fascinates them, leading them into self-destructive behavior and ultimately bringing about their demise.

This fascination is linked for Dunbar (as it is for Dreiser) to the space of the theater, a space that, though pernicious for men, enchants women in a more productive way. When the Hamiltons attend their first show, Joe becomes "lost, transfixed": "His soul was floating on a sea of sense. He had eyes and ears and thoughts only for the stage. His nerves tingled and his hands twitched. Only to know one of those radiant creatures, to have her speak to him, smile at him! If ever a man was intoxicated, Joe was" (44). Kitty, too, is captivated by "the mystery and glamour that envelops the home of the drama," viewing her surroundings "with the fascination that one always experiences for what either brings near or withholds the unknown," but the yearning kindled in her by this captivation is very different from that kindled in Joe (43). For while Joe wants to pursue the actresses romantically, to become the object of their "smiles," Kitty wants to become an actress herself, exclaiming to her companion, Mr. Thomas: "This is grand. How I'd like to be an actress and be up there!" (44). Indeed, while Kitty is not taken in by the apparent glamour of everyday New Yorkers—she has "that critical faculty that kept her from thinking a five-cent cheese-cloth any better in New York than it was at home"—she is "enchanted" by the theatricalized bodies onstage: "The cheap dresses on the street had not fooled Kitty for an instant, but take the same cheese-cloth, put a little water starch into it, and put it on the stage, and she could see only chiffon" (38, 44). Thus while the stage figures as a space of erotic enticement for Joe, it figures as one of self-fashioning for Kitty. Like Carrie, she catches a desire to perform from the actresses as if by contagion, instilled by the theater's fascination with a desire to become fascinating herself.

This is, of course, what happens, and she becomes, like Carrie, a successful actress who enchants spectators with her theatrical movements. After all, the novel makes it clear that, as in *Sister Carrie*, movement is what captures and retains attention. During the Hamiltons' trip to the theater, it is the lively dancing that wins Fannie over: while she is at first "surprised" at the other theatergoers' "enthusiasm over just such dancing as she could see any day from the loafers on the street corners down home," she eventually "c[omes] around to the idea that it was she who had always been wrong in putting too low a value on really worthy things. So she laughed and applauded with the rest" (45). Kitty's first audition also revolves around dance, for, though her actual performance is a vocal one—a popular song accompanied by a pianist—it takes place in the midst of a dance rehearsal, and the first directive she is given upon landing a part as a chorus girl is to "watch these girls close and see what they do, and tomorrow be prepared to go into line and move as well as sing" (71). She of course is only given the opportunity to audition in the first place by impressing Hattie—an actress whose Dreiserian personality gifts her with "the faculty of attracting a good deal of attention"—with her "simple manner" of performing (64, 40). Like Carrie, it is her natural ability to perform naturalness that secures her a job as an actress, a position that highlights and intensifies the fascinating quality of her "manner." Catching the attention of Hattie and the manager with her simple performing style, she is allowed to become an actress because of the pleasing way she carries herself.

Though fascinating theatrical movement plays an important role in the rise of both Carrie and Kitty, the two women's narratives ultimately take different shapes. This is due to the difference in their races. After all, while *Sister Carrie* is almost overwhelmingly white, *The Sport of the Gods* is populated with sites and scenes of specifically Black performance.[29] The show to which Mr. Thomas takes the Hamiltons, for example, is a coon show in which the Black performers "sing" with "their voices, their bodies, their souls," "thr[owing] themselves into" the caricaturally lively figure of the "coon," a popular minstrel character type that "both evoke[s] and parodie[s] the plantation tradition" (Dunbar 44; Scruggs 46).[30] It is this kind of performance that Kitty admires, and she quickly "drop[s] the simple old songs she knew to practise the detestable coon ditties which the stage demanded" (54). Consequently, the arc of Kitty's development as an actress runs contrary to Carrie's: whereas Carrie begins her career as a kind of stilted somnambulist and slowly learns how to carry herself more naturally, Kitty begins her career as a paragon of theatrical simplicity and must learn how to adopt the aesthetics of the coon show, developing in herself what Sianne Ngai calls "animatedness," a quality of "liveliness, effusiveness, spontaneity, and zeal" that goes into troubling constructions of nonwhite subjects as "unusually receptive to external control" (*Ugly* 95, 91). If Carrie's success relies on her ability to perform naturalness, Kitty's relies on her ability to perform the unnatural caricature of the coon, to move in an exaggeratedly lively way.

This perhaps explains the difference in the two characters' broader patterns of geographic movement. While Carrie begins her adult life as quite the traveler, moving from city to city and apartment to apartment, her narrative leaves her settled in New York; as her onstage movements become more reserved, so, too, do her geographic movements. Kitty, on the other hand, decides to tour, leaving New York to circulate the country with her show; as her movements onstage become larger and more animated, her scope of geographic movement grows as well. The difference in the theatrical aesthetics allowed each of these women onstage, then, also appears to dictate the way they move offstage, a point that seems particularly significant when we remember that *The Sport of the Gods* represents a seminal example of the Great Migration novel.[31] Kitty's narrative of geographic mobility thus not only becomes emblematic of the way minstrel performance "afforded black performers the room to move, socially, economically, and geographically" in the late nineteenth century, "to transport themselves literally across the country, to new economic heights"; it also becomes synecdochic for the narrative form of the Great Migration novel and the historical narrative of the Great Migration itself (Brooks 214). Unlike Carrie, whose movements grow more restrained the more successful she becomes, Kitty uses the caricatural aesthetics of the coon show to expand her scope of movement. Transforming a seemingly restrictive standard of performance into a source of at least partial agency, her racialized style of theatrical gesture models the generative possibilities of social, literary, and historical movement for Black subjects.

In her role as an actress, then, Kitty takes up the racist figure of the animated coon and turns it toward productive ends, transforming a trope meant to police Black agency into a tool of social and geographic mobility. If, as Atkinson claimed, the "excitable, emotional colored man" is supposed to be especially susceptible to fascination, readily "'tak[ing]-on' the mental states of those around him," Kitty makes the most of this susceptibility, harnessing the power of theatrical gesture to become just as fascinating as she is fascinated (*Mental Fascination* 133–34). This strategy affects the structure of *The Sport of the Gods*, which at least in part traces the increasing scope of Kitty's movements, mapping, as equal parts Black naturalist novel and Great Migration narrative, the geographic circulation of her body onto her trajectory of socioeconomic ascent. Her movements thus index the way Blackness itself is constructed in the novel: the cause of both Joe's fall and Kitty's rise, a central element of both the racist discourse of animatedness and the socioeconomic opportunities of migration, theatricalized movement grants a modicum of power to an otherwise powerless figure.

From Animatedness to Animacy: The Naturalist Actress and Feminist New Materialisms

If we typically think of agency as the property of a conscious, rational, volitional subject, naturalist novels such as *Sister Carrie* and *The Sport of the Gods* invite us to think again. For it is not the strong wills of Carrie and Kitty that propel them to stardom; in fact, it is their exceptionally weak wills, their ability to hand the burden of agency over to the nonconscious processes of their bodies. Such an approach to agency identifies the very liveliness of the body itself as a kind of power—what Dierdre Sklar, borrowing a term from Daniel Stern, might call its "vitality affect"— suggesting that "bodies" might be able to "communicate with other bodies through their gestures and conduct to arouse visceral responses and prompt forms of judgment that do not necessarily pass through conscious awareness" (Sklar 95–96; Coole and Frost 20). Even if Kitty and Carrie may not seem to qualify as fully rational, autonomous subjects, then, this is precisely what facilitates their social mobility: from this perspective, "freedom" (to borrow a phrase from Elizabeth Grosz) "is . . . not primarily a capacity of mind but of body: it is linked to the body's capacity for movement, and thus its multiple possibilities of action" (Grosz, "Feminism" 152). Eminently capable of fascinating movement, Carrie and Kitty invite us to rethink what it means to be an effective social agent.

As my nod to Grosz suggests, this reading of Carrie and Kitty is very much in line with recent attempts to theorize agency beyond the mind-body split, to rethink it not as the property of a conscious subject but as an effect of what Mel Y. Chen calls "animacy" (5). A "quality of agency, awareness, mobility, and liveness," animacy designates a kind of nonconscious capacity for movement, the ability to, in affect theoretical terms, "affect the world" and "be affected by it" (Chen 2; Hardt ix). Interested in the way "matter that is considered insensate, immobile, deathly, or otherwise 'wrong' animates cultural life in important ways," critics such as Chen suggest that we discard "binary systems of difference" (such as "dynamism/stasis, life/death," and "subject/object") in order to rethink agency in terms of an "animacy hierarchy," a phenomenon that is not "all or nothing" but "more or less" (2, 3). By thinking of agency as a spectrum or a scale, they argue, we might, on the one hand, develop a more accurate and nuanced account of how agency works and, on the other, distribute care and value more equitably to those inhuman actors with which humans regularly interact (as well as those human actors that have historically been considered sub- or inhuman). Framing agency not as a capacity of the rational subject but as a property of matter itself, Chen and their cohort aim to broaden our understanding of what constitutes a social actor.

In certain explicit ways, then, Chen's work embraces what Jane Bennett would call a kind of "vital materialism," an understanding of matter not as dead or inert but as "vibrant, vital, energetic, lively, quivering, vibratory, evanescent, and effluescent" (*Vibrant* 112). Driven, like Chen, by a desire "to distribute value more generously" across animacy hierarchies—"to bodies as such" rather than "a particular (Euro-American, bourgeois, theocentric, or other)" version of the subject—Bennett and her fellow vital materialists celebrate the "vitality" of apparently inanimate things, their "capacity . . . to act as quasi agents or forces with trajectories, propensities, or tendencies of their own" (13, viii). Such an understanding of matter as "vibrant"—as an "enchanting and dangerous matter-energy"—invites us, as Chen's theory of animacy does, "to horizontalize the relations between humans, biota, and abiota," to locate agency somewhere other than the rational mind (xix, 112). Arguing that matter itself is imbued with a kind of "enchanting," affective power, Bennett offers up a theory of agency that, like Chen's, is more or less indifferent to the phenomena of rationality, intentionality, and consciousness.

This turn toward the vibrancy of matter is emblematic of a broader trend in feminist philosophy and cultural criticism that has come to be identified by the pluralizing label of "feminist new materialisms." Attempting to account for "twentieth-century advances in the natural sciences" in a rigorous, philosophical way, feminist new materialists work to "discern emergent, generative powers (or agentic capacities) even within inorganic matter, and they generally eschew the distinction between organic and inorganic, or animate and inanimate, at the ontological level" (Coole and Frost 5, 9). Arguing that "matter is not immutable or passive," thinkers such as Karen Barad, Donna Haraway, and Rosi Braidotti—as well, of course, as Grosz, Bennett, and Chen—aim to "describe nonhuman agency in a scientific context": "articulat[ing] the liveliness of matter as both a novel and liberatory idea," they suggest that the overlooked effectivity (and affectivity) of things represents a pressing political and philosophical problem (Barad 139; Alaimo and Hackman 7; Schuller 212). Rejecting binary logics that split the world into active subjects and passive objects, such thinkers use the figure of lively matter to rethink the very terms of feminist liberation.

Such a perspective casts a new light on the relationship between race, gender, movement, and agency that has been the central focus of this chapter. After all, it would seem that Bennett and her intellectual cohort are interested in describing—and, more importantly, validating—precisely the kind of "impersonal agency" that Carrie and Kitty embody (Bennett, *Vibrant* 75). For just as both characters use their bodies' enchanting movements to affect others, so, too, does vibrant or vibratory matter—in other words, matter that moves—have the surprising capacity to act as an agent.

This convergence between naturalist agency and feminist new materialist agency could, of course, lead our analysis in one of two directions. On the one hand, we might use the rubric of feminist new materialisms to more clearly explain the survival strategies employed by Kitty and Carrie. Pushing back, as Michael Datcher does, against the idea "that subjects positioned at the bottom of the human animacy scale have relatively little power to . . . affect subjects on the animacy scale above them," we might use the language of vital materiality to articulate how and why Carrie and Kitty—two figures of animate unconsciousness—come to function as effective social agents (12). Adopting the stance that matter itself has certain enchanting powers, we might use Carrie and Kitty to illustrate the social and political potential of feminist new materialist thought.

On the other hand, we might use the work of Dreiser and Dunbar—two writers who, like the feminist new materialists, went to great lengths to account for the "advances in the natural sciences" of their day—to develop a more nuanced understanding of what it means to embrace a certain kind of materialist feminism. For even as feminist new materialists may celebrate matter's animacy, its capacity for powerful and agential movement, they seem to prefer certain kinds of animacy to others. After all, it does not seem like a coincidence that Bennett is particularly drawn to *vibrant* matter, to the "live presence" of "vibratory" objects that, she claims, are often so "fascinating to people" (*Vibrant* 5, 10). Claire Colebrook, too, claims that feminist new materialisms allow "matter to vibrate without forward movement, production, creation, or relation," causing "the world itself" (in Grosz's words) "to vibrate with its possibilities for being otherwise" (Colebrook 81–82; Grosz 153). For Bennett, Colebrook, and Grosz, feminist possibility lies in the vibratoriness of matter, its latent (but, importantly, unrealized) potential for broader movement; it is matter's kinetic *restraint*—its tendency to vibrate, to move in place—that imbues it with its limitless potential. If we were to put this position in naturalist terms, we might say that thinkers such as Bennett value vibrant matter for its *grace*, the way it, like Carrie (but, significantly, not Kitty), is capable of making minimalist movements, of employing a restrained gestural aesthetic.

Even, then, as this brand of feminist materialism may claim to tip standard animacy hierarchies on their sides, to extend value to a broader array of bodies and "set up a kind of safety net for those humans who are now . . . routinely made to suffer because they do not conform to a particular . . . model of personhood," I would argue that it simply uses a new rubric—that of animacy or vibrancy—to define certain implicitly racialized kinds of matter as more interesting, valuable, and rich with potential than others (Bennett, *Vibrant* 13). This is, I think, because scholars such as Chen and Bennett base their work on one tenuous assumption: that the white, male, Enlightenment subject has historically distinguished itself from objects, animals, and racialized (sub)human beings on the basis of its animacy, its greater awareness and agency relative to other beings. If this were true, of course, it would make a great deal of political sense to argue that matter it-self is animate and therefore worthy of value, respect, and care. The claim that animacy has historically been bound up with power or autonomy, however—that, in the words of Grosz, "freedom" is synonymous with "the capacity for action"—is not, as Dreiser and Dunbar show, necessarily true (140). For while Kitty and Carrie may both employ theatrical gesture as a survival strategy, Kitty employs an animated, excessively lively aesthetic, and Carrie is lauded for her gestural restraint. In other words, whiteness appears in naturalist writing not as a capacity for action but as the power to limit action, to restrain one's liveliness according to the gestural aes-thetics of grace.

Thus while the metaphysics of feminist new materialisms may indeed help us to understand the kind of agency exhibited by Carrie and Kitty—two figures rendered as more matter than consciousness, more body than mind—Carrie and Kitty themselves help to clarify the racialized and racial-izing logic implicit in the recent critical turn to vibrant matter. For vibrant materialism in many ways rehearses the turn-of-the-century discourse of whiteness as gestural restraint, calling for renewed attention to and care for those types of matter that, like Carrie, are capable of containing their movements. Even, then, as such work claims to redistribute value and care to bodies historically denied recognition as subjects, it obfuscates the fact that, at least at the turn of the twentieth century, racialized bodies were not denied such recognition because they were considered insufficiently animate but because they were considered too animate, imbued with a capacity for movement that exceeded rational control. Shedding light on the way movement itself can be (and often is) racialized, Carrie and Kitty help us to see the limitations of theorizing agency as an effect of animacy.

Naturalism, Fascination, Movement

"I tell you," says the journalist Skaggs in *The Sport of the Gods*, "dancing is the poetry of motion." "Yes," replies his drinking partner, Sadness, "and dancing in rag-time is the dialect poetry" (Dunbar 82). This laconic ex-change illustrates just the kind of uneasy alliance I have been tracing between the different kinds of fascinating movements employed by white and Black actresses. Yes, both Carrie and Kitty harness the superhuman forces of naturalist fiction and put them to their own uses, exerting a hypnotic influence over their audiences. And yes, they both exert this influence by carefully choreographing their movements, kinetically charging their bodies with something like a vitality affect or a mesmeric vital principle. The specific kinds of gestures allowed each of them, however, are racially determined: whereas Carrie fascinates through grace and restraint, Kitty, constrained as she is by the aesthetic idiom of the coon show, fascinates with exaggerated movement and excessive animatedness. These racialized aesthetic conventions, moreover, map onto Carrie's and Kitty's different modes of geographic movement, and, while Carrie becomes more stationary the more famous she becomes, Kitty tours the country, suturing the narrative of the combine actress to the literary and historical narrative of Black migration.

By way of a conclusion, I would like to suggest that these racialized kinetic practices in fact play a central role in the way naturalist fiction itself is structured. For it is not simply the figure of the actress that has historically fascinated readers; it is also the restless, wandering plot of naturalist fiction itself. A number of critics, after all, have noted the important role rhythmic, repetitive movement plays in the plotting of *Sister Carrie*: F. O. Matthiessen, for example, famously claimed that Dreiser's writing aims to render "the *movement* of life as he feels it," and one early critic of Dreiser maintained that "to tell you the plot of the story would be to destroy for you that inestimable pleasure which comes with perusing any slow revelation of relentless tragic forces" (Matthiessen 183; Lyon 163).[32] This slow-moving process of revelation has, for decades, seemed to cast a kind of spell over Dreiser's readers, another early critic going so far as to note that, despite its everydayness, Dreiser's writing exerts a kind of "fascination": "The tragedy and romance is of the commonest kind of common people, yet the spell is there" (Reedy 159). Like Carrie's gestures, the very prose of *Sister Carrie* seems to be imbued with an enchanting vitality, a "quality of life—shifting, elusive, unaccountable—that," in the words of Charles C. Walcutt, inexorably "*holds our attention*" (Walcutt 496, my emphasis).

Dunbar, of course, has received less critical praise for his experimentation with naturalist form: while Dreiser is often seen as one of the great masters of the naturalist novel, Dunbar has historically received more attention for his dialect poetry. Gathered in such well-received collections as *Oak and Ivy* (1893) and *Majors and Minors* (1895), his poetry largely pleased its white readers for the way it presented animated caricatures of Black life. In a review of *Majors and Minors*, for example, William Dean Howells praised Dunbar's writing for the "jolly rush of its movement, its vivid picturesqueness," the way it expressed a particular "race-life": "Mr. Dunbar's race is nothing if not lyrical, and he comes by his rhythm honestly" (Life 630). This is to say nothing of the popularity of the coon songs Dunbar wrote, which appeared in the first all-Black Broadway musical, *Clorindy; or, The Origin of the Cakewalk,* and explicitly employed minstrel aesthetics.[33] In some ways, the public enthusiasm for Dunbar's dialect poetry and coon songs may help to explain why readers have historically found *The Sport of the Gods* less fascinating than *Sister Carrie*: just as the decadent aspects of Chesnutt's writing have often been overlooked because decadent taste is considered incompatible with Blackness, so, too, has the potential fascination of Dunbar's writing been obfuscated by certain racialized expectations about his relationship with minstrel aesthetics and naturalist form. In other words, while Dunbar's contemporary readers (and subsequent generations of critics) may have been captivated by the animated aesthetics of his dialect poetry and coon songs, *The Sport of the Gods* may have seemed too graceful, too restrained—to put it simply: too white—to be worthy of much attention. Even, then, as the novel could easily be called just as fascinating as *Sister Carrie*, it is precisely its similarities to Dreiser's novel that have prevented it from being seen this way. Following the wandering structural conventions of naturalism a little too neatly, it is not imbued with the unrestrained animatedness and wild vitality that white readers have long come to expect from Black writers.

In some ways, then, this chapter represents a kind of polemic, a call to read Dreiser and Dunbar in similar terms. Rather than view *Sister Carrie* and *The Sport of the Gods* as different kinds of novels simply because one was written by a white man and one was written by a Black man, it might be more productive to let our attention linger on their similarities, to allow the issue of racial difference to lend nuance to rather than dominate our understandings of the novels. As I hope to have shown, taking such an approach helps to shed new light on the way race, theatrical movement, and aesthetics have historically interacted with one another. On the one hand, this approach cautions us to be skeptical of theoretical accounts of movement that gloss over racial difference and equate increased animacy with increased freedom; on the other, it demonstrates that movement may indeed provide figures refused recognition as rational, modern subjects—those figures, such as Carrie and Kitty, around which so much naturalist fiction revolves—with a certain amount of agency, mobility, and power. Ultimately, then, it allows us to describe more clearly the ambivalent position occupied by the figure of the actress in naturalist fiction: contagiously imitative, both fascinated and fascinating, this figure is capable of affecting audiences, suitors, and even the structure of the fiction in which she appears (and, by extension, the readers of this fiction), using the power of gesture to carve out a space for herself in the modern world.

4

Primitive Flatness and
Early Ethnographic Cinema

IN A 1910 EDITION of the *New York Dramatic Mirror*'s Spectator's Comments, the anonymous Spectator offered an early polemic for aesthetic verisimilitude in what was, at the time, the still relatively new medium of film. Arguing that the "strange power of attraction" exerted by moving pictures "lies in the semblance of reality which the pictures convey," he claimed that, when crafted properly, a realistic film "exerts on the minds of the spectators an influence akin to hypnotism or magnetism by visual suggestion." This "sort of limited hypnotic influence," moreover, "is capable of more powerful exertion through the medium of motion pictures than is possible in any sort of stage production or in printed fact or fiction": "It is therefore the part of wisdom to cultivate absolute realism in every department of the motion picture art" (Spectator's 18). Realistic cinema, he suggested, could fascinate audiences just as well as any hypnotist; indeed, it was precisely its ability to indexically document the world that was the source of its entrancing power. Capable of absorbing spectators in a cinematic world almost as real as our own, film promised to be one of the great technologies of fascination of the twentieth century.

In a strange historical coincidence, the birth of this technology coincided in the United States with the birth of academic anthropology, a discipline whose aims were strikingly similar to those of realistic cinema. Guided by a conviction that the Indigenous peoples of North America were on the verge of extinction, early anthropologists made it their task to generate a record of so-called primitive life; indeed, if film provided a new means by which to document the world, anthropology provided one important subject to be documented.[1] Thus was born the medium of ethnographic film, a mode of cinematic representation that combined the indexical capacities of film with the preservative project of anthropology. Such a project, of course, was destined to be fascinating from the start: overlaying the hypnotic allure of the cinematic screen with the kind of fascination that, as we saw in chapter 1, white Americans had long associated with the figure of the Indian, ethnographic film married the alluring powers of filmic indexicality to those of primitive culture.

Much like the vitalist philosophy of William James and Henri Bergson, then, the genre of ethnographic film occupies a transitional place in the history of fascination. For while fascination was largely understood in the nineteenth century as an embodied experience, one rooted in the material presence of a person or object, twentieth-century thinkers began to understand it as an effect of surface and the simulacrum, a "passion for the image" (Blanchot 32).[2] What, we might ask, changed between these two historically distinct moments? What shifted the locus of fascination from the material to the immaterial, from the body to the image of the body? The emergence of cinema, of course, is one possible answer to such questions. I would like to suggest, however, that the emergence of ethnographic cinema in particular was instrumental to this shift, as the genre self-consciously employed both modern and premodern techniques of fascination. Blending the enchanting power of the primitive subject with the allure of modern surface, ethnographic cinema dematerialized fascination, shifting its locus from the body to the image.

To understand how this happened, we must first examine the critical discourse surrounding early film, a medium whose aesthetic practices relied upon and operationalized the fascinating powers of surface. These practices, of course, intersected with those of early academic anthropology, a field that embraced a uniquely flat aesthetic, one that rendered primitive culture not in terms of historical or evolutionary depth but in terms of lateral cultural relation and geographic spread. Bringing these two discourses into conversation with one another, I would like to bring them to bear on two early examples of ethnographic film: Robert J. Flaherty's *Nanook of the North* (1922) and Edward S. Curtis's *In the Land of the Head-Hunters*

(1914). *Nanook,* an ostensibly true depiction of Eskimo life on Canada's Hudson Bay, is considered by many to be the first true ethnographic film, and *Head-Hunters,* though structured by a melodramatic narrative filled with witchcraft and revenge, faithfully depicts many aspects of Kwakiutl life (a fact that led many of its contemporary viewers to see it as a work of ethnography). These films, I argue, map the alluring power of the film screen onto the alluring surface of the primitive body, inviting viewers to project their own values and feelings onto the virtual subjects they display. This practice, moreover, encourages us to rethink the concept of virtuality itself. Ultimately, I suggest that ethnographic cinema reduces the primitive body to its own kind of entrancing, virtual screen, relocating fascination from the body to its twentieth-century simulacrum—the cinematic image.

Primitive Cinema and the Aesthetics of Display

Oddly enough, the story of cinema's rise in the United States uncannily parallels the story of mesmerism's rise. In the first place, many of early cinema's most prominent acolytes were Frenchmen—often affiliated with the Lumière company—whose spectacular demonstrations so impressed American audience members that, like Charles Poyen's mesmeric converts, they themselves took up filmmaking. In the second, the technologies and viewing practices of cinema borrowed from and extended a long history of visual illusion that, much like animal magnetism, blended elements of occult enchantment with the most cutting-edge discoveries in medical and physical science.[3] Indeed, as Tom Gunning puts it, early cinema emerged from a "diverse genealogy of optical fascinations" that "twin[ned] about the separate poles of optical entertainment and scientific demonstration," toeing the line between natural science and supernatural spectacle in much the same way Poyen's demonstrations did ("'Animated'" 106).

Perhaps because of this, early cinema was often thought by its contemporary critics to exert a supernatural power over its audiences, to be capable of captivating minds and moving bodies. Maxim Gorky, for example, described the experience of watching a Lumière film as a kind of enchantment, writing that, even as the spectral image of Parisian life on-screen made "you feel as though Merlin's vicious trick is being enacted before you," "as though [a wizard] had bewitched the entire street," the screen itself entranced you, causing "strange imaginings" to "invade your mind" and leading "your consciousness . . . to wane and grow dim" (408). The spell of the cinema was so complete for early spectators that, according to popular legend, those who attended the first screening in 1895 of the Lumière brothers' *l'Arrivée d'un train en gare de La Ciotat*—which depicted a train appearing to barrel toward the audience as it pulled into a station—screamed and jumped out of their seats, moved corporeally by the immaterial images on the screen.[4] This kind of uncanny power over viewers' bodies and minds was a central element of what Gunning has famously termed "the cinema of attractions," an early mode of film that, rather than absorb viewers in its narrative diegesis, "directly solicit[ed] spectator attention, inciting visual curiosity, and supplying pleasure through an exciting spectacle" ("Cinema" 383).[5] Seizing the bodies and minds of audiences as if by magic, early cinema fascinated with its illusionistic ability to replicate reality.

Though the language of enchantment may have played a privileged role in popular accounts of early cinema, clinical psychologists such as Hugo Münsterberg were more interested in the medium's concrete effects on the mind. Writing less than twenty years after the Lumières first terrified audiences with their arriving train, Münsterberg, like the anonymous Spectator, attributed the power of film to its unusually potent powers of suggestion. Like a hypnotic subject, "the spellbound audience in a theater or in a picture house is certainly in a state of heightened suggestibility and is ready to receive suggestions." This is because the very purpose of the cinema is to conjure images that are then "forced on us": just as "the hypnotizer . . . awakens in the mind of the hypnotized person ideas which he cannot resist," so, too, does the screen present the audience with images that are irresistibly linked together in chains of association (108). Working not through magic but through the power of suggestion, cinema, Münsterberg suggested, affected audiences in much the same way hypnotists affected their subjects.

This hypnotic power was closely linked for him to two traits that distinguished early film from live theater: its flatness and its use of close-ups.

While critics have long celebrated film's fascinating ability to depict lifelike movement, Münsterberg pointed out that this was not a property unique to film, as it was shared by both film and theater; indeed, the novel power of cinema "does not consist in imitating the movements of nature"—"it's a matter of *making images seen*" (Léger 21).[6] Even if, as we saw in the previous chapter, theatrical movement exerted its own fascination over turn-of-the-century pleasure-seekers, it was the strange play of surface and depth that primarily characterized the psychological experience of early cinema. After all, films produced before 1915 were largely characterized by what Noël Burch calls a "visual flatness," or, even more tellingly, a "primitive externality": rather than aim for an illusion of depth—for the impression that they took place in Renaissance space—these films were composed according to the conventions of portraiture and *tableaux vivants* (164, 188). Because the clunkiness of early cameras required that they remain stationary while filming and early filmmakers frequently used painted backdrops, most films appeared two-dimensional, presenting themselves not as an immersive, illusionistic art form but as true *moving pictures* (Burch 164). And, while this two-dimensionality may have been the result of technological limitations, it came to be a central formal concern of early film theorists such as Münsterberg. For, he suggested, when such films offer us the illusion of depth, "*we cannot accept it*": they may purport to depict "*reality with all its true dimensions; and yet it keeps the fleeting, passing surface suggestion without true depth and fullness*" (56). This, he claimed, played a "not unimportant part in the mental make-up of the whole photoplay," as the projection of depth onto an objectively flat screen was a fundamental element of cinematic spectatorship (57). For Münsterberg, the hypnotic suggestiveness of film was closely related to its aesthetic and psychological flatness, its ability to *suggest* depth. Positioning early cinema's two-dimensionality as a formal precondition for its ability to entrance, he framed its aesthetics of primitive externality as a way to attract and hold spectatorial attention.

While flatness may indeed have been an essential trait of early cinematic aesthetics, the technique that most differentiated film from live theater, Münsterberg believed, was the close-up. As Gunning points out, close-ups were used in early films as "an attraction in their own right," directing the audience's attention in a way that theater was fundamentally incapable of replicating ("Cinema" 384). This, for Münsterberg, was an aesthetically revolutionary technique, for if good visual and theatrical artworks overwhelmed the "voluntary attention" of spectators with a kind of involuntary attention that "receives all its cues from the work of art itself," film achieved this effect in a uniquely totalizing way (76). Insofar as the close-up forced the audience to look at and dwell on the small details of a scene, he suggested, it *has objectified in our world of perception* the very *mental act of attention and by it has furnished art with a means which far transcends the power of any theater stage* (88). As Jean Epstein would later put it: "The closeup limits and directs attention . . . I don't have the right nor the means to be distracted. Imperative present of the verb 'understand'" (98).[7] This is because the close-up did not merely highlight a detail against a less important background; it eliminated this background from the frame altogether, manipulating spectatorial attention in a previously unimaginable way. Forcing on the viewer a kind of Jamesian involuntary attention, the close-up solicited, held, and guided the gaze of the audience.

The aesthetics of early film, of course, soon gave way to the aesthetics of classical cinema, which replaced the flatness of early film with its own illusory depth and subordinated the close-up to the necessities of diegetic development. Indeed, classical filmmakers treated the cinematic screen not as a flat surface across which two-dimensional images moved but as a window into a three-dimensional world populated by three-dimensional characters. Carefully engineering the illusion of both spatial and psychological depth, classical cinema turned away from the primitive aesthetics of display and toward an aesthetics that privileged narrative over spectacle.

The aesthetics of display, however, proved difficult to shake, and much classical film and film theory continued to be haunted by early cinema's techniques of attraction. Christian Metz, for example—one of classical film's most influential theorists—viewed flatness, like Münsterberg, as one of film's defining aesthetic characteristics, distinguishing cinema from live performance by pointing out that theater and opera "do not consist of *images*": "The perceptions they offer to the eye and the ear are inscribed in a true space" (43). Laura Mulvey, too, turned to the exhibitionary tech-

niques of early film when formulating her famous feminist theory of spectatorship, which argued that the spectacle of women's bodies—particularly
close-ups of their legs and other eroticized body parts—tends not only "to
work against the development of a story line, to freeze the flow of action
in moments of erotic contemplation," but to "destroy . . . the Renaissance
space, the illusion of depth demanded by the narrative" as well (837, 838).
For theorists of classical cinema such as Metz and Mulvey, what Burch
termed early cinema's "primitive mode of representation" seemed to have
the nasty habit of popping up in purportedly narrative films, foregrounding, when it did, the artificiality of the diegesis and the two-dimensionality
of the screen. Thus even as the conventions of classical cinema came to
dominate film production in the 1910s and 1920s, the fascinating techniques of a more primitive representational mode were never fully ban-
ished from the medium.

In both its primitive and its classical incarnations, then, early cinema
actively solicited and manipulated the attention of spectators. This was
linked both to its overt two-dimensionality and to its capacity for guiding
viewers' attention with carefully framed close-ups. Because both of these
traits characterized the formal nature of the cinema in a fundamental way,
the medium seemed to objectify the very act of attending, offering the
cinematic screen up as a surface onto which audience members could ex-
ternalize the psychic mechanism of attention. And even as primitive film,
with its aesthetics of surface and spectacle, slowly gave way to the spatial
and psychological depth of classical cinema, the fascinating techniques
of the cinema of attractions continued to haunt the medium, resurfacing
even in the most narrative of films, capturing audiences' attention and
interrupting the forward movement of the diegesis. Foregrounding its status as a medium that dealt in images, early cinema held and directed its
audiences' gazes in carefully orchestrated ways.

Early Anthropology and the Aesthetics of Cultural Relativism

While it may seem like another historical coincidence, the American public began to fall under the spell of primitive film at precisely the same

moment they were falling under the spell of another fascinating object: primitive culture itself. Even as they were flocking to the film screen to marvel at the technology of the future, so, too, were they flocking to anthropological exhibits in order to marvel at the cultures of the past; at the great fairs and expositions of the turn of the century, they could marvel at both. And just as film exerted a kind of hypnotic influence over its audiences, so, too, did public displays of primitive culture; indeed, as Jonathan Crary points out, "both hypnosis and the material life of colonial peoples" came to be exhibited in similar ways and similar spaces, and a certain elision of the two in popular culture caused "displays and representations of the 'primitive'" to become viewed as "objects of fascination" in their own right (231, 236). In fact, primitive film and displays of primitive culture functioned as surprisingly similar sources of visual pleasure for turn-of-the-century spectators: attracting and manipulating attention in comparable ways, they employed many of the same representational techniques to captivate curious audiences.

These techniques largely had their roots in the earlier display practices of the folk museum, a kind of national cultural museum that functioned as a site of both education and entertainment. Such museums—which first appeared in the late-to-industrialize Scandinavian nations—were largely created, as Mark B. Sandberg notes, to display "ethnographic collections of folk costumes, furniture, and tools from rural districts," to "preserve a concentrated, frozen, tableau-like image of traditional culture at the very moment that culture seemed most threatened by the changing conditions called modernity" (320). This image typically incorporated lifelike wax figures positioned in dramatic scenes from everyday folk life. Consequently, many people visited these museums not to learn about national history but to gawk at the uncanny *tableaux vivants*, and, when similar exhibits made an appearance at the Philadelphia Centennial Exposition in 1876, American viewers were, in the words of Bill Brown, "entranced" by their "realistic effect" (*Sense* 93). By the end of the nineteenth century, such exhibits were common at major expositions, and visitors, whether they encountered such displays at the fair or in the folk museum, approached them primarily as forms of entertainment, bringing to bear on them "composite viewing habits" drawn from "a variety of late-nineteenth-century attractions," including film (Sandberg 321). By depicting absorbing, dramatic scenes from folk life, the folk museum offered visitors many of the same kinds of pleasure afforded by early cinema.

The cultural impact of this kind of museum was wide-ranging, and it was, in fact, the folk museum that Franz Boas—commonly considered the founder of academic anthropology in the United States—took as his model when he introduced the idea of the "life-group" display to American museums. Until the late nineteenth century, museums tended to display their primitive artifacts not as parts of cultural wholes but as rungs on an evolutionary ladder: arranging material so as to demonstrate the development of universal "inventions," they placed "specimens from diverse cultures . . . together" to illustrate, in the words of Ira Jacknis, "the putative evolution of a technological type" ("Franz Boas" 77). Boas, however, argued that artifacts should be displayed, as in the folk museum, within their proper cultural context. Instead of arranging them as parts of an evolutionary series, he thus incorporated them into lifelike scenes of the primitive everyday. Rather than situate artifacts temporally, he situated them geographically, refusing the dominant tendency of the day to curate exhibits according to abstract evolutionary laws. Using the representational practices of the folk museum to vividly depict scenes from primitive life, Boas injected an element of visual pleasure into the practice of museum curation.[8]

The aesthetics of the resulting exhibits had much in common with those of primitive cinema. In the first place, they drew (as early film did) on the compositional techniques of *tableaux vivants*, arranging their subjects in carefully curated, static scenes. In the second place, Boas's model of curation involved a certain flattening of cultural artifacts and their meaning: if the evolutionary model of display lent objects a kind of visible historical depth, the life-group model erased this depth, built, as it was, upon the assumption that the significance of artifacts arose from their lateral relations with other artifacts. Lastly, the life-group exhibit was explicitly crafted with the intention of catching, holding, and directing the attention of museumgoers in particular ways. Just as the early film screen entranced viewers by allowing them to project their internal mental processes onto it, so, too, did life-group exhibits invite spectators to, in the words of Bill Brown, "imaginatively inhabit the local scene" they depicted (*Sense* 95). When arranged carefully, a series of such exhibits was capable of manipulating attention in much the same way Münsterberg suggested film was, working, in the words of Jacknis, "to gain the attention of the viewer, to concentrate it upon a single point, and then guide it systematically to the next in a series of points": "The constant danger was the loss of attention" ("Franz Boas" 90). Characterized by the same kind of visual flatness that characterized early film, the life-group exhibit harnessed the aesthetics of primitive externality to attract and direct the attention of visitors.

This flat aesthetic, of course, played an important role in Boas's general approach to culture as well. After all, his preference for the life-group over the evolutionary series was symptomatic of a deeper methodological and epistemological shift he hoped to facilitate, a shift that reframed the task of the anthropologist not as the application of evolutionary laws to individual cultures—a task famously embraced by Edward Burnett Tylor and shaped by the work of Charles Darwin and Herbert Spencer—but as the particularistic description of cultures in their own right.[9] Such a shift represented a radical flattening of the idea of culture, for if evolutionists like Tylor believed that the key to understanding a culture was in understanding its relative historical *depth*, Boas argued that it was just as important to understand the *breadth* of a culture's relations with "its near and distant neighbors" ("Anthropology" 278). This was particularly important when studying primitive cultures, for anthropologists could observe "only their present status" and had no empirical data about their historical or evolutionary development ("Mythologies" 135). Such a lateralizing of cultural relations allowed Boas to both embrace an early kind of cultural relativism and reject popular hierarchical models of racial difference. Indeed, even as the racist eugenics movements of the early twentieth century began to gain scientific traction, his 1911 *Mind of Primitive Man* made one primary assertion: "There is no fundamental difference in the ways of thinking of primitive and civilized man" (v).[10] Polemicizing against the popular tendency to describe a race or culture "as lower, the more fundamentally it differs from our own," he urged readers to view Western cultures not as higher than non-Western ones but as different from them (5). Shifting his attention from temporal depth to geographic breadth and flipping civilizational hierarchies on their sides, Boas flattened the idea of primitive culture in much the same way film flattened live performance.

There is, of course, one caveat to this description of Boas's work as an aesthetic and methodological flattening; this has to do with Boas's relationship with history. If, on the one hand, Boas vigorously rejected the evolutionist model of culture propounded by Tylor, he also, on the other, rejected the purely comparative approach of Adolf Bastian, who argued that disparate cultures developed similar technologies and belief systems because all humans share innate, psychological propensities for things like language and religious belief. This was because, for Boas, both these schools of thought relied too heavily on deductive reasoning, on the application of abstract explanatory models and preexisting hypotheses to highly particularized individual cultures. As an alternative, he offered what he called the "historical method," a method that involved inductive rather than deductive reasoning, that centered on the detailed observation and description of cultural phenomena "in their bearings to the total culture of the tribe practicing them, and in connection with an investigation of their geographical distribution among neighboring tribes" ("Limits" 905).[11] Thus even as he called for a flattening of culture and an increased attention to cultures' lateral relations with one another, he also called for an increased attention to the way these relations were historically situated.

This kind of historicism, which relied heavily on the analysis of ongoing cultural interaction and change, was central to Boas's project of cultural relativization. For if, as he suggested, cultures do not develop according to some predetermined evolutionary sequence but in response to the exigencies of their particular histories, it would simply make for bad anthropology to evaluate the merits of primitive cultures according to the values of Western civilization. Though anthropologists may take for granted that Western habits and values represent the pinnacle of civilization, he argued, this is simply because they lack critical distance, shaped, as they are, by the influences of Western culture. In order to "draw conclusions about the development of mankind as a whole," he suggested, "we must try to divest ourselves of these influences, and this is only possible by immersing ourselves in the spirit of primitive peoples whose perspectives and development have almost nothing in common with our own" (Boas, "Aims" 71). In other words, it is neither ethically permissible nor method-ologically sound to measure other cultures against Eurocentric standards, to project the values and ideals of one's own culture onto a culture with a radically different history. So even as he called for a flattening of primitive culture and an increased attention to its lateral (rather than evolution-ary) relations, he cautioned other anthropologists not to treat it as a blank screen. No matter how tempting it might be to project Western ideals onto non-Western cultures, he claimed, this actually compromised objective an-thropological understandings of both the primitive and the civilized world.

The techniques Boas and his followers used to represent primitive culture, then, resembled the representational techniques of primitive cin-ema in several ways. On the one hand, the life-group exhibit transformed primitive culture into an object of display and fascination, functioning for the public as a kind of attraction analogous to film. On the other, the fas-cination exerted by primitive culture was predicated upon its flatness at both the aesthetic and the epistemological level, its potential for present-ing itself as a screen onto which the fairgoer or the anthropologist might project his own psychic life. Boas, of course, viewed this kind of projection as problematic, and, even though he capitalized on the fascinating flatness of his museum exhibits to guide and educate visitors, he encouraged other anthropologists to guard against Eurocentric evaluations of culture by em-ploying his "historical method." First transforming primitive culture into a kind of screen and then cautioning Westerners against projecting them-selves onto it, Boas drew the world of primitive culture and the world of primitive film into surprising proximity with one another.

Ethnographic Film and the Legacy of the Actuality

If Boas was cautious about projecting Western values onto primitive peoples, those admirers of his who explicitly mapped the flatness of primitive cul-ture onto the flatness of the film screen—early ethnographic filmmakers—

had no such qualms. Framing the Indigenous subjects they filmed not as representatives of real, historically situated cultures but as timeless images of noble savagery, these filmmakers stripped them of their particularity, transforming them and their environments into flat, aestheticized objects of visual pleasure. Encouraging audiences to project Western emotions, social structures, and civilizational ideals onto the image of the primitive other, early ethnographic films constructed the figure of the native as a kind of fascinating and impenetrable surface, an image that captured spectatorial attention with its illusion of depth.

Before we turn to the history and aesthetics of ethnographic cinema, however, a word is in order about the term's definition. While I use the phrase *ethnographic film* to describe the films discussed in the remainder of this chapter, the term is in some ways both too capacious and too specific. The production of *Nanook of the North*, after all, tends to be viewed as an inaugural moment not only for ethnographic cinema but for the broader genre of documentary as well.[12] And, while *In the Land of the Head-Hunters* employed Indigenous actors and was careful to depict Kwakiutl rituals in accurate ways—facts that have made the film of genuine use to anthropologists—it overlaid these documentary elements with an entirely fabricated narrative of romance and revenge. Indeed, both films freely used elements of fictional storytelling (such as renaming actors and staging scenes), and, if we wanted to be more precise, we might actually describe them as "*documentaires romancés*," fictionalized travelogues that use exotic actors and scenery to achieve picturesque effects.[13] Someone like Flaherty, however, was less concerned with painting a verisimilitudinous picture of Eskimo life than with spinning a story out of what he saw as the heart of Eskimo culture, using, in the words of one Flaherty enthusiast, "artifice to assert truth" (Heider 22). I thus use the term *ethnographic cinema* in much the same way Fatimah Tobing Rony uses it: to designate a genre of cinema that takes a racial or cultural other as its subject; purports to tell some kind of truth about this other; and identifies this other as a remnant of a primitive past, thereby "situat[ing] indigenous peoples in a displaced temporal realm" (8). Combining the scientific descriptivism of ethnography with the representational conventions of early narrative film, such cinema brought an apparently hyperrealistic depiction of primitive culture to early-twentieth-century audiences.

In many ways, then, early ethnographic cinema represented the legacy of the actuality film and the travelogue. The oldest genre of film, the actuality simply recorded events from everyday life, displaying for audiences familiar scenes made strange; *L'Arrivée* is perhaps the best-known example of this. Not all actualities, however, depicted such domestic content, and the subgenre of the "foreign view," which offered viewers a peek into the everyday life of exotic locales, enjoyed immense popularity around the turn of the century (Gunning, "Aesthetic" 125). With the decline of the cinema of attractions around 1907, the foreign view was replaced by the travelogue, a genre of film that, while more protracted and narratively cohesive, largely appealed to audiences as a mode of virtual tourism (Barnouw 19). It was not until 1922, when *Nanook* appeared, that ethnographic film coalesced as a distinct genre. What differentiated this kind of cinema from the travelogue or the foreign view was, on the one hand, its intensified narrativity (for it used the cinematographic conventions of fictional cinema and aimed to tell a story rather than simply exhibit exotic attractions) and, on the other, its pretension to anthropological objectivity, centering, as it did, not the experiences of the filmmaker but those of the native people he encountered.[14] In fact, when Flaherty's first batch of footage from his time on the Hudson Bay was destroyed in a fire, he was reportedly unfazed, as it felt "too much like a travelogue"—"a scene of this and that, no relation, no thread" (Barnouw 35; R. Flaherty, "Talking" 12). Combining the exotic attractions of the foreign view and the travelogue with the narrative cohesiveness of fiction film, ethnographic cinema employed both primitive and classical filmic techniques to entertain audiences.

Because of this, early ethnographic film developed an aesthetic uniquely its own, one that drew on the representational logic of both cinema and Boasian anthropology. As its subject matter, it took the everyday life of primitive peoples and their "natural . . . surroundings for their own sake," often treating its human subjects as themselves a kind of picturesque scenery (Barsam, *Nonfiction* 18). This is because the genre's focus was not on the native actors' psychological character but, as in the life-group

display, on their physical attributes, "the anatomy and gestures of the indigenous person . . . and . . . the body of the land" this person "inhabit[s]"
(Rony 111). Paradoxically, this fixation on corporeality involved a demateri-
alization of the very bodies filmed, for, on the one hand, turn-of-the-century
ethnography depicted the native subject as on the verge of extinction,
"the romantic hero of a 'vanishing race'"; and, on the other, early film technology worked to flatten this subject out, to transform him into a lifeless
image (93). Indeed, as David MacDougall puts it, documentary film "gives
us the bodies of those we have filmed, yet those same bodies dissipate or
are transformed before our eyes" into nothing more than "a set of broken
images" ("Fate" 25). Overlaying the gaze of the ethnographer with the gaze
of the camera, early ethnographic film reduced subjects to bodies and bodies to images. Transforming the primitive body into a kind of immaterial
phantom, an index of a culture already (or soon to be) extinct, it framed
primitive life as always already a simulacrum of itself.

This demateralization of primitive life was in many ways an extension
of a general anthropological tendency in the early twentieth century toward salvage ethnography. Salvage ethnography, a mode of anthropology
that was built upon the assumption that certain cultures were in the process of going extinct and therefore needed to be indexed for posterity, was
largely Boas's methodology of choice (Rony 91). Ethnographic film, itself
a kind of "salvage operation," was therefore a direct extension of Boas's anthropological project; in fact, Boas himself even dabbled in ethnographic
filmmaking near the end of his life (Weinberger 139).[15] As soon as film
technology had advanced enough for cameras to be taken easily into the
field, they were put to use "collect[ing] and preserv[ing] human behaviors"; to quote Eliot Weinberger, "the only good Indian" quickly became
"a filmed Indian" (139). As this pithy remark suggests, however, ethnographic film had a vested interest in the disappearance of actual Indigenous people, for if these people were not in the process of vanishing, there
was no need for them to be salvaged. In other words, the literal violence
against Indians advocated by Philip Sheridan ("the only good Indian is
a dead Indian") became, in the age of ethnographic film, a kind of representational violence: in order to preserve the image of Indigenous life

as a state of noble savagery—an image that held a great deal of Romantic value for Americans—filmmakers had to replace actual native individuals with flattened-out, archetyped versions of themselves. They thus reduced primitive culture to a collection of readily consumable images, enabling white viewers to participate in what Rony calls "fascinating cannibalism," or the consumption of "the images of the bodies—as well as actual bodies on display—of native peoples offered up by popular media" (10). By replacing historically situated cultures and people with flat images impervious to the ravages of time, ethnographic film helped to realize the dream of anthropology. Substituting the changeless image for the changeable body, it represented the aesthetic culmination of salvage ethnography's scientific project.

What made ethnographic films such as *Nanook* and *Head-Hunters* more popular with the general public than written ethnographies, of course, was the way they operationalized the fascination of the screen, offering multiplying surfaces onto which audiences could project their psychic life. After all, ethnographic film "has always," in the words of MacDougall, "produced a fascination that seems disproportionate to taking the measure of human societies"; this, I would argue, is because of the canny way it maps the flatness of the primitive subject onto the flatness of the screen ("Ethnographic" 187). If, as Münsterberg suggested, film appeals to us because it objectifies the phenomena of perception and attention, early filmic representations of native bodies intensified this experience, soliciting (and, in fact, requiring) an increased psychic investment from white viewers. For while all filmic images of bodies require the viewer to "'fill . . .' or replenish . . . the image with his or her own bodily experience, inhabiting the absent body represented on the screen," images of native bodies—being doubly absent—invited a kind of projective identification on multiple levels (Mac-Dougall "Fate" 53). Thus even as ethnographic films claimed to give audiences a glimpse of the unknown, a point of access to the primitive other, they encouraged viewers to see this other as a reflection of themselves. Indeed, even though they may have asserted what Bill Nichols has called a "transparency between what is seen and the knowable," what was seen was typically a distorted reflection of Western culture; rehearsing "some version of the family-of-man myth," such films suggested not only that the peoples they portrayed were, in the end, just like Western viewers but that, because this commonality bore "a one-to-one correlation to the visible," it was a matter of empirical record (*Ideology* 274). Enticing white audiences with the promise of a peek into an exotic culture, these films instead gave their viewers a literal and figurative screen onto which they could project their own cultural expectations.

This is, of course, why representational distortions are so rampant in a film such as *Nanook*. Glossing over the realities of Eskimo culture and the lived experiences of Nanook (who was played by a man actually named Allakariallak), the film transforms Nanook and his "improbably nuclear family of good-looking protagonists" into "an uncorrupt example of all the values of the West—independence, perseverance, and patriarchy" (Saunders 89; Rony 108). Nichols goes so far as to suggest that the film does not belong to the cinema of documentary social representation but to "the cinema of wish-fulfillment," being, in many ways, "a fiction about the kind of peoples and cultures someone like Flaherty wished to find in the world" (*Introduction* 4). Transposing "his potential audiences' own narrative expectations onto the northern lands," Flaherty domesticated Eskimo culture, making of it simply another iteration of American ideals (Saunders 89).

Ethnographic film as a genre thus transformed the salvage operation of ethnography into a form of entertainment, blending the fascinating representational techniques of Boasian anthropology with the fascinating representational techniques of early film. Mapping the flatness of primitive culture onto the flatness of the screen, it equated the aims of anthropology (the preservation of culture) with the aims of cinema (the preservation of images). It is perhaps fitting, then, that ethnographic film worked not only to salvage representations of primitive peoples but to salvage the representational practices of primitive cinema. For even as it borrowed certain narrative techniques from classical fiction film, the cinema of attractions played a larger role in its aesthetics. Indeed, just as salvage ethnographers viewed primitive peoples as survivals from an earlier era, so, too, did the conventions of primitive cinema live on as survivals in the purportedly narrative genre of ethnographic film. Offering audiences a range of surfaces onto which they could project themselves, ethnographic cinema fascinated viewers with its doubly primitive aesthetics.

Nanook of the North and the Surface of the Primitive Face

If we are to examine the fascinating aesthetic practices of ethnographic film in detail, we could find no better case study than Flaherty's *Nanook of the North,* a film that many identify as the first true product of the genre. Much, of course, has been made of the film's propensity for Romantic fabrication, the way it depicts its subjects not as they actually were when Flaherty encountered them but as he imagined they might have been before the encroachment of Western civilization.[16] Flaherty, however—a true salvage ethnographer at heart—was adamant that "sometimes you have to lie": "One often has to distort a thing to catch its true spirit" (qtd. in Calder-Marshall 97). Even, then, if *Nanook* may seem to be more fiction than fact, this is actually one of the reasons it offers us such a useful example of ethnographic cinema.

Another reason is that the film looms large in the developmental history of cinematography. *Nanook,* after all, pioneered the use of the gyrohead tripod, a device that allows the camera to pan and tilt simultaneously (R. Flaherty, "Talking" 13). Flaherty was also the first to overlay the realistic content of the actuality or travelogue with the dramatic structure of fictional cinema; indeed, critics have long marveled at his effective use of narrative suspense, exemplified perhaps most clearly in the igloo-building scene in which Nanook cuts and polishes a block of ice whose function— that of a window—is only revealed at the end of the scene.[17] What interests me most about *Nanook,* however, is not its technical innovations; it is the way its narrative structure remains punctuated by moments of spectacle, moments in which the representational techniques of classical, narrative film are replaced by those of what would already have been seen in 1922 as a more primitive mode of cinematic representation. Relying just as much on the primitive aesthetics of flatness and display as on the classical aesthetics of depth and diegesis, *Nanook,* I suggest, represents primitive culture in the idiom of primitive film.

Though Flaherty does at times make effective use of Renaissance space (particularly in the scenes in which Nanook and his party sledge toward or away from the camera), the film remains haunted by the flatness of primitive cinema. As Richard Barsam points out, one of the primary problems with the film—according to the standards of classical cinema, at least—is its frequent use of "static tableaux" (*Vision* 24). The trading post scene, for example, in which a white trader demonstrates for Nanook the use of a gramophone, is composed of a single shallow, frontal shot that positions Nanook and the trader alongside one another. Such staging is even more evident in the igloo scenes, which were filmed in a specially built cutaway igloo and, by necessity, lack any significant depth. In them, Nanook and his family are lined up next to each other and displayed to the audience as they go about their morning and evening routines—laying out blankets, eating, dressing and undressing. Movement aside, the family almost looks as if it could be an exhibit in Boas's National Museum, a life-group display come to life. Borrowing from the staging conventions of primitive film, Flaherty poses his subjects as if they were in a museum display or a *tableau vivant*.

Such tableaux are emblematic of the film's broader investment in display and surface, an investment that cannot seem to be recuperated for the sake of the film's overarching narrative. This is perhaps best exemplified in Flaherty's use of intertitles, that device that so typically drives narrative development in silent films. While it is true that, with the onset of winter in the second half of the film, the intertitles come to function according to the logic of fictional cinema—linking events together in a causal way and building narrative suspense—they are largely descriptive in the first half, sprinkled throughout a series of unrelated vignettes of Eskimo life.[18] Rather than suture the film's disparate shots into a cohesive narrative, they merely redescribe the contents of these shots. Thus after we see a band of Eskimo carrying their *omiak* (a kind of canoe) on their shoulders, the following intertitle simply reads, "The omiak, of driftwood frame, covered with the hides of seal and walrus"; after a shot of sealskin boots being dried in the sun, the intertitle reads, "On harpoon points, boots of sealskin drying in the sun." The intertitles function in the first half of the film almost like museum labels, speaking in the voice not of a storyteller but of an ethnographer. And while they do eventually slip into a more overtly narrative mode, *Nanook* begins in the mode of ethnography, describing rather than narrating, offering up and expanding upon the surface of Eskimo life instead of plumbing its depths.

Such a fixation on surface is nowhere more evident than in the sequence that introduces the film's main characters, Nanook and Nyla. Offering the audience a kind of visual *dramatis personae*, this sequence dwells on Nanook's and Nyla's faces in prolonged shots that resemble photographic portraits or, as one critic puts it, "postcards" (Winston 108). When we are introduced to Nanook, an intertitle describes him as "Chief of the 'Itivimuits'"—"a great hunter famous throughout Ungava—Nanook, The Bear"—then the camera cuts to a nearly fifteen-second close-up of Nanook's face, impassive and unsmiling; he does nothing but blink at (or perhaps past) the camera. An intertitle then introduces "Nyla—The Smiling One," and we are offered a similar (though slightly shorter) close-up of her smiling and rocking, looking past the camera. While this sort of introductory sequence is common in early fictional films and is likely a convention that Flaherty borrowed from D. W. Griffith, what is remarkable about these postcard shots is their static quality: whereas Griffith would typically depict his characters engaged in some sort of characterizing action, Nanook, critics like to point out, "is doing nothing—nothing, that is, apart from being viewed, allowing himself to be viewed by the camera" (Rothman 6). Introducing Nanook and Nyla with portrait-style shots reminiscent of salvage ethnographic photography, Flaherty positions them not as subjects of action but as objects of display.[19] Fixing the camera on the passive—and impassive—surface of their faces, these postcard shots emphasize that Nanook and Nyla are there to be observed, their features there to be scrutinized.

This capacity for exhibiting the impassive surface of the primitive face was, for Flaherty, one of film's compelling characteristics. In an interview for the BBC, Flaherty once claimed that film is "very well-suited to portraying the lives of primitive people whose lives are simply lived and who feel strongly, but whose activities are external and dramatic rather than internal and complicated"; "I don't think you could make a good film of the love affairs of an Eskimo . . . because they never show much feeling in their faces" (qtd. in Rotha, *Robert* 36). It is precisely the impassiveness and impenetrability of the primitive face, Flaherty believed, that makes it a good subject for film. Even when Nanook laughed during filming—and this did not happen infrequently—Flaherty took it not as an expression of emotion but as a symptom of Nanook's childish simplicity, a surface phenomenon that paradoxically signaled his *lack* of psychological complexity, his *lack* of depth.[20] Thus whereas film theorists such as Münsterberg and Epstein valued the close-up of the face for its intense emotional expressivity, Flaherty employed it to different ends. Rather than use the close-up to suggest psychological depth, he used it to present the primitive face as a curiosity, an object of display.

Strangely enough, then, the postcard sequence actually evacuates Nanook and Nyla of psychological depth, treating them, one might argue, like mannequins in a Boasian museum exhibit. Indeed, Rony suggests that Flaherty "portrayed natives . . . in the mode of *taxidermy*," handling them not as subjects but as lifelike objects. After all, the taxidermist's job is to use "artifice and reconstruction in order to make the dead look alive," and this task in many ways resembles what Flaherty saw as his own cinematic project (14). Using the artifice of film to reconstruct a bygone way of life, Flaherty, Rony suggests, was engaged in precisely the same kind of work as Boas and his followers.

I am not sure, however, that this is quite the case. For while the taxidermic life-group exhibit may have employed artificial bodies, these bodies were nonetheless three-dimensional, presented, in Rony's own words, "in the round"; *Nanook*, on the other hand, deals in flat, two-dimensional images (14). And while there are clearly continuities between the nineteenth-century practices of museum curation and the twentieth-century practices of ethnographic filmmaking, these continuities, I would argue, are less significant to *Nanook* than the historical and technological discontinuities that separate Flaherty from Boas. After all, encountering primitive bodies and faces on-screen is, as Münsterberg would have pointed out, fundamentally different from encountering them in three dimensions, and, rather than present Nanook and Nyla in the round, the postcard sequence flattens them out. Indeed, it constructs the primitive face as pure surface, a kind of screen, uniting the cinematic externality Flaherty attributed to the primitive subject with the primitive externality Burch attributed to early cinema. Functioning in the film as moments of flat display, these shots, like those arresting shots that meant so much to Mulvey, resist narrativization, catching and holding the spectator's gaze with their powers of attraction. Rather than engage the viewer's attention according to the logic of taxidermy, the postcard sequence offers up a kind of screen within a screen, binding the fascination exerted by the primitive face to the fascination exerted by primitive cinema.

The face, however, is not the only fascinating surface to appear in *Nanook*: the land itself is also rendered in alluring, superficial terms. As Rony points out, Flaherty develops a certain equivalence between the surface of Nanook's face and the surface of the land he occupies, going so far as to claim that the film actually begins by "introducing . . . two main landscapes": "the land of Inuit Quebec, and the face of Nanook" (111). After all, the first shot of the film is a prolonged establishing shot of the Hudson Bay, sunlight glimmering on its reflective surface. This opening shot is followed up in the second half of the film with several wide shots of snow-covered landscapes, shots that minimize the presence of human subjects and that likely draw their aesthetic inspiration from Eskimo art.[21] This alternation between sweeping establishing shot and intense close-up, between landscape and face, establishes a kind of analogy between the two surfaces, an analogy that recalls Gilles Deleuze and Félix Guattari's claim that "the close-up in film treats the face primarily as a landscape; that is the definition of film" (172). The slippage that film enables between face and landscape thus positions the Hudson Bay in much the same way it positions Nanook and Nyla, and it would not be farfetched to suggest that the shot of the bay does not simply precede the film's postcard sequence but actually functions as an extension of the sequence. Reducing both the primitive face and the primitive landscape to a collection of postcardlike snapshots, *Nanook* replaces its subjects—both human and inhuman—with flat images of themselves, photographic souvenirs of Eskimo life.

This proliferation of flat surfaces invites, as I have already hinted, a kind of projective identification with the film's subjects, encouraging white viewers to see Nanook and his family as reflections of themselves. After all, when Flaherty's wife, Frances, was told by two German filmmakers that, forty years after its release, *Nanook* was still playing in Germany, one of the filmmakers attributed this to the fact that "we can identify with these people on the screen" (22). Flaherty himself credited the film's success to the way it humanized its subjects, presenting "not a freak . . . but a real person after all, facing the perils of a desperate life and yet always happy" ("Talking" 18). Hence the marketing campaign booklet distributed to ex-hibitors of the film that advised the best way to attract viewers was to highlight *Nanook*'s sentimental elements, to "emphasize the human angle" (*Campaign* 63). The numerous taglines the booklet offered foregrounded how familiar Nanook's family life should be to Western audiences, calling the film's characters "Pa Eskimo, Ma Eskimo," and "all the Eskimo kids" and asking, "Is mother love any different in the Arctic than in your home town?" (66, 67). One promotional photo of Nyla and her child was even captioned "A Madonna of the Arctic" (71). Thus even as Flaherty purported to offer audiences a window into the real lives of Indigenous subjects, to give them "a real person after all," he and his promoters at Pathé delivered highly Westernized depictions of Eskimo life, a cast of characters onto which viewers could project Western social structures (such as the bour-geois family) and emotions (such as hometown "mother love"). The great appeal of the film in the early twentieth century, it would seem, was that it allowed audiences to "identify" with their own reflection, with a West-ernized image of the primitive that they themselves had projected onto the screen. It drew viewers in with the titillating promise that they would receive a glimpse of the exotic other, then reassured them that this other was not so different after all, that it was merely a distorted iteration of Western values.

Thus goes one possible reading of *Nanook*. I would, however, like to complicate this reading, for even as Flaherty's contemporary audiences may have seen themselves in Nanook's and Nyla's smiling faces, they must also have sensed a residual otherness there, an uncannily persistent ele-ment of real and genuine difference. It is all well and good, after all, to laugh at Nanook when he tries to bite into a gramophone record, but what is a white spectator to do when Nanook turns to the camera in close-up, smiles, and swallows a piece of raw seal meat? In the words of Siegfried Kracauer, viewers may "laugh," but "at the same time they feel a shudder," for the pleasure of spectatorship is accompanied by a suppressed feeling of horror, an uncanny feeling that one is "glimps[ing] a moment of time past, a time that passes without return" ("Photography" 424). Even as the film invites white viewers to identify with Nanook, then, this identification remains haunted by its own incompleteness, the fact that Nanook's way of life is always just out of historical reach.

This sense of temporal alienation—a constitutive characteristic of film (and especially ethnographic film)—is compounded in *Nanook* by the alienating effect of the protagonist's racial difference. For while the primitive face may indeed provide a screen for the identificatory projections of white audiences, it also, as Kathryn Bond Stockton points out, "blocks our sight" of the individual to which it is attached, offering viewers merely an image of a psyche, a simulacrum of subjectivity ("Queer" 506). A flat, impenetrable signifier, the face "meets and defeats [the] gaze at every turn," denying spectators access to the psychic world that lurks behind it (517). Shielding the primitive subject's interior life from the white audience's prying gaze, it produces what Christopher Freeburg, in his work on photographic representations of lynching victims, calls a feeling of *"epistemic estrangement"* (3). Even, then, as the surface of the primitive face doubles the surface of the film screen, inviting audiences to project their own fantasies and psychic processes onto it, it functions as a kind of protective wall between the white observer and the nonwhite subject of observation. Simultaneously soliciting attention and refusing penetration by the white gaze, the filmic representation of the primitive subject oscillates between the seductions of the flat screen and the discomfiting barrier of the nonwhite face.

This combination of allure and impenetrability is, of course, the essence of fascination. Both capturing the gaze of the white spectator and blocking this spectator's ability to know the subject on the screen, the close-up of the primitive face captivates with more than the mere promise of identification. Rather than present taxidermied bodies for scopophilic consumption or surfaces onto which white audiences might project primitivist fantasies, *Nanook* solicits attention and inhibits rational thought the same way the Spectator's figurative hypnotist did.

It is no wonder, then, that the campaign booklet for *Nanook* suggested the film was "more spellbinding than hypnotism," for spellbinding it was: screened across the Western world, the film enjoyed a six-month run when it premiered in London and Paris, and it ran "even more sensationally" (according to Flaherty) in Berlin and Rome (*Campaign* 62; R. Flaherty, "Talking" 18). While American critics paid less attention to it than Flaherty or his biographers would have liked, it was, from the moment it was released, a popular success, and it is still played in American classrooms today as an example of good ethnography and cinematography.[22] It is no exaggeration, then, to suggest—as many scholars do—that the film incited a kind of "Nanookmania," an international craze for all things Eskimo that lasted for several years.[23] In fact, when Frances visited Berlin a decade after *Nanook*'s release, she bought an Eskimo pie in the Tiergarten and discovered, to her delight, that it was called a "Nanuk," the wrapper printed with Nanook's smiling face (22). The film's reliance on primitive cinematic aesthetics, then, did not hinder its popularity: fans flocked to screenings despite Flaherty's alleged artistic shortcomings. Capitalizing on those fascinating qualities Münsterberg suggested were unique to cinema, the film attracted massive audiences throughout the West.

This is, in the end, one of *Nanook*'s most interesting achievements: while it did, as critics are quick to point out, bring the techniques of classical cinema to bear on a new kind of story—one purportedly drawn from the fabric of everyday life—it also managed to revive, operationalize, and monetize the outmoded representational practices of preclassic cinema, breathing new life into the aesthetics of primitive film. Mapping the flatness of early cinematic aesthetics onto the flatness of the primitive face, *Nanook* provided audiences with an array of surfaces that both solicited their gaze and blocked their scopic mastery. Catching and holding the attention of viewers with images of Nanook's impenetrable face (as well as with the vast, shining landscape of the Hudson Bay), the film used flat aesthetics to fascinate audiences.

In the Land of the Head-Hunters, Surface, and Shine

While Flaherty is typically seen as the first true ethnographic filmmaker, an increasing number of scholars have suggested that he was actually beaten to the punch by Edward S. Curtis, whose *In the Land of the Head-Hunters* re-created the ceremonial elements of Kwakiutl life in painstaking detail.[24] Even though *Head-Hunters* is structured by a Romantic plotline of Curtis's own devising, Curtis was adamant that he "regarded the work from a purely educational standpoint," as the film's primary purpose was to preserve a record of Kwakiutl life ("Filming" 121). The film, in fact, influenced Flaherty significantly, and Flaherty even visited Curtis in New York while he was working on *Nanook.*[25] Both men, moreover, employed much the same method in their filmmaking—fabricating and staging certain elements of their films in the service of supposedly telling a larger truth—and, however much Flaherty apologists may claim some kind of unique documentary status for *Nanook* based on its less overtly Romantic overtones, *Nanook* and *Head-Hunters* are, as George Irving Quimby puts it, largely "the same kind of motion picture" ("Mystery" 50).[26]

There are, however, significant differences between the two films. In the first place, *Head-Hunters* was produced and released much earlier than *Nanook,* a product of, on the one hand, the late stages of primitive cinema and, on the other, an early-twentieth-century vogue for "films with Indian themes" (Holm and Quimby 32).[27] In the second place, Curtis never pretended that the plot of his film was true to Kwakiutl life; though he took great pains to ensure that the dances and rituals he depicted were reproduced accurately, it was clear to viewers from the beginning that he was offering a *documentaire romancé* or a "*fiction ethnographique*" rather than a truly documentary film (Maurel 220). Finally, while *Nanook* was an international blockbuster, *Head-Hunters* was a financial failure. This was, in some ways, due to historical bad luck: whereas *Nanook* was released during the early 1920s—a time of prosperity and cinematic innovation—*Head-Hunters* appeared shortly after the commencement of World War I, when public tastes abruptly shifted from Indian films to war films (Quimby, "Mystery" 53). The film was, in fact, so quickly and completely forgotten that, until it was rediscovered and rereleased in 1973 with a new soundtrack as *In the Land of the War Canoes,* it was thought to be lost to history.[28] It is no wonder, then, that scholars tend to cite the release of *Nanook* as ethnographic cinema's inaugural moment: both overtly fictionalized and a box office flop, *Head-Hunters* had a much smaller direct effect on subsequent documentary filmmakers. It did, however, represent primitive culture in ways strikingly anticipatory of Flaherty and reminiscent of Boas, linking primitive culture to aesthetic flatness and doubling the surface of the primitive body with the surface of the primitive film screen.

Curtis, of course, exhibited a predilection for aesthetic display even before he started filming *Head-Hunters.* He began his career, after all, as a still photographer, and he continues to be best known for having produced a twenty-volume collection of Indian portraits titled *The North American Indian.* Taking an overtly salvage ethnographic approach to his subjects in these portraits, he dressed them in primitive costumes to enhance their Indianness and erased from the photos all traces of modern life. Meant to be of both artistic and anthropological value, *The North American Indian* exhibited its subjects' faces in much the same way Flaherty's postcard shots exhibited Nanook and Nyla, crossing elements of pictorialist art photography with the "craniometric gaze" of the ethnographer and the racial pseudoscientist (Wakeham, *Taxidermic* 105–6). The project, which took several decades and a great deal of money to complete, led Curtis to offer a series of illustrated lectures on Indian life (largely as a means of fundraising for further fieldwork), and, in 1911, he premiered the Curtis "Musicale" or "Picture Opera," which integrated still and moving images with a lecture and live music to create a sort of ethnographic *Gesamtkunstwerk* (108).[29] Treating primitive culture as itself an attraction, Curtis's Indian portraits and lectures blended the methods of salvage ethnography with the primitive cinematic aesthetics of display.

Head-Hunters expanded upon this aesthetic project, presenting audiences with a collection of visual attractions only loosely held together by a diegetic narrative. After all, the purpose of the film was to display Kwakiutl artifacts and rituals, and the parts of the film that its contemporary audiences found "most fascinating" were "the spectacle of ceremonial dances, religious objects, [and] 'vision quests'" (Hearne 313). This spectacular aesthetic significantly shaped *Head-Hunters*'s cinematography, resulting in a film that, like *Nanook*, is largely composed of long shots taken from a static camera angle, its subjects arranged in *tableaux vivants* with "little depth of field" (Russell 101).[30] Several of the dances, for example, are clearly staged for the film, the dancers' range of movement limited by the camera's visual scope, and in the scene that depicts the traditional gambling game of *lehal*, the players are shown not in two parallel lines (as they should be for the sake of ethnographic accuracy) but in a single, tableau-like row that faces the audience (Wakeham, *Taxidermic* 115). This investment in display reduces the film's Romantic narrative to an afterthought; in fact, one contemporary reviewer went so far as to suggest that "the story . . . is a minor detail, the real object of the film being to show the customs, amusements, fights, domestic life, and sports of the North American Indians" ("Filming" 125). Employing the static camerawork and exhibitionary aesthetics of primitive cinema, Curtis depicts his subjects less as psychologically complex characters and more as objects of ethnographic display.

This tendency toward display is evident, as in *Nanook*, in the portrait sequence that introduces the film's main characters, visually establishing the *dramatis personae*. Though all but one of Curtis's introductory portraits have been lost (and the portraits that appear in *War Canoes* are simply photographs Curtis took of the lead actors during the filming of *Head-Hunters*), the one original that has survived—a profile shot of Naida—is telling.[31] Entirely static, it looks as if it could have been pulled directly from *The North American Indian*, displaying the immobile head and shoulders of Naida. Whereas Flaherty's postcard shots of Nanook and Nyla incorporate movement, rendering their faces passive but animate, Curtis's portrait freezes Naida completely, offering her up as an object for the "craniometric gaze" to inspect, an aestheticized attraction utterly removed from the film's diegesis. Reducing Naida's face to an inanimate object, Curtis outdoes even Flaherty in his flattening of the primitive face.

Curtis's investment in primitive flatness, however, does not stop at the face; indeed, *Head-Hunters* is in many ways about the proliferation of surfaces. Whereas Flaherty merely focuses on the topography of the face,

Curtis also presents the bodies of his subjects for inspection. In the film's opening scene, for example, in which the protagonist, Motana, dances and sleeps on a mountain, he is half-naked, nothing but a cedar bark robe wrapped around his waist; he remains in this exposed state as he travels to the Island of the Dead, hunts sea lion and whale, and rescues Naida from her captors. In fact, the only sequence in which his torso is covered occurs when he returns from his vision quest, and he appears fully clothed for no more than fifteen seconds in the entire film. This nudity is largely a cinematic contrivance, as the Kwakiutl had given up the traditional cedar bark robe long before Curtis began filming; he actually had to commission local women to braid cedar bark specifically for the film (Holm and Quimby 55). Beneath the gaze of Curtis's camera, however, Motana becomes an object of titillating display, his exposed chest and arms glinting in the natural light of the mountaintop and the seashore. Capitalizing on the temperate climate of the Pacific Northwest, the film expands Flaherty's investment in surface from the Indigenous face to the entire Indigenous body.

The only time the shine of Motana's body is eclipsed during the film is when the camera focuses on the shimmering surface of the ocean itself. As one reviewer put it, Curtis "is not afraid to point his camera at the sun, contrary to the instructions of the kodak primer"; indeed, "the scenes that elicited most applause from the audience were after all not those of Indian combats, but those of waves and clouds at sunset" ("Ethnology" 72). As in *Nanook,* one of the great attractions in *Head-Hunters* is the land itself. But, whereas Flaherty presents the land largely unaltered by special effects, Curtis uses the unique perceptual apparatus of the camera to highlight the ocean's surface, to capture and intensify its reflectivity. Just as Motana's bare body catches the sunlight in tantalizing ways, so, too, does the water itself, dazzling the eye with its reflective brilliance. The shine of the primitive body and the shine of the ocean actually combine in the final scene of the film, in which the villain Yaklus, thrown from his canoe by rough waves, drowns: first we see him lying on his back in the water, nothing but his face (and briefly his feet) exposed; then we are shown a prolonged shot of the same stretch of ocean with no Yaklus in it, the implication, of course, being that the water has swallowed him whole. Here the face and the land merge, literalizing the slippage noted by Deleuze, Guattari, and Rony, subsuming one shining surface into another. Shifting its attention from surface to surface, the camera highlights the reflectivity of the primitive body, face, and landscape, drawing attention to the way they catch and release the light.

Much of the film's appeal, then, lies in the shine produced by its surfaces. As Anne Anlin Cheng has shown in her work on early classical cinema, the shine of surface—particularly the shine of the nonwhite body's surface—has a strangely alluring quality to it; it "beckons us to plunge into a flat and reflective interiority" (1030). This shine, while primarily located on the body proper, can be intensified and extended through the addition of ornament, a technique that multiplies the surfaces upon which light can play, "expanding bodily periphery through the extension of inanimate objects" (1035). The effect of this kind of shine in narrative film is to interrupt the flow of the story, "activat[ing] cognitions that reach beyond the explicit domain of the diegesis": "In the superluminous moments when light seems to exceed the frames of the film, the viewer is moved furthest from the plot and transported . . . into another realm of seeing, hearing, and feeling" (1033). Such an understanding of shine, of course, usefully illuminates several aspects of *Head-Hunters*. It explains, for example, the particular fascination exerted by Motana's naked skin as well as the appeal of those dazzling shots of the sunlit ocean. It also sheds new light on the preponderance of ceremonial masks, costumes, and jewelry in the film—those artifacts that so intrigued the film's contemporary viewers—and frames them as methods not for concealing the primitive body but for extending it, for multiplying its surfaces. Perhaps most interestingly, however, this formulation explains Vachel Lindsay's famous claim that, because the Indian film should be "planned as bronze in action," *Head-Hunters* represented an aesthetic triumph, "abound[ing]," as it does, "in noble bronzes" (69). Presenting its audience with a proliferation of surfaces, *Head-Hunters* uses the alluring power of shine to capture spectatorial attention. Expanding its attention from the surface of the face to the surface of the body and its prosthetic ornaments—as well, of course, as the surface of the land—the film invites the eye to lose itself in the play of light.

Curtis thus takes the aesthetics of display and primitive externality to an extreme. While Flaherty's representational strategy relies primarily on static tableaux and the flatness of the face and the land, Curtis multiplies the surfaces in his film, inviting viewers to lose themselves not only in the primitive face and landscape but also in the primitive body and its ornaments. Combined with the overt fictitiousness of the film's narrative, this flattening of the primitive world constructs *Head-Hunters*'s Indigenous subjects as even more immaterial than *Nanook*'s, even less fleshy. Reducing Motana to a sheer surface for light to play upon, it foregrounds his virtuality: disappearing before the camera lens, he becomes an exemplary member of a vanishing race.

Virtuality and the Indigenous Subject

Before I conclude this chapter, I would like to think seriously for a moment about the way *Head-Hunters* virtualizes Motana. For this is indeed what Curtis does: he virtualizes the actors before his camera lens, reducing them to immaterial simulacra of themselves. This practice, as we have already seen, is borrowed, in part, from the salvage ethnographic methods of early-twentieth-century anthropology. But does it not also seem strangely postmodern, a precursor to the decorporealizing logic that, around the turn of the twenty-first century, gave rise to such phenomena as virtual reality and the internet? Indeed, it is a small step, I think, from the fascinating screen of the ethnographic film to the fascinating screen of the computer or smartphone (two devices that, like the ethnographer's camera, are often used to document and archive even the most banal of day-to-day events). For the next few pages, then, I would like to explore what it might mean to approach ethnographic film as a technology of virtualization, to ask how the historical practices of ethnographic filmmakers might reorient contemporary critical conversations about the nature of virtuality.

Perhaps unsurprisingly, such critical conversations often borrow from the work of Henri Bergson. After all, Bergson was deeply invested in the space of "the virtual," a concept that he theorized as an unrealized "*dimension* of [everyday] reality," an aspect of existence that, though lacking in material form, still had its own kind of reality (Massumi, "Envisioning" 55). For thinkers such as Brian Massumi and Elizabeth Grosz—two philosophers with whom we are by now quite familiar—this understanding of the virtual holds a great deal of heuristic value, as it helps to explain (and in some ways even justify) recent postmodern celebrations of the immaterial. Indeed, it helps them to locate postmodern culture within a long, legible history of technological and philosophical innovation: even if, for example, today's digital technologies may seem unprecedented in the history of the West, the Bergsonian notion of virtuality reassures us that "the real" is, in fact, "saturated with the spaces of projection, possibility, and the new that we now designate as virtual in order to keep them contained behind the glassy smoothness of the computer screen" (Grosz, *Architecture* 75, 78). Bridging the epistemological gap between early-twentieth-century philosophy and the postmodern present, the virtual signifies for contemporary philosophers those aspects of existence that are real but immaterial.

This concept has proven particularly appealing for cultural critics because of the way it aligns immateriality with radical change; indeed, "the base definition of the virtual in philosophy," according to Massumi, "'is potentiality'" ("Envisioning" 55). Insofar as it designates that which is real but not (yet) actual, it "teach[es] us that this reality always has the potential of being radically different from what it actually is" (Nusselder 82). For Massumi, this means that it designates a kind of "abstract event potential," that intangible quality of existence that makes it possible for the world to be otherwise (*Semblance* 16). For Grosz, "the unactualized potential of the virtual" is actually "the condition of all radical politics," for a truly radical politics "more or less accepts as desirable a dislocation or incoherence between the present and the future"; indeed, "the future as surprise is welcomed" (*Nick of Time* 253, 258).[32] Like affect, the virtual represents a force of emergent futurity: it reveals the contingency of the world that is and points the way toward a world that could be. It is, in the words of Grosz, that "spark of indetermination" that makes meaningful change possible ("Feminism" 153).

Paradoxically, however, the future engendered by the virtual is always a product of the past. As Grosz puts it, "The virtual" is, in fact, "another name for the inherence of the past in the present, for the capacity to become other"; because the past "is the condition of innovation and the new," "the new can be formed only through a kind of eruption or interruption of the present that . . . is a reworking of the past so that the present is different from itself" (*Nick of Time* 252). In other words, it is the "inherence of the past in the present" that invests the present with its productive instability: it "layers and resonates the present, refuses to allow the present the stability of the given or the inevitable" (*Architecture* 111). For Massumi, this lends a certain "untimeliness" to the virtual, a quality of always being "*too early* or *too late* (perhaps even both at once)"; indeed, the virtual reaches out toward both past and future, transforming the latent potential of the past *into* the emergent future ("Envisioning" 56). Not only does it signify the real but not yet actual, then; it also signifies the real but *no longer* actual, a past that is no longer present but that might be reanimated in—or, more precisely, as—the future. Balanced between the no-longer and the not-yet, the virtual represents the site where the past becomes the future.

One thing to keep in mind, of course, is that, from the Bergsonian point of view, the virtual never actually realizes itself as a concrete past or future; if it did, it could no longer be called the virtual. Instead, it occupies a position of perpetual indetermination between the no-longer-actualized past and the future-not-yet-actualized-as-present. Indeed, Massumi aligns the virtual with "nonlinear processes: resonance and feedback that momentarily suspend the linear progress of the narrative present from past to future"; "it is a state of suspense," "a temporal sink" or "a hole in time" (*Parables* 26). Not only, then, is the virtual untimely; it is also in a sense timeless, existing beyond—beneath, above, and beside—the homogeneous time and space of actual reality. Even as its function is to translate the past into the future, the virtual itself resists concrete temporalization.

Though what I am about to suggest may sound strange, I would like to argue that this kind of virtuality—the virtuality of Grosz and Massumi—is precisely the kind of virtuality at play in films such as *Nanook* and *Head-Hunters*. After all, what kind of world does Motana occupy if not one that has "a kind of reality" but "is not . . . actual," a world that hyperrealistically indexes our own but that, nonetheless, exists only on-screen (Nusselder

75)? Does this world not also mediate between past and future the way the Bergsonian virtual does, transforming the premodern figure of the primitive body into a hypermodern representation of itself? If this chapter's central claim has been that ethnographic cinema maps the fascination of the Indigenous subject onto the fascination of the cinematic image (and, in so doing, transports audiences into fascinated states of temporal suspension), it would not be farfetched to suggest that the virtuality of Motana and Nanook is, indeed, the virtuality of Grosz and Massumi.

From these thinkers' perspectives, then, Nanook and Motana might look like figures of radical futurity, symbols of modern technology's creative power. After all, they did provide Flaherty and Curtis—two of cinema's most celebrated innovators—with the visual material they needed to hone their craft, the motivation to explore film's technical and representational possibilities. Approaching Nanook and Motana from this perspective, however, raises one important question: *for whom* were these possibilities explored? For while it is certainly possible to approach the virtualization of the Indigenous subject as an example of cultural preservation or technological innovation, such an approach glosses over the very real violence done to Indigenous subjects that, as we have already seen, such virtualization facilitates and even relies upon. Indeed, if the virtual signifies reality's potential to be "radically different from what it actually is," *Nanook* and *Head-Hunters* show us that the realization of this potential is not always ethically or politically desirable. We might even go so far as to say that the recent critical turn toward the virtual simultaneously relies upon and obfuscates a distinctly salvage ethnographic mindset, the kind of colonial worldview that, in the early twentieth century, reduced the Indigenous body to an image with which filmmakers like Flaherty and Curtis could experiment.

While this line of analysis may seem largely theoretical in nature, it is also deeply historical, for the virtual technology of film and the figure of the vanishing Indian emerged alongside one another in roughly the same historical moment. This moment, moreover, was the moment in which fascination began to be understood not as a material, embodied phenomenon but as an immaterial emanation of surface. Ethnographic cinema capitalized upon all three of these developments: shifting the locus of fascination from the Indigenous body to the image of the Indigenous body, it mapped the premodern enchantment of the Indian onto the modern enchantment of the cinematic screen. The medium thus functioned as a chiasm between premodern and modern modes of fascination, between embodied and disembodied entrancement. Capturing spectatorial attention with its multifaceted flatness, it pivoted fascination out of the materialist world of the nineteenth century and into the immaterial world of the twentieth.

This immaterial world, of course, is largely the world in which we still live, and this understanding of fascination—as a property of the virtualizing screen—is certainly the understanding embraced by most Americans today. After all, one need only flip through the "Opinions" section of the *Washington Post* or the *New York Times* to see that, as a culture, we are still exceedingly anxious about our screens' powers of entrancement, even if this anxiety is expressed in terms of "screen time" and "phone addiction" rather than hypnotic suggestion. Indeed, fascination is experiencing a kind of renaissance in our present historical moment, as we are increasingly finding ourselves surrounded by proliferating technologies of captivation and perceptual manipulation. This technological proliferation, moreover, has been paralleled by a proliferation of scholarly work on nonrational experience and inhuman agency, the kind of posthumanist, new materialist, and affect theoretical work toward which I have gestured at various points throughout this book. For much of the twentieth century, however, Americans seemed to lose interest in perceptual fixation and compulsive attention, at least as theorized by the likes of Bergson and James. By way of a conclusion, then, let us return to the early decades of the twentieth century and explore how and why this came to pass.

CONCLUSION

From Modern Fascination to Modernist Fascination

IF HENRY ADAMS WAS overwhelmed at the Great Exposition of 1900 by the sheer modernity of the dynamo—a machine whose powers of attraction left his "historical neck broken"—the hypermodern world of the 1920s and 1930s would have broken much more than his historical neck (382). After all, the cultural milieu that produced both *Nanook of the North* and some of high modernism's most famous formal experiments would have been unrecognizable to a genteel nineteenth-century intellectual like Adams. Not only did these years bestow a certain high-cultural validation on phenomena (such as film) that had previously been considered popular, low, or unseemly; they also witnessed a dramatic shift in the way Americans thought and wrote about those supersensual forces that Adams spent his life trying to theorize.

Indeed, by the 1920s and 1930s, many Americans had traded in the mysticism of vitalist psychology for a more psychosexual understanding of the self. To a certain extent, there was good reason for this: while the romantic oblivion of the *durée réelle* was all well and good, the comparatively scientific disciplines of sexology and psychoanalysis purported to offer a less metaphysical—and therefore more therapeutically practical—theory of the unconscious. Describing the motivations behind human behavior not in terms of an élan vital but in terms of sex, they reduced Adams's supersensual forces of attraction and stupefaction to the hypersensual force of the libido. They spoke not of the mystical powers of fascination, then, but of fetishism and sexual fixation, terms that diminished the language of enchantment to a metaphor for sexual desire. One benefit of such psychosexual models of the self was their psychiatric efficacy: whereas Bergson vaguely suggested that one needed to engage "intuition" to access the liberating forces of the *durée réelle*, Sigmund Freud and his followers offered a therapeutic practice that manipulated the unconscious in a more systematic way. It is thus no surprise that psychoanalytic (and, later, sexological) ideas proved influential in the United States, a nation already familiar—thanks to its long romance with mesmerism and mind-cure—with the basic tenets of the talking cure. While vitalist thought certainly did not vanish after the turn of the twentieth century, then, it was largely overshadowed in the public eye by the emergent psychology of sex.

It was also in the early decades of the twentieth century, of course, that modernism emerged.[1] Just as turn-of-the-century theories of fascination gave way to psychosexual theories of fetishism and fixation, so, too, did the fascinating aesthetics of decadentism and naturalism give way to the aesthetics of modernist experimentation. Indeed, if the discourse of fascination had long tended to blur the line between modern present and premodern past, this tendency found its culmination in the primitivist practices of modern art and literature, practices that, for better or worse, could not help but attract attention. Not only, then, did fascination pave the way for sexological and psychoanalytic theories of mind; it also laid the aesthetic foundations for American modernism.

Critical common sense, of course, dictates that modernism owes more of a debt to its discursive contemporaries, sexology and psychoanalysis, than to the historical discourse of trance. As Joseph Allen Boone and Michael Trask put it, modernism's "crises of narrative authority" in many ways represent "an extension of the irregular or perverse desires that sexology liberated" (Boone 10; Trask 1).[2] According to this view, the primary irrational force that modernist writers aimed to harness was sex, as the libido provided them with a useful tool for disrupting narrative and experimenting with formal fragmentation. I would like to suggest, however, that neither modernism nor the psychology of sex were ever fully able to rid themselves of the specter of fascination, offering accounts of the unconscious mind that were strangely haunted by the language of enchantment and entrancement. By way of a conclusion, then, I would like to look briefly at Djuna Barnes's *Nightwood* (1936), a formally experimental novel that, in recounting the disastrous love affair between two women—Nora Flood, a circus promoter, and Robin Vote, a "true born invert"—draws on both the psychosexual ideas of early sexologists and the vitalist discourse of fascination to craft a distinctively entrancing high modernist aesthetic (Faderman 364). Depicting the relationship between Nora and Robin in terms of both queer sexual attraction and compulsive attention, the novel exemplifies the way modernist writing blurred the line between the "perverse desires" unleashed by sexology and the compulsive forms of attention theorized by vitalist thinkers.

From the very beginning of the novel, it is clear that Robin—*Nightwood*'s most overtly sexologized character—is a "born somnambule." When we first meet her, she is passed out in a hotel room, her legs "spread as in a dance," her "thick-lacquered pumps looking too lively for the arrested step" (Barnes 38). This fainting spell—which uncannily freezes her body in the "arrested step" of a somnambulic "dance"—recalls "the fainting spell of a hysteric," that pose "so often depicted as the death-like throws of ecstasy in the photographic images of Charcot's patients at the Salpêtrière" (Hutchison 219). This is because even as Barnes draws on the sexological discourse of sexual inversion to characterize Robin, her "intellectual origins are [also] to be found" in "Anton Mesmer's experiments with hypnotism" and the "intellectual history of 'somnambulism'" (Marcus, *Hearts* 108, 107, 108). Rendered in the language of both inversion and entrancement, Robin appears throughout the novel as a kind of queer magnetic somnambule.

Robin's propensity for somnambulism helps to explain another of her defining character traits: her penchant for drink. For in almost every scene, "she [is] drunk" (52). And while we could simply chalk this up to a characteristically modernist interest in alcohol and alcoholism on the part of Barnes, we might be better served to remember that drunkenness was also a pet interest of nineteenth-century theorists of fascination.[3] Indeed, for someone like George Miller Beard, inebriation and somnambulism represented different manifestations of the same psychic phenomenon. While trance states could "be produced naturally by an immense variety of causes" (such as "epilepsy, hysteria, or insanity, or simple neurasthenia"), they could be produced "just as well" by "alcohol" (Introduction 7). Robin's drunkenness thus might be understood as another manifestation of her affinity for trance.

This affinity, of course, lends her a certain fascination. Nora, after all, is consumed throughout the novel by an obsessive, monomaniacal love for Robin, one that leaves her "mind . . . so transfixed that . . . Robin seem[s] enormous and polarized" (Barnes 62). Even when Robin does something as mundane as get ready in another room, Nora cannot tear her attention away from her: she "tabulate[s] by the sounds of Robin dressing the exact progress of her toilet; chimes of cosmetic bottles and cream jars; the faint perfume of hair heated under the electric curlers; seeing in her mind the changing direction taken by the curls that hung on Robin's forehead . . . Half narcotized by the sounds" (64). Her obsession culminates in a scene in which she is physically overwhelmed by her attraction to Robin. When, one night, Nora sees Robin in the courtyard of their home, she finds herself fascinated by Robin's gaze: "Standing motionless, straining her eyes, she saw emerge from the darkness the light of Robin's eyes, the fear in them developing their luminosity until, by the intensity of their double regard, Robin's eyes and hers met. So they gazed at each other" (69). Nora then sees that Robin is there with another woman, "her arms about Robin's neck, her body pressed to Robin's, her legs slackened in the hang of the embrace": "Unable to turn her eyes away, incapable of speech, experiencing a sensation of evil, complete and dismembering, Nora fell to her knees, so that her eyes were not withdrawn by her volition, but dropped from their orbit by the falling of her body" (70). In this moment, Nora is literally overpowered by the sight of Robin: thrust into a state of unconscious automatism, she loses control of her body, collapsing against her will. Just as entrancing in this scene as she is entranced, Robin overwhelms Nora with her gaze, literally bringing her to her knees.

This moment is uncannily reminiscent of the late nineteenth century. For in it, Robin resembles any number of the fascinating and fascinated characters we have examined in the foregoing chapters: like Spofford's Yone, she casts a spell over her lover, thrusting Nora into a kind of horrific dream; like Dreiser's Carrie or Dunbar's Kitty, this power to entrance is facilitated by her own entrancement. Even, then, as she may embody the sexological figure of the true born invert, she also conjures up a variety of nineteenth-century figures of fascination. In so doing, she knits together the discourses of sexuality and entrancement, using her susceptibility to fascination to capture the sexual attentions of Nora. Shaped in equal parts by the discourses of fascination and inversion, she bridges the gap between trance and sex.

If Robin, one of *Nightwood*'s most important characters, wanders through much of the novel in a trance, it should perhaps come as no surprise that, for many readers, Barnes's style itself seems to be imbued with a certain fascination. Critics have long commented on the idiosyncratic diction and syntax of the novel, variously calling Barnes's language "lavish," "too stylized," (neo)baroque, and even decadent (Baxter 1176; Caselli 156).[4] One particularly Jamesian critic, for example, suggests that the novel has "minimal plot and character" but plenty of "exotic rhetoric"; another describes *Nightwood*'s form as "spatial," driven not by narrative necessity but by the "interweaving of images and phrases independently of any time-sequence" (Singer 66; Frank 456). Take, for example, the sentence that introduces Robin: "On a bed, surrounded by a confusion of potted plants, exotic palms and cut flowers, faintly over-sung by the notes of unseen birds, which seemed to have been forgotten—left without the usual silencing cover, which, like cloaks on funeral urns, are cast over their cages at night by good housewives—half flung off the support of the cushions from which, in a moment of threatened consciousness she had turned her head, lay the young woman, heavy and disheveled" (37–38). Like Spofford's writing, it is both elaborately descriptive and syntactically difficult: in fact, "by the time the reader reaches the end of this split independent clause, it is easy to forget who or what topic we encountered" at its beginning (Herring 184). Strung together, we might say, "like beads on a leash," *Nightwood* takes up the ornamental techniques of decadent description and uses them to disrupt the teleological movement of its narrative (H. James, review of *Azarian* 270).

Consequently, the novel's form is strangely repetitive and nonlinear, moving, like the naturalist novels we encountered in chapter 3, for the sake of movement. After all, much of the novel follows Robin as she "go[es] from table to table, from drink to drink, from person to person," moving "in a formless meditation," "her thoughts . . . themselves a form of lo-comotion" (64). Simultaneously devastated by and fixated upon Robin's faithlessness, Nora, too, wanders the streets at night, compulsively looking for "traces of Robin" (66). Even after Robin has left Nora for a new lover, the two women cannot seem to help circling back to and around one an-other. Indeed, the second half of the novel largely focuses on Nora com-pulsively retelling the story of their affair, and the narrative concludes with Robin leaving her new lover, Jenny Petherbridge, to "circle . . . closer and closer" to Nora, ending her wanderings on Nora's figurative doorstep (177). This structure, of course, is strikingly similar to what I called in chapter 3 the restless, wandering form of naturalist fiction. And while Robin's and Nora's wanderings are, in part, motivated by sexual desire, they are just as much driven by Robin's penchant for sleepwalking. Imperfectly translating the hypnotic movements of Carrie and Kitty into the discourse of same-sex attraction, *Nightwood*'s itinerant plot is propelled in equal parts by trance and sexual desire.

If Barnes's style is as decadent as Spofford's and her plot as peripatetic as Dreiser's, it makes sense that critics should often be struck by the strange temporality of *Nightwood*, its failure to move forward according to the real-ist logic of narrative progress. In the words of Kathryn Bond Stockton, the novel "seems not to move at all . . . to many readers": as it progresses, its "sense of chronological time . . . gradually reced[es]," and "the fifth section of *Nightwood*, 'Watchman, What of the Night?' is out of time altogether" (Stockton, *Queer* 106; Kannenstine 92).[5] This sense of "being out of time altogether," I suggest, is closely linked to what Jeanette Winterson calls the "narcotic quality" of Barnes's writing: by piling long, convoluted sentence upon long, convoluted sentence, "Barnes attempts to overwhelm the reader, so we become as drunken and disoriented as Robin Vote" (Winterson x; Loncraine 301). Like "The Amber Gods" or *Sister Carrie*, the novel aims to entrance its readers, to lull them into a state of suspended consciousness.

This fascinating style borrows at least some of its force from its exper-imental engagement with cubist aesthetics. After all, "*Nightwood* is governed, not by the logic of verisimilitude, but by the demands of the decor necessary to enhance the symbolic significance of the characters"; "we are asked only to accept their world as we accept an abstract painting . . . as an autonomous pattern giving us an individual vision of reality, rather than what we might consider its exact reflection" (Frank 435, 438). The novel's "sense of suspended motion" thus comes from its "refraction of key actions through Cubist-inspired verbal repetitions," a technique that "resists the insistent forward march of history" and makes "time itself seem . . . to fracture into many pieces" (Boone 220; Glavey 49; Boone 241). Such temporal disruption, of course, is one of cubism's primary objectives, as cubist painting aims, in the words of Guillaume Apollinaire, to "embrace at a glance the past, present and future" (9). Rejecting the progressive imperatives of narrative form, *Nightwood* uses the representational practices of abstract art to suspend the movement of linear time.

This ultimately brings us back to the allure of surface that was the central focus of chapter 4. For if, as we saw there, early ethnographic cinema captivated audiences by mapping the fascinating surface of the primitive body onto the fascinating surface of the cinematic screen, cubism aims to do something strikingly similar. Indeed, the defining characteristic of cubist painting is its disdain for perspectival illusionism, its rejection of "linear perspective" in favor of "the two-dimensional picture surface" (Cooper 19). This privileging of surface, moreover, represents a self-consciously primitivist representational strategy, one borrowed, in the words of one art historian, from "the more primitive, less naturalistically subservient art of ancient Mediterranean civilizations, of early Greek art and of Egyptian art" (20). Like ethnographic cinema, cubism mobilizes the flat aesthetics of primitive culture, emphasizing the superficiality of the canvas itself.

To put things simply, *Nightwood* takes up, modifies, and employs the strategies and techniques of fascination that have been the focus of this book as a whole. In Barnes's writing, the captivating, accretive style of decadent fiction becomes a cubist multiplication of lines and planes; the compulsive, repetitive movements of the naturalist actress crystallize into the recursive structure of spatial form; and the flatness of the ethnographic film becomes the superficiality of the abstract work of art. The effect of these representational practices, moreover, is a collapse of linear time, both the historical time that separates the modern from the primitive and the narrative time of realist form. Twisting its ornamental language into elaborate narrative loops, the novel weaves itself into an impenetrable surface—the fascinating surface of modern art.

Nightwood, of course, merely represents one example of modernism's aesthetic investment in fascination. For another example, we might look to someone like Gertrude Stein, who was even more notorious than Barnes for employing cubist techniques in her writing and whose prose was often driven by the same kind of stylized plotlessness that characterizes *Nightwood*.[6] We might also look to the flat, journalistic prose of many of Barnes's other expatriate peers (such as F. Scott Fitzgerald and Ernest Hemingway) as well as the "dry, hard" imagery of the Imagist poets (Hulme 79).[7] For as Hugh Kenner famously put it, "the language flattened, the language *exhibited*, the language staunchly condensing information while frisking in enjoyment of its release from the obligation to do no more than inform: these are the elements of a twentieth-century poetic, a pivotal discovery of our age" (106). Yet insofar as this exhibitionary language borrowed its fascinating representational techniques from decadentism, regionalism, naturalism, and ethnographic cinema, we might more accurately call this "twentieth-century poetic" a *rediscovery*. For if, as a writer like Adams knew, modernization was just as much about reviving the old, the outmoded, and even the archaic as it was about "making it new," modernism might best be understood as an extension of—rather than a break from—the fascinating aesthetic schools that preceded it.

To put things simply: modernist aesthetics emerged from those turn-of-the-century practices of enchantment and entrancement that have been the central concern of this book. If modernism indeed borrowed its difficult style, its descriptivism, and its obsession with surface from nineteenth-century literary movements such as decadentism and naturalism, it also, I hope to have shown, borrowed these traits from the aesthetics of fascination. Just as the thoroughly nineteenth-century practices of mesmerism and hypnotism ultimately gave rise to the proto-modernist philosophies of James and Bergson (as well as, a century later, the postmodern philosophies of affect theory, posthumanist theory, and feminist new materialist theory), so, too, did the thoroughly nineteenth-century aesthetics of Spofford, Chesnutt, Dreiser, and Dunbar lay the groundwork for the fascinating formal innovations of modernist literature. Emerging in the mid-nineteenth century as a way to describe and critique the conditions of modern life, the discourse of fascination eventually culminated in the impenetrable, primitivist art of the twentieth century, a kind of art whose enchantment and allure endure to this day.

NOTES

Introduction: The Fascination of Modern Life

1. For more on interest, see Ngai, *Our Aesthetic Categories* 110–73.

2. For more on the sublime, see Kant 75–189.

3. For more on glamour, see J. Brown, especially the introduction (1–19).

4. For more on wonder, see Bennett, *Enchantment,* especially the first chapter (3–16).

5. For a more or less arbitrary example of this genre of think piece, see Rose.

6. For more on the conceptual history of fascination, see Degen, "Concepts" and *Ästhetische Faszination*; Baumbach; Seeber, "Magic"; Weingart; and Gregory.

7. For a broad overview of this transformation, see two classic works, Trachtenberg; and Kern.

8. See Weber 35.

9. See, for example, Owens; Albanese; and McGarry; as well as any number of essays in the 2013 special issue of *American Literary History* on (post)secularity, *American Literatures / American Religions* (especially Ebel and Murison; Fessenden; and Modern, "Commentary").

10. See Fretwell 12–19; and Gaskill 21–31.

1. From Mesmerism to Mind Cure: A History of American Fascination

1. Spiritualism may, in the context of these other movements, seem like a glaring omission from this project, as it grew out of and closely resembled the trance-based practices of animal magnetists; for more on this relationship, see Taves, *Fits* 166–206; R. Fuller 95–100; and Braude. The reasons I do not address it here are twofold: first, spiritualists, unlike animal magnetists, by and large did not claim to be practicing any sort of science, attributing somnambulic phenomena like clairvoyance and telepathy not to the physiology of the human body but to the work of spirits; and second, spiritualist séances typically involved the self-entrancement of a single medium, a practice that did not involve (and in fact foreclosed the possibility of) the action of one human mind or body upon another.

2. Though scholars such as Britt Rusert have persuasively argued against using the term *pseudoscience* to describe nineteenth-century science (because the term has historically been

used to discount the epistemic practices of marginalized communities and because it discursively positions a supposedly objective, empirical present against a benighted, unscientific past), I intentionally use the term here for two reasons. First, several of the practices addressed throughout this book (such as mesmerism and New Thought) were in fact considered pseudoscientific by many late-nineteenth- and early-twentieth-century Americans. These practices, moreover, did not belong to the marginalized; they were largely developed and embraced by white men, and they were often used to position women, Indigenous people, and people of color as irrational, subhuman, and improperly modern. Second, my aim in this chapter is to show how particular forms of institutionalized philosophy and science have their roots in those practical and popular forms of pseudoscience that we—as good modern subjects—like to disavow. Thus while Rusert suggests that "the deployment of *pseudoscience* tries to imagine a scientific present unencumbered by an embarrassing scientific past," I use the term to opposite effect: both to signal the way turn-of-the-twentieth-century science and philosophy tried to distance themselves from their antebellum pasts and to demonstrate how this strategy of disavowal was necessarily compromised, partial, and incomplete (6).

3. I use the terms *mesmerism* and *animal magnetism* interchangeably as, while *mesmerism* may in its most technical sense refer only to the collection of ideas and practices pioneered by Franz Anton Mesmer and *animal magnetism* refers to the slightly wider array of theories and practices that sprang from Mesmer's work, many nineteenth-century writers used these terms to describe the same phenomenon.

4. For more on Mesmer's actual practices (which can only be described as absolutely bizarre, including, as they did, the wearing of a lilac cape, the playing of a glass harmonica, and the touching of patients with an iron wand), see Hart, "Hypnotism" 1215; as well as R. Fuller 6–7.

5. While Joseph du Commun, an otherwise unremarkable French professor, also gave a series of lectures on mesmerism at New York's Hall of Science as early as 1829, these lectures did not take hold of the public's imagination the way Poyen's did. For more on du Commun, see Nygren 100.

6. For more on the life and work of Charles Poyen, see Carlson; Ogden, "Beyond"; Quinn; Ayer 248–50; and Poyen's own account of his life in *Progress* (39–56).

7. For more on the relationship between mesmerism and ether, see Schmit 418; as well as Quinn 246. For various accounts of teeth being extracted and tumors excised from magnetized patients, see, again, Schmit 413; Carlson 125; and Poyen, *Progress* 73–76, 178, 188–90.

8. See, too, Schmit 407.

9. For a few examples of women convulsing, see Poyen, *Progress* 69, 85, 172, 202; for Poyen's account of Gleason's nonconsensual magnetization, also see *Progress* 124–25.

10. Accounts of such experiments appear throughout Poyen's text, performed in various places by various magnetists. For an example of the use of pins and hair pulling, however, see Poyen, *Progress* 210; for an example of the use of gunshots and ammonia, also see Poyen, *Progress* 131.

11. For more on Deleuze's extensive influence, see Lind 1078.

12. Both Poyen and Deleuze, for example, instruct their audience to establish "the same degree of heat" between the hands of operator and subject as well as to bring one's

hands "down . . . before the face, at a distance of one or two inches" (Poyen, "M. Poyen's" 9; J. Deleuze 41).

13. For more on classical and medieval ideas about action at a distance, see Kovach; and Weingart 77–81.

14. See, for example, Gauld 264–67.

15. On ether, see, again, Schmit 418; and Quinn 246. On the rise of spiritualism and its relationship with animal magnetism, see Taves, *Fits* 167–68; and Gauld 192–93.

16. The belief that snakes entrance through smell was held at least as early as 1851, when Hawthorne, in *The House of the Seven Gables*, made mention of the "serpent, which, as a preliminary to fascination, is said to fill the air with his peculiar odor" (168). Poyen also gestures to the idea that magnetic fluid is in fact vaporous in his letter to Col. William L. Stone, in which he claims that "an emanation of some kind . . . springs from the brain" of magnetist and magnetic subject, forming "about them a peculiar atmosphere" (10).

17. I borrow the term *antimodernist* from Lears, *No Place*.

18. For more on the debate that took place between Charcot and what has come to be known as the Nancy school (usually associated with Ambroise-Auguste Liébeault and Hippolyte Bernheim), see Hart, "Schools"; as well as Gauld 306–56.

19. For more on the way animal magnetism was "reconstituted . . . as hypnotism in order to divest it of its popular connotations," see Taves, *Fits* 122.

20. See Taves, *Fits* 253–54.

21. See also Beard, Introduction 7–8.

22. See the *New York Times* article of January 11, 1881, titled "The Science of Trance: Dr. Beard Repeats His Mesmeric Seances."

23. See the *New York Times* article of January 7, 1881, titled "Mesmeric Experiments: Dr. George M. Beard and His Four Young Men."

24. Today's reader might still detect a homoerotic element in Beard's experiments, as it is hard not to read sexual overtones into one observer's report that, to wake a subject, Beard "smoothed his forehead as affectionately as a woman" ("Science of Trance" 2). This erotic element, however, did not seem to register with Beard's contemporaries in the way the sexual and moral dangers of mesmerism registered with Poyen's.

25. For more on the use of hypnotism as a party trick, see the *New York Times* article of April 3, 1881, titled "Mesmerism in Society." As Gauld points out, Beard in fact was, "among the American neurologists, the only one who showed significant interest in hypnotism" (351).

26. See the *British Medical Journal* articles of 1891 titled "Hypnotism in America" and "Dangers of Hypnotism."

27. See P. Quimby 30; as well as R. Fuller 119.

28. Some attempts were made by early hypnotists to connect serpentine fascination to hypnosis, but these attempts made no mention of vapors or atmospheres; see, for example, Wright.

29. See, for example, P. Quimby 43–56.

30. The language (and even the strange gnostic style) of the Bible recur so often in Quimby's manuscripts that it would be difficult to pinpoint just one illustrative moment.

Two sections that are particularly biblical in tone and content, however, are "Questions and Answers" and "Christ or Science" (P. Quimby 165–78, 179–229).

31. For more on the lantern model of the eye (which held that, rather than receive impressions from the outside world, the eye projected a kind of light onto objects of perception), see Gregory 145–47.

32. See, for example, Gale.

33. See W. James, *Varieties* 379–429, 387–89; as well as Bordogna 519.

34. On James's presidency of the SPR, see Murphy and Ballou's edited volume of James's writing (55–63). On his belief in telepathy, see Bordogna 518. On his interest in spirit mediums and séances, see, for example, sections 3 and 4 of Murphy and Ballou, "Clairvoyance, Levitation, and 'The Astral Body'" and "William James and Mrs. Piper" (71–210).

35. On James's meeting with Janet, see Bordogna 515. On James's general interest in Janet's work, see Taves, "Religious Experience" 306–11; and any number of chapters in W. James, *Principles*, especially chapter 10, "The Consciousness of the Self" (188–259); as well as Gale 261. James was actually a member of the Society for Psychical Research's Committee on Hypnotism; his articles in the *Proceedings* include *Report of the Committee on Hypnotism* (coauthored with M. Carnochan) and "Reaction-Time in the Hypnotic Trance."

36. On the "cash value" of ideas, see, for example, W. James, *Pragmatism* 21.

37. While James does discuss the possible existence of magnetic fluid in *The Principles of Psychology* only to immediately discount it, his belief in an animating spiritual force embraces the same sort of vitalist thought that shaped the theories of Deleuze and Poyen (838–39).

38. For more on the personal relationship between James and Bergson, see Perry 338–52; and McGrath 610; as well as the correspondence between the two men in volumes 10–12 of W. James, *Correspondence*; and Bergson, *Mélanges* (roughly) 566–816). For more on the intellectual relationship between the two men, see Girel; Worms; and Herwig.

39. While Bergson's disparagement of everyday consciousness is quite evident in his first major work, *Time and Free Will*, he came in his later work to acknowledge that everyday consciousness and intuitive experience—which he associated with the *durée réelle*—simply represent different (but equally useful) modes of being in the world. For more on the relative usefulness of intuition and everyday intellection, see McGrath 609–12.

40. This position on free will, which Bergson explains in *Matter and Memory*, is an abrupt reversal of the one he took seven years earlier in *Time and Free Will*, in which he claimed that "to act freely is to recover possession of oneself, and to get back into pure duration" (232). This shift in position is due, I would suggest, to a shift in methodology between the two books: while *Time and Free Will* is, at its core, a critique of time and space—one that only employs the idea of consciousness insofar as this idea serves the book's deeply metaphysical project—*Matter and Memory* is much more psychologically driven, a project whose primary goal is to define the nature of consciousness and its relation to the world.

41. For more on the emergence and rise of affect theory, see Reber; Fischer; and Clough 1–33; as well as "An Inventory of Shimmers" in Seigworth and Gregg.

42. It is generally agreed that there are two schools of affect theoretical thought: the materialist Tomkinsean-Ekmanian school, which builds on the "basic emotions" paradigm of psychologist Silvan S. Tomkins (and which is perhaps best represented by the work of Eve Sedgwick); and the more metaphysical Spinozist-Deleuzean school, which often explicitly draws on the ideas of James and Bergson (and which is perhaps best represented by the work of Brian Massumi) (Leys 434–44; Seigworth and Gregg 5–6). It is the Spinozist-Deleuzean school with which I am primarily concerned here.

43. For more on Massumi's "speculative pragmatism," see "The Ether and Your Anger: Toward a Speculative Pragmatism," the second chapter of *Semblance* (29–38).

44. For definitions of these terms, see Massumi, *Semblance* 85.

45. For more on the essential relationship Massumi posits between affect and futurity, see "The Future Birth of the Affective Fact: The Political Ontology of Threat," in which he positions the rationalism of political discourse against "the more compelling, future-oriented, and affective register" (58).

46. This is the central tenet of what we might call the identity-political critique of affect; for more on this critique, see Hsieh 231; as well as Wetherell 60–61.

2. Amuletic Aesthetics and the Fascination of Decadent Style

1. Throughout this chapter, I use the term *decadentism* (rather than the simpler *decadence*) as a rough synonym for *decadent style*. This is because the term *decadentism* signals, for me, a self-conscious, aestheticized engagement with decadent values, whereas *decadence*—which has historically been levied as a kind of exonymic insult against decadent artists and writers—implies less cultural self-awareness. Even, then, if *decadentism* is perhaps most often associated with a distinctly Italian manifestation of decadent aesthetics, I use it to signify any kind of elaborate style that self-reflexively conceptualizes itself as decadent.

2. For more on Nietzsche's treatment of Socrates's decadence, see Degen, "Sokrates."

3. See "Fascinum, Fascinus."

4. On the evil eye's catastrophic consequences, see the *Dictionnaire des antiquités:* "D'une façon générale le mauvais œil détruisait tout le bonheur de la victim; il pouvait l'atteindre non seulement dans sa personne, mais dans ses biens et dans tout ce qui lui était cher" (984). On the overlap between fascination and the evil eye, see "Fascinum," *Dictionary;* as well as Degen, "Sokrates" 9.

5. The *Paulys Realencyclopädie der classischen Altertumswissenschaft* calls fascination a kind of charm that "jeder ausüben kann" (2009). For more on the fascination worked by jealous gods, see "Fascinum, Fascinus" 983.

6. For more on the use of the term *fascinum*, see "Fascinum," *Paulys* 2009; and *Dictionary* 234. For more on commonly used apotropaic images, see the entries for *fascinum* in the *Dictionary of Classical Antiquities*, the *Dictionnaire des antiquités*, and the *Paulys Realencyclopädie;* as well as Clerc 642. For more on the apotropaic powers of amber and coral, see Jahn 43–44;

and *Paulys* 2010. Interestingly enough, both of these substances still play an important role in apotropaic folk practices today. Amber, for example, is still used as a supernatural prophylactic in certain Jewish belief systems; see Moss and Cappannari 8; Lykiardopolous 226; and "Evil Eye." In Italy and Spain, amber and coral are both still incorporated into protective amulets; see Hildburgh 147–48.

7. The general purpose of the amulet was to break or redirect an envious glance by any means necessary ("die schädliche Kraft des neidischen Blicks . . . euf irgend eine Weise [zu] stör[en]"); grotesque or fearful images (such as beasts of prey or medusae) achieved this not by attracting the gaze but by terrifying onlookers ("schrecken") (Jahn 57).

8. For more on Spofford's conventional association with the Romantic and the gothic, see Bendixen xi; Bode 234; Logan 37; and St. Armand 102.

9. Instead, critics tend to focus on the story's relationship with genre and/or race. On genre, see, again, Bendixen; Bode; and St. Armand; as well as Bernardi 139, 141–42. On race, see, again, Logan; as well as Ellis.

10. See Luciano, "Geological"; as well as the chapter on Spofford in Beam (131–63).

11. On the sunlight theory, see Rogers and Beard 273; and Pliny 10:191. On the Phaethon theory, see Burnham 7–8; and Pliny 187. Other theories maintained that amber was composed of the tears of various other mythical figures (or even of "certain sea-birds") (Burnham 8), that it was solidified lynx urine (Pliny 189), and, in consonance with modern scientific opinion, that it was hardened tree resin (Pliny 195–97).

12. On the electric properties of amber, see Converse 599; as well as Burnham 345–46.

13. Converse also notes the connection between amber and specifically feminine ornament (599).

14. On Spofford's education, see, for example, Fetterly 262.

15. Though the story does not reference *Lalla-Rookh* by name, Rose borrows from it the phrase "loveliest amber that ever the sorrowing sea-birds have wept" (56).

16. For more on the particularly strong apotropaic power the ancients associated with "fremde[n] Gottheiten" and "fremden Göttern," see, respectively, *Paulys* 2014; and Jahn 46. On the more general use of syncretic and gnostic imagery in *fascina,* see Jahn 46; *Paulys* 2014; and especially Burnham 106–7, 165.

17. Bode discusses this difference at length.

18. Chesnutt himself was ambivalent about the efficacy of conjure: while his expository work clearly frames it as nothing more than a collection of superstitions and folk practices, his conjure tales paint a more optimistic portrait of its potential for social resistance and subversion. For more on Chesnutt's ambivalence about conjure, see his essay "Superstitions and Folk-Lore of the South"; as well as Minnick 77–98.

19. For more on the conjure tales' relation to plantation fiction, a subgenre of regionalism that romanticized the antebellum South (and that found its clearest articulation in Joel Chandler Harris's Uncle Remus stories), see Gilligan; G. Martin; Nowatzki; Piacentino; Fleissner, "Earth-Eating"; and Andrews.

20. In Chesnutt's tale "The Gray Wolf's Ha'nt," for example, a slave who has killed the son of a conjure man purchases a protective "life charm" made from his hair "en a piece er

red flannin, en some roots en yarbs . . . put . . . in a little bag made out'n 'coon-skin" (98). In "Hot-Foot Hannibal," the eponymous Hannibal is made "light-headed en hot-footed" by his proximity to a doll with red peppers for feet (112).

21. Indeed, numerous critics have pointed out that the story's central conceit is a pun on "the curse of Ham"; for more on this, see Swift and Mamoser; Christopherson 213; Harding 242; and Sundquist 382.

22. For more on Chesnutt's evocation of lynching, see Wood 204; as well as Sundquist 382.

23. For more on Julius's economic gains, see E. Hewitt; as well as virtually any other critical treatment of the conjure tales.

24. For some representative theories of Black humanity and agency that do not privilege the rational subject, see Weheliye; Keeling; Allewaert; A. Musser; and, of course, the seminal essay "Mama's Baby, Papa's Maybe" in Spillers.

3. Gesture, the Actress, and Naturalist Fiction

1. See also Schmit 417–18.

2. For more on these demonstrations, see M. Evans xiii; Hunter 1; and Gauld 307–8.

3. For an extensive treatment of Charcot's theatrics, see J. Marshall, particularly the introduction and the seventh chapter, "Hysterical Hypnosis and Infectious Theatre" (1–18, 157–86).

4. For more on the theatricality of hysteria (and particularly Charcot's treatment of it), see McCarren, "'Symptomatic Act'" 765.

5. See Gordon 529; as well as M. Evans xiii.

6. For more on Beard's relationship with Charcot's work, see *Study of Trance* 36–40.

7. For a particularly blistering accusation of charlatanry leveled against Beard, see J. Browne.

8. Compare Beard's *Study of Trance*, which asserts that "the artificial trance—so-called hypnotism—is but the artificial induction of the natural trance" (8), to Janet's *Major Symptoms of Hysteria*, which claims "there is no reason for making a special place for the hypnotic state; it is a somnambulism analogous to the preceding [spontaneous] one" (115).

9. For more on the retraction of the field of consciousness, see the fifth lecture in Janet, *Major Symptoms* (293–316).

10. For more on this practice, see "Mental Architecture," the seventh lesson in Atkinson, *Secret* (215–57).

11. See also Hart, "Hypnotism" 1218.

12. Atkinson was quite fond of citing James as an authority, also quoting him, for example, in a manual titled *Practical Mind-Reading* (5–6).

13. See Roach 179–81.

14. For more on Fuller, see her memoir, *Fifteen Years of a Dancer's Life* (25–38); as well as McCarren, "Symptomatic Act." The popular association of hypnotism with vaudeville performance persisted well into the twentieth century; indeed, a 1930 article in the *Scien-

tific Monthly claimed that "hypnotism acts are always headliners at vaudeville shows" (M. Stein 87).

15. James was not alone in framing emotion as the sensation of movement. Henry Rutgers Marshall, for example—writing one year before *Principles of Psychology* was published—reduced emotion to "muscular sensation" (536).

16. For more on the rise of the combination system, see Johnson 50; and Strang 2: 195.

17. For more on Bernhardt's perpetual touring, see Blum 51, 117; as well as B. Hewitt 43.

18. For more on the comparative popularity of actresses, see T. C. Davis 105–36.

19. For more on Dreiser's theory of magnetic personality, see Diebel; as well as Lears, "Dreiser" 75.

20. For more on Dreiser's romance with biological determinism (particularly as it appears in the work of Herbert Spencer), see Pizer; Gerber 21–24; Lehan 68; Moers 140; and Sloane 27.

21. Several of the essays in *The Cambridge Companion to Theodore Dreiser*, for example—a representative sampling of Dreiser criticism—use some variation of the word *fascinated* to describe Dreiser's work; see Cassuto and Eby 6; Eby 143; and B. Brown, "Matter" 87, 91.

22. For classic treatments of the novel's commodities, see Kaplan 140–60; and Michaels 29–58. For a more recent discussion of the novel's things, see Lemaster.

23. For more on the link between imitation and hysteria, see Gordon.

24. As Diebel points out, this paradoxical performance of naturalness was in fact expected of women around the turn of the century: "if you want to succeed," went the common advice, "you should . . . both be yourself and play a part—that is, be someone else. Women in particular were advised, in *Success, Ev'ry Month,* and other popular magazines, to act *naturally*" (134, my emphasis).

25. A brief note on terminology: throughout this chapter, I use the terms "coon" and "coon show" somewhat freely. While I acknowledge that this language is now outdated and even offensive, these terms were used in a specialized way to describe a specific genre of racialized performance around the turn of the century; there are thus no exact synonyms with which these words might be replaced.

26. For more on the relationship between Dreiser's and Dunbar's brands of naturalism, see Larson; Brezina; Hurd 91; and Rodgers 44.

27. For more on the novel as a narrative of decline, see Bone 42; Dudley 144; and Morgan, "Black Naturalism" and "City."

28. For more on Dunbar's association of actresses with prostitutes, see Turner 10; and Thomas 171. For more on the general nineteenth-century tendency to conflate these two professions, see Johnson, especially the first chapter, "Enter the Harlot" (3–36); and T. C. Davis, especially the section on "Actresses and Prostitutes" (78–86).

29. For more on the whiteness of *Sister Carrie,* see Gair.

30. For more on the role of the coon show in the novel, see Von Rosk; as well as Thomas 160.

31. For more on the text as a Great Migration novel, see Murphy; as well as Rodgers.

32. For more on rhythm and movement in *Sister Carrie,* see Markels; Fleissner, *Women* 161–200; and Moers, "Finesse" 202.

33. For more on Clorindy, see Londré and Watermeier 220; Thomas 160; and Von Rosk.

4. Primitive Flatness and Early Ethnographic Cinema

1. A brief note on terminology: throughout this chapter, I use the term *primitive* without enclosing it in quotation marks, and I use the terms *Indian, Eskimo,* and *Kwakiutl,* rather than *Native American, Inuit,* or *Kwakwaka'wakw.* While I acknowledge that this language is both exonymous and outdated, it is the language used by this chapter's primary texts (as well as many of its secondary texts), and, for the sake of clarity and consistency, I have decided to use the terms these texts use.

2. For more on the relationship between fascination and the image, see Abbas; Van Imschoot; Massey; Seeber, "Surface"; and Declercq and Spriet; as well, of course, as Blanchot 32–33.

3. For more on this history, see Gunning, "'Animated Pictures.'"

4. Gunning points out in "An Aesthetic of Astonishment: Early Film and the (In)Credulous Spectator" that because they were accustomed to the optical illusions of things like the magic lantern show and the kinetoscope, it is unlikely that audience members actually thought they were in danger of being run over. The legend, however, usefully dramatizes the genuine, visceral shock that many early cinemagoers likely did experience.

5. For more on the history of the cinema of attractions, see C. Musser.

6. For more on cinema and movement, see the classic treatment in Epstein 94; as well as more recent work, including Charney 287; Doane 22; and Gunning, "Aesthetic" 119.

7. This is my translation. The original: "Le gros plan limite et dirige l'attention . . . Je n'ai ni le droit, ni les moyens d'être distrait. Impératif present du verbe comprendre."

8. For more on Boas's curatorial practices, see B. Brown, *Sense* 92–927; and Jacknis, "Franz Boas" 77–83.

9. For more on Tylor, Darwin, and Spencer (as well as Boas's critique of them), see Boas, "Anthropology" 274–77 and *Mind*—particularly the chapter titled "The Interpretations of Culture" (175–96)—as well as Stocking 1–6.

10. In "Anthropology," Boas claims that academic anthropology is positioned to "teach . . . better than any other science the relativity of the values of civilization" (280). He also discusses, in "The Aims of Ethnology," "the *relative* correctness of emotions which seem so natural to us" (71).

11. For more on Boas's relationship with history, see Stocking 12–13.

12. For more on *Nanook*'s place in the history of documentary film, see Aufderheide 1–55, 106–24; Barnouw 31–50; Nichols, *Introduction* 1–28; Saunders 11–101; Warren 1–21; and Barsam, *Nonfiction.*

13. For more on *documentaires romancés* and their relation to ethnographic film, see Heider 20; and Rony 85.

14. For more on the narrative difference between documentary and travelogue, see Winston 107–12. On the decentering of the filmmaker in documentary film (especially in Flaherty's work), see Sherwood 4; and Burton and Thompson 76.

15. For more on Boas's limited use of film, see Ruby.

16. For more on Flaherty's generally Romantic tendencies as a filmmaker, see, most notably, Grierson 148; and Kracauer, *Theory* 247; as well Rotha, *Documentary* 119; Matheson; Gray 41; Aufderheide 28–32; Barnouw 45; Nichols, *Ideology* 275; Rony 89; and Warren 4. For more on the fabricated elements of *Nanook*, see R. Flaherty, *My Eskimo Friends* 139–40 and "Life"; as well as Barnouw 36–37; and Saunders 88–99. The most famous of these fabrications, of course, include the renaming of the Indigenous actors in the film (which transformed Allakariallak into Nanook, Alice into Nyla, and so forth); the construction for the film of an oversized, cutaway igloo (because real igloos were too small and dark to allow for filming); the staging of a walrus hunt using harpoons rather than rifles (even though rifles had long been in use among the Eskimo); and the staging of the scene in which Nanook, apparently baffled by the magic of modern technology, attempts to divine the nature of a phonographic record by biting it (many of the Eskimo with whom Flaherty worked were more adept at operating and maintaining his camera than he was). Less commonly cited but perhaps more unsettling is the fact that the women who appear in the film were not romantically involved with Allakariallak but were, in fact, common-law wives of Flaherty (Rony 123).

17. For more on Flaherty's strategic building of suspense, see Rotha, *Robert J. Flaherty* 38; and MacDougall, "Subjective" 103–5; as well as Heider 23; and Winston 111.

18. For more on Flaherty's narrative use of intertitles, see Winston 109–11.

19. Flaherty himself took apparently ethnographic photos of Eskimo subjects before and during the filming of *Nanook*. For more on these photos, see Danzker.

20. For more on the illegibility of Nanook's laughter and its connection to his supposed childishness, see Grace; Raheja 1159–60; Huhndorf 134; and Bitomsky 183; as well as Matheson 13; and Rony 111.

21. For more on the influence of Eskimo art on Flaherty's cinematography, see F. Flaherty 59; as well as Barsam, *Nonfiction* 128–29 and *Vision* 19; Rotha, *Robert J. Flaherty* 49; and Calder-Marshall 69.

22. *Nanook's* continued presence in both anthropology and film classes is noted by virtually every scholar who writes about ethnographic film.

23. For more on Nanookmania, see Rony 99–100; Barsam, *Vision* 26; and Huhndorf 125.

24. See, for example, MacDougall, "Ethnographic" 179; and Rony 90–98.

25. For more on Flaherty's personal contact with Curtis (as well as the line of aesthetic influence between the two), see Hearne 318; C. Browne 183–84; and Holm and Quimby 30; as well as Danzker 15; Burton and Thompson 77; and Winston 12.

26. Because Curtis's intention was not to show the Kwakiutl as they lived at the time of filming but to give audiences "a glimpse of the primitive Americans as they lived in the Stone Age," he had to incorporate even more artificial elements than Flaherty did (Curtis vii). He gave his male actors long wigs to cover up their modern haircuts, for example, and he had to have a great deal of Indigenous artwork purchased or created for the film. Like

Flaherty, he constructed artificial cutaway dwellings that would allow sunlight in for film-ing, and, also like Flaherty, he staged a hunting scene using an animal that was already dead (Flaherty used a seal; Curtis used a whale). Curtis also inexplicably had multiple actors play the same role—there were three different Naidas—and he sometimes cast the same actor in multiple lead roles (for example, the same man played both Naida's father, Waket, and her kidnapper, Yaklus). For more on these artifices, see Holm and Quimby (who document the entire process of filming *Head-Hunters* in great detail); as well as Wakeham, "Becoming" and *Taxidermic* 87–127; Bryant-Bertail 51; Glass and Evans 11–12; and G. Quimby "Curtis."

27. For more on *Head-Hunters* in the context of Indian-themed films, see B. Evans.

28. There has been some critical controversy about the historical faithfulness of *War Canoes,* as the film's editors, Bill Holm and George Irving Quimby, not only added a soundtrack and rewrote the intertitles but did some trimming of repetitive sequences and incorporated their own re-creation of a (very brief) scene they could not recover; for more on these changes, see Holm and Quimby; Wakeham, "Becoming"; and Russell, *Experimental Ethnography* 98–115. *War Canoes* is, however, the only version of the film that is widely accessible, and, as Holm and Quimby's most significant intervention—the alteration of the intertitles—has little to do with my argument, I will be using *War Canoes* for my analysis.

29. For more on Curtis's musicale, see Gidley 51–54; and Jacknis, "Chamber" 115–17.

30. The primitive cinematic aesthetics of the film are touched on in both Wakeham, *Taxidermic* 114–15; and Russell 101–3.

31. For more on the discrepancies between the portraits in *Head-Hunters* and those in *War Canoes,* see Russell 101; and Holm and Quimby 65.

32. Both Grosz and Bergson, of course, are careful to distinguish between the "potential" (which is a property of the virtual) and the "possible" (which is the product of a retroactive mapping of cause and effect onto events that, at a metaphysical level, actually occurred spontaneously); see, for example, Bergson, "Possible." Because this difference is somewhat tangential to my own argument, however, I use these words more colloquially (that is, as rough synonyms for one another).

Conclusion: From Modern Fascination to Modernist Fascination

1. I use the term *high modernism* intentionally, for while "the new modernist studies" may take as its object any writing, music, or art produced between the middle of the nine-teenth century and the present moment, I am primarily interested here in the formally inventive writing that flourished during the first few decades of the twentieth century. For more on the new modernist studies, see Mao and Walkowitz, "New Modernist Studies"; as well as their introduction to *Bad Modernisms* (1–18).

2. For other treatments of sexology's influence on modernism, see Peppis; and Salvato.

3. For more on Robin's alcoholism, see Lansky; and Goodspeed-Chadwick 27.

4. For more on the (neo)baroque qualities of the novel, see Kaup; and Armond. For more on Barnes's decadence, see Carlston 42–85; Danzer; Blyn; Azzarello; and Marcus, "Mousemeat."

5. See also Miller 121–68; and Smith 203.

6. For evidence of this, one need only look at Stein's short story "Melanctha," which tells the tale of a woman who "liked to wander, and to stand by the railroad yard," drawn there, like Robin, by "a ceaseless fascination."

7. See, too, Weir, *Decadence*.

WORKS CITED

Abbas, Ackbar. "On Fascination: Walter Benjamin's Images." *New German Critique* 48 (1989): 43–62. JSTOR, https://doi.org/10.2307/488232.

Adams, Henry. *The Education of Henry Adams.* 1907. Boston: Houghton Mifflin, 1961.

Alaimo, Stacy, and Susan Hackman. "Introduction: Emerging Models of Materiality in Feminist Theory." In *Material Feminisms,* edited by Alaimo and Hackman, 1–19. Bloomington: Indiana University Press, 2008.

Albanese, Catherine L. *A Republic of Mind and Spirit: A Cultural History of American Metaphysical Religion.* New Haven, CT: Yale University Press, 2007.

Allewaert, Monique. *Ariel's Ecology: Plantations, Personhood, and Colonialism in the American Tropics.* Minneapolis: University of Minnesota Press, 2013.

Andrews, William L. "The Significance of Charles W. Chesnutt's 'Conjure Stores.'" *Southern Literary Journal* 7. no. 1 (1974): 78–99. JSTOR, www.jstor.org/stable/20077505.

Apollinaire, Guillaume. "Aesthetic Meditations on Painting: The Cubist Painters." In *Cubism,* edited by Dorothea Eimert, 8–36. New York: Parkstone International, 2010.

Armond, Kate. "Allegory and Dismemberment: Reading Djuna Barnes' *Nightwood* through the Forms of the Baroque Trauerspiel." *Textual Practice* 26, no. 5 (2012): 851–70. doi.org/10.1080/0950236X.2012.669400.

Asad, Talal. *Formations of the Secular: Christianity, Islam, Modernity.* Stanford, CA: Stanford University Press, 2003.

Atkinson, William Walker. *Mental Fascination.* Chicago: Masonic Temple, 1907.

———. *Practical Mind-Reading.* Chicago: Advanced Thought Publishing, 1907. Internet Archive, archive.org/details/PracticalMindReading.

———. *The Secret of Mental Magic.* 1907. Reprint, Hollister, MO: YOGeBooks, 2010.

Aufderheide, Patricia. *Documentary Film: A Very Short Introduction.* New York: Oxford University Press, 2007.

Ayer, Hugh M. "Nineteenth Century Medicine." *Indiana Magazine of History* 48, no. 3 (1952): 233–54. JSTOR, www.jstor.org/stable/27788045.

Azzarello, Robert. *Queer Environmentality: Ecology, Evolution, and Sexuality in American Literature.* London: Taylor & Francis, 2012.

Barad, Karen. "Posthumanist Performativity: Toward an Understanding of How Matter Comes to Matter." In *Material Feminisms,* edited by Stacy Alaimo and Susan Hackman, 120–54. Bloomington: Indiana University Press, 2008.

Barnes, Djuna. *Nightwood.* 1936. New York: New Directions, 2006.

Barnouw, Erik. *Documentary: A History of the Non-Fiction Film.* 2nd rev. ed. New York: Oxford University Press, 1993.

Barsam, Richard Meran. *Nonfiction Film: A Critical History.* Boston: E. P. Dutton & Co., 1973.

———. *The Vision of Robert Flaherty: The Artist as Myth and Filmmaker.* Bloomington: Indiana University Press, 1988.

Baudelaire, Charles. "The Painter of Modern Life." In *The Painter of Modern Life and Other Essays,* by Baudelaire, edited and translated by Jonathan Mayne, 1–41. New York: Phaidon Press, 1964.

———. "Three Drafts of a Preface." Translated by Jackson Matheus. *The Flowers of Evil,* by Baudelaire, edited and selected by Marthiel and Jackson Matheus, xxv–xxxi. New York: New Directions, 1955.

Baudrillard, Jean. "On Seduction." In *Jean Baudrillard: Selected Writings,* edited by Mark Poster, 149–65. Stanford, CA: Stanford University Press, 1988.

Baumbach, Sybille. "The Medusa's Gaze and the Aesthetics of Fascination." *Anglia* 128, no. 2 (2010): 225–45. MLA International Bibliography, doi:10.1515/ANGL .2010.029.

Baxter, Charles. "A Self-Consuming Light: *Nightwood* and the Crisis of Modernism." *Journal of Modern Literature* 3, no. 5 (1974): 1175–87. JSTOR, www.jstor.org /stable/3831003.

Beam, Dorri. *Style, Gender, and Fantasy in Nineteenth-Century American Women's Writing.* Cambridge: Cambridge University Press, 2010.

Beard, George Miller. *American Nervousness: Its Causes and Consequences.* New York: G. P. Putnam's Sons, 1881. Internet Archive, archive.org/details/american nervousnoobearuoft.

———. Introduction. *The Trance State in Inebriety: Its Medico-Legal Relations.* Hartford, CT: Case, Lockwood, and Brainard Co., Printers, 1882. Internet Archive, archive.org/details/cu31924024903704.

———. *The Scientific Basis of Delusions: A New Theory of Trance and Its Bearing on*

Human Testimony. New York: G. P. Putnam's Sons, 1877. Internet Archive, archive.org/details/b2244323x.

———. *The Study of Trance, Muscle-Reading, and Allied Nervous Phenomena in Europe and America, with a Letter on the Moral Character of Trance Subjects and a Defence of Dr. Charcot.* 1882. Internet Archive, archive.org/details/studyoftrance musoobear.

Bendixen, Alfred. Introduction to *The Amber Gods and Other Stories*, by Harriet Prescott Spofford. Edited by Bendixen, ix–xxxiv. New Brunswick, NJ: Rutgers University Press, 1989.

Benjamin, Walter. "The Work of Art in the Age of Mechanical Reproduction." *Illuminations*, by Benjamin, edited by Hannah Arendt, translated by Harry Zohn, 219–54. New York: Schocken Books, 1969.

Bennett, Jane. *The Enchantment of Modern Life: Attachments, Crossings, and Ethics.* Princeton, NJ: Princeton University Press, 2001.

———. *Vibrant Matter: A Political Ecology of Things.* Durham, NC: Duke University Press, 2010.

Bentley, Nancy. *Frantic Panoramas: American Literature and Mass Culture, 1870–1920.* Philadelphia: University of Pennsylvania Press, 2009.

Bergson, Henri. *Matter and Memory.* Translated by Nancy Margaret Paul and W. Scott Palmer. New York: Doubleday Anchor Books, 1959.

———. *Mélanges.* Edited by André Robinet. Paris: Presses Universitaires de France, 1972.

———. "The Possible and the Real." *The Creative Mind.* Translated by Mabelle L. Andison, 107–25. New York: Philosophical Library, 1946.

———. *Time and Free Will: An Essay on the Immediate Data of Consciousness.* Translated by F. L. Pogson. New York: Harper Torchbooks, 1960.

Bernardi, Debra. "'A Bit Sensational' or 'Simple and True': Domestic Horror and the Politics of Genre." *Legacy* 16, no. 2 (1999): 135–53. JSTOR, www.jstor.org/stable /25679299.

Bitomsky, Hartmut. "Nanooks Lächeln." In *Schreiben Bilder Sprechen: Texte zum essayistischen Film*, edited by Christa Blümlinger and Constantin Wulff, 179–92. Vienna: Sonderzahl, 1992.

Blanchot, Maurice. *The Space of Literature.* Translated by Ann Smock. Lincoln: University of Nebraska Press, 1982.

Blum, Daniel. *A Pictorial History of the American Theatre, 1860–1970.* Enlarged and revised by John Willis. 3rd ed. New York: Crown Publishers, 1971.

Blyn, Robin. "*Nightwood*'s Freak Dandies: Decadence in the 1930s." *Modernism/*

modernity 15, no. 3 (2008): 503–26. Project MUSE, doi.org/10.1353/mod.0
.0004.

Boas, Franz. "The Aims of Ethnology." In *The Shaping of American Anthropology,
1883–1911: A Franz Boas Reader,* edited by George W. Stocking Jr., 67–71. New
York: Basic Books, 1974.

———. "Anthropology." In *The Shaping of American Anthropology, 1883–1911: A Franz
Boas Reader,* edited by George W. Stocking Jr., 267–81. New York: Basic Books,
1974.

———. "The Limitations of the Comparative Method of Anthropology." *Science* 4,
no. 103 (1896): 901–8. JSTOR, www.jstor.org/stable/1623004.

———. *The Mind of Primitive Man.* Rev. ed. New York: Macmillan, 1938.

———. "The Mythologies of the Indians." In *The Shaping of American Anthropology,
1883–1911: A Franz Boas Reader,* edited by George W. Stocking Jr., 135–48. New
York: Basic Books 1974.

Bode, Rita. "Narrative Revelations: Harriet Prescott Spofford's 'Amber Gods' Revisited." *ESQ: A Journal of the American Renaissance* 50, no. 4 (2004): 233–67.

Bone, Robert. *The Negro Novel in America.* New Haven, CT: Yale University Press,
1958.

Bonner, Campbell. *Studies in Magical Amulets, Chiefly Graeco-Egyptian.* Ann Arbor:
University of Michigan Press, 1950.

Boone, Joseph Allen. *Libidinal Currents: Sexuality and the Shaping of Modernism.*
Chicago: University of Chicago Press, 1998.

Bordogna, Francesca. "Inner Division and Uncertain Contours: William James and
the Politics of the Modern Self." *British Journal for the History of Science* 40, no.
4 (2007): 505–36. JSTOR, www.jstor.org/stable/30160835.

Bourget, Paul. "Charles Baudelaire." In *Essais de Psychologie Contemporaine,* 3–32.
Paris: Plon-Nourrit et cie. Internet Archive, archive.org/details/essaisdepsycho
102bourgoog.

Braid, James. *Neurypnology, or the Rationale of Nervous Sleep Considered in Relation to
Animal Magnetism or Mesmerism and Illustrated by Numerous Cases of Its Successful Application in the Relief and Cure of Disease.* Edited by Arthur Edward Waite.
London: George Redway, 1899. Internet Archive, archive.org/details/braidon
hypnotismoobrai.

Braude, Ann. *Radical Spirits: Spiritualism and Women's Rights in Nineteenth-Century
America.* Bloomington: Indiana University Press, 1989.

Breuer, Joseph, and Sigmund Freud. *Studies on Hysteria.* Edited and translated by James
Strachey. New York: Basic Books, 1957. Internet Archive, archive.org/details
/studiesonhysterio37649mbp/page/n9.

Brezina, Jennifer Costello. "Public Women, Private Acts: Gender and Theater in Turn-of-the-Century American Novels." In *Separate Spheres No More: Gender Convergence in American Literature, 1830–1930,* edited by Monika M. Elbert, 225–42. Tuscaloosa: University of Alabama Press, 2014.

Brodhead, Richard H. Introduction to *The Conjure Woman and Other Conjure Tales,* by Charles W. Chesnutt. Edited by Brodhead, 1–21. Durham, NC: Duke University Press, 1996.

Brooks, Daphne. *Bodies in Dissent: Spectacular Performances of Race and Freedom, 1850–1910.* Durham, NC: Duke University Press, 2006.

Brown, Bill. "The Matter of Dreiser's Modernity." In *The Cambridge Companion to Theodore Dreiser,* edited by Leonard Cassuto and Clare Virginia Eby, 83–99. Cambridge: Cambridge University Press, 2004.

———. *A Sense of Things: The Object Matter of American Literature.* Chicago: University of Chicago Press, 2003.

Brown, Judith. *Glamour in Six Dimensions: Modernism and the Radiance of Form.* Ithaca, NY: Cornell University Press, 2009.

Browne, Colin. "Unmasking the Documentary: Notes on the Anxiety of Edward Curtis." In *Return to the Land of the Head Hunters: Edward S. Curtis, the Kwakwaka'wakw, and the Making of Modern Cinema,* edited by Aaron Glass and Brad Evans, 167–89. Seattle: University of Washington Press, 2014.

Browne, J. Crichton. "Dr. Beard's Experiments with Hypnotism." *British Medical Journal* 2, no. 1078 (1881): 378–79. JSTOR, www.jstor.org/stable/25257736.

Bryant-Bertail, Sarah. "Old Spirits in a New World: Pacific Northwest Performance: Identity, Authenticity, Theatricality." In *Native American Performance and Representation,* edited by S. E. Wilmer, 40–60. Tucson: University of Arizona Press, 2009.

"Bulla." *A Dictionary of Classical Antiquities: Mythology, Religion, Literature and Art.* London: William Glaisher, 1895. Internet Archive, archive.org/details/cu31924028214652.

Burch, Noël. *Life to Those Shadows.* Edited and translated by Den Brewster. London: BFI Publishing, 1990.

Burnham, S. M. *Precious Stones in Nature, Art, and Literature.* Boston: Bradlee Whidden, 1886. Internet Archive, archive.org/details/preciousstonesinooburnrich.

Burton, John W., and Caitlin W. Thompson. "Nanook and the Kirwinians: Deception, Authenticity, and the Birth of Modern Ethnographic Representation." *Film History* 14, no. 1 (2002): 74–86. JSTOR, www.jstor.org/stable/3815582.

Calder-Marshall, Arthur. *The Innocent Eye: The Life of Robert J. Flaherty.* New York: Harcourt, Brace & World, 1963.

Campaign Book for Exhibitors. Studies in Visual Communication 6, no. 2 (1980): 61–76.

Carlson, Eric T. "Charles Poyen Brings Mesmerism to America." *Journal of the History of Medicine and Allied Sciences* 15, no. 2 (1960): 121–32.

Carlston, Erin G. *Thinking Fascism: Sapphic Modernism and Fascist Modernity.* Stanford, CA: Stanford University Press, 1998.

Carroy, Jacqueline. *Hypnose, suggestion, et psychologie: l'invention de sujets.* Paris: Presses Universitaires de France, 1991.

Caselli, Daniela. *Improper Modernism: Djuna Barnes's Bewildering Corpus.* Farnham, UK: Ashgate, 2009.

Cassuto, Leonard, and Clare Virginia Eby. Introduction. In *The Cambridge Companion to Theodore Dreiser,* edited by Cassuto and Eby, 1–12. Cambridge: Cambridge University Press, 2004.

Charney, Leo. "In a Moment: Film and the Philosophy of Modernity." In *Cinema and the Invention of Modern Life,* edited by Leo Charney and Vanessa R. Schwartz, 279–94. Berkeley: University of California Press, 1995.

Chen, Mel Y. *Animacies: Biopolitics, Racial Mattering, and Queer Affect.* Durham, NC: Duke University Press, 2012.

Cheng, Anne Anlin. *Ornamentalism.* New York: Oxford University Press, 2019.

———. "Shine: On Race, Glamour, and the Modern." *PMLA* 126, no. 4 (2011): 1022–41.

Chesnutt, Charles W. "Dave's Neckliss." In *The Conjure Woman and Other Conjure Tales,* edited by Richard H. Brodhead, 123–35. Durham, NC: Duke University Press, 1996.

———. "The Gray Wolf's Ha'nt." In *The Conjure Woman and Other Conjure Tales,* edited by Richard H. Brodhead, 94–106. Durham, NC: Duke University Press, 1996.

———. "Hot-Foot Hannibal." In *The Conjure Woman and Other Conjure Tales,* edited by Richard H. Brodhead, 107–20. Durham, NC: Duke University Press, 1996.

———. "Sis' Becky's Pickaninny." In *The Conjure Woman and Other Conjure Tales,* edited by Richard H. Brodhead, 82–93. Durham, NC: Duke University Press, 1996.

———. "Superstitions and Folk-Lore of the South." In *Charles W. Chesnutt: Essays and Speeches,* edited by Joseph R. McElrath Jr. et al., 155–61. Stanford, CA: Stanford University Press, 1999.

Christopherson, Bill. "Conjurin' the White Folks: Charles Chesnutt's Other 'Julius' Tales." *American Literary Realism* 18, nos. 1–2 (1985): 202–18. JSTOR, www.jstor.org/stable/27746183.

Clerc, Jean-Benoît. "Pour se protéger du fascinum (Pline le Jeune, *Lettres*, VI, 2)." *Latomus* 57, no. 3 (1998): 634–43. JSTOR, www.jstor.org/stable/41538373.

Clough, Patricia Ticineto. Introduction. In *The Affective Turn: Theorizing the Social*, edited by Clough, with Jean Halley, 1–33. Durham, NC: Duke University Press, 2007.

Colebrook, Claire. "On Not Becoming Man: The Materialist Politics of Unactualized Potential." In *Material Feminisms*, edited by Stacy Alaimo and Susan Hackman, 52–84. Bloomington: Indiana University Press, 2008.

Connor, Stephen. "Fascination, Skin and the Screen." *Critical Quarterly* 40, no. 1 (2003). Wiley Online Library, https://doi.org/10.1111/1467-8705.00142.

Constable, Liz, Matthew Potolsky, and Dennis Denisoff. Introduction. In *Perennial Decay: On the Aesthetics and Politics of Decadence*, edited by Constable, Potolsky, and Denisoff, 1–32. Philadelphia: University of Pennsylvania Press, 1999.

Converse, Emma M. "Amber." *Appleton's Journal* 8, no. 192, November 30, 1872, 599–601. *Making of American Journals*, quod.lib.umich.edu/m/moajrnl/acw84 33.1-08.192/603.

Coole, Diana, and Samantha Frost. "Introducing the New Materialisms." In *New Materialisms: Ontology, Agency, and Politics*, edited by Coole and Frost, 1–43. Durham, NC: Duke University Press, 2010.

Cooper, Douglas. *The Cubist Epoch*. New York: Phaidon, 1971.

Crane, Stephen. *Maggie: A Girl of the Streets*. 1893. Reprint, New York: Scholars' Facsimiles & Reprints, 1966.

Crary, Jonathan. *Suspensions of Perception: Attention, Spectacle, and Modern Culture*. Cambridge, MA: MIT Press, 1999.

Curtis, Edward S. *In the Land of the Head-Hunters*. Chicago: World Book Co., 1915.

Dames, Nicholas. "'The Withering of the Individual': Psychology in the Victorian Novel." In *A Concise Companion to the Victorian Novel*, edited by Francis O'Gorman, 91–112. Hoboken, NJ: Wiley-Blackwell, 2004.

"Dangers of Hypnotism." *British Medical Journal* 1, no. 1578 (1891): 714. JSTOR, www.jstor.org/stable/20242181.

Danzer, Ina. "Between Decadence and Surrealism: The Other Modernism of Djuna Barnes." *AAA: Arbeiten aus Anglistik und Amerikanistik* 23, no. 2 (1998): 239–57. JSTOR, www.jstor.org/stable/43025576.

Danzker, Jo-Anne Birnie. "Robert Flaherty/Photographer." *Studies in Visual Communication* 6, no. 2 (1980): 5–32.

Datcher, Michael. *Animating Black and Brown Liberation: A Theory of American Literatures*. Albany: State University of New York Press, 2019.

Davis, Theo. *Ornamental Aesthetics: The Poetry of Attending in Thoreau, Dickinson, and Whitman.* New York: Oxford University Press, 2016.

Davis, Tracy C. *Actresses as Working Women: Their Social Identity in Victorian Culture.* New York: Routledge, 1991.

Debord, Guy. *Society of the Spectacle.* Detroit: Black & Red, 1983.

Declercq, Gilles, and Stella Spriet. *Fascination des images, images de la fascination.* Paris: Sorbonne Nouvelle, 2014.

Degen, Andreas. *Ästhetische Faszination: Die Geschichte einer Denkfigur vor ihrem Begriff.* Berlin: Walter de Gruyter GmbH, 2017.

———. "Concepts of Fascination, from Democritus to Kant." *Journal of the History of Ideas* 73, no. 3 (2012): 371–93. JSTOR, www.jstor.org/stable/23253880.

———. "Sokrates fasziniert: Zu Begriff und Metaphorik der Faszination (Platon, Ficino, Nietzsche)." *Archiv für Begriffgeschichte* 53 (2011): 9–31. JSTOR, www.jstor.org/stable/24361879.

Deleuze, Gilles, and Félix Guattari. *A Thousand Plateaus: Capitalism and Schizophrenia.* Translated by Brian Massumi. Minneapolis: University of Minnesota Press, 1987.

Deleuze, Joseph Phillipe François. *Practical Instruction in Animal Magnetism.* Translated by Thomas C. Hartshorn. Providence, RI: B. Cranston & Co., 1837.

Diebel, Anne. " 'That Indescribable Thing': Personality in Dreiser's Early Journalism and *Sister Carrie.*" *Studies in American Naturalism* 9, no. 2 (2014): 123–46. Project MUSE, doi.org/10.1353/san.2014.0018.

Doane, Mary Ann. *The Emergence of Cinematic Time: Modernity, Contingency, the Archive.* Cambridge: Harvard University Press, 2002.

Dreiser, Theodore. *Hey Rub-a-Dub-Dub: A Book of the Mystery and Wonder and Terror of Life.* New York: Boni & Liveright, 1920. HathiTrust, hdl.handle.net/2027 /loc.ark:/13960/t2g74276g.

———. "Reflections." March 1896. In *Theodore Dreiser's Ev'ry Month*, edited by Nancy Warner Barrineau, 52–61. Athens: University of Georgia Press, 1996.

———. *Sister Carrie.* 1900. New York: Holt, Rinehart, & Winston, 1957.

———. "Transmutation of Personality." *Notes on Life.* Edited by Marguerite Tjader and John J. McAleer, 165–76. Tuscaloosa: University of Alabama Press, 1974.

Dudley, John. *A Man's Game: Masculinity and the Anti-Aesthetics of American Literary Naturalism.* Tuscaloosa: University of Alabama Press, 2004.

Dunbar, Paul Laurence. *The Sport of the Gods.* 1902. Reprint, Overland Park, KS: Digireads, 2010.

Ebel, Jonathan, and Justine S. Murison. "American Literatures / American Religions." *American Literary History* 26, no. 1 (2013): 1–5.

Eby, Clare Virginia. "Dreiser and Women." In *The Cambridge Companion to Theodore Dreiser*, edited by Leonard Cassuto and Eby, 142–59. Cambridge: Cambridge University Press, 2004.

Eliot, T. S. Introduction to *Nightwood*, by Djuna Barnes, xvii–xxii. 1936. Reprint, New York: New Directions, 2006.

Ellis, R. J. "'Latent Color' and 'Exaggerated Snow': Whiteness and Race in Harriet Prescott Spofford's 'The Amber Gods.'" *Journal of American Studies* 40, no. 2 (2006): 257–82. JSTOR, www.jstor.org/stable/27557792.

Epstein, Jean. "Bonjour, Cinéma." In *Écrits sur le cinéma, 1921–1953*, edited by Pierre Lherminier, 1:71–104. Paris: Seghers, 1974.

"Ethnology in Action." Review of *In the Land of the Head-Hunters*, directed by Edward S. Curtis. *Independent*, January 11, 1915.

Evans, Brad. "Indian Movies and the Vernacular of Modernism." In *Return to the Land of the Head Hunters: Edward S. Curtis, the Kwakwaka'wakw, and the Making of Modern Cinema*, edited by Aaron Glass and Evans, 190–211. Seattle: University of Washington Press, 2014.

Evans, Martha Noel. Preface. In *The Makings of Dr. Charcot's Hysteria Shows*, edited by Dianne Hunter, xi–xv. Lewiston, NY: Edwin Mellen Press, 1998.

"Evil Eye." *Jewish Encyclopedia*, 1906. www.jewishencyclopedia.com/articles/5920 -evil-eye.

Faderman, Lillian. *Surpassing the Love of Men: Romantic Friendship and Love between Women from the Renaissance to the Present*. London: Women's Press, 1985.

"Fascinum." *A Dictionary of Classical Antiquities: Mythology, Religion, Literature and Art*. London: William Glaisher, 1895. Internet Archive, archive.org/details/cu 31924028214652.

———. *Paulys Realencyclopädie der classischen Altertumswissenschaft*. Stuttgart, Germany: J. B. Metzler, 1909.

"Fascinum, Fascinus." *Dictionnaire des antiquités grecques et romaines, d'après les textes et les monuments*. Paris: Librairie Hachette, 1896. Internet Archive, archive.org /details/pt2dictionnairedo2dare.

Fessenden, Tracy. "The Problem of the Postsecular." *American Literary History* 26, no. 1 (2013): 154–67.

Fetterly, Judith. Introduction to "Circumstance," by Harriet Prescott Spofford. In *Provisions: A Reader from 19th Century American Women*, edited by Fetterly, 261–68. Bloomington: Indiana University Press, 1985.

"Filming the Head-Hunters: How 'The Vanishing Race' Is Being Preserved in Moving Pictures." 1915. In *Edward S. Curtis in the Land of the War Canoes: A Pioneer Cinematographer in the Pacific Northwest*, by Bill Holm and George Irving Quimby, 121–25. Seattle: University of Washington Press, 1980.

Fischer, Clara. "Feminist Philosophy, Pragmatism, and the 'Turn to Affect': A Genealogical Critique." *Hypatia* 31, no. 4 (2016): 810–26.

Flaherty, Frances Hubbard. *The Odyssey of a Film-Makers: Robert Flaherty's Story.* Centennial ed. New York: Threshold Books, 1984.

Flaherty, Robert J. "Life among the Eskimos." *World's Work* 44 (1922): 632–40. HathiTrust, hdl.handle.net/2027/njp.32101075886489.

———. *My Eskimo Friends: "Nanook of the North."* New York: Doubleday, Page, & Co., 1924.

———. "Robert Flaherty Talking." In *The Cinema 1950*, edited by Roger Manvell, 11–29. New York: Penguin, 1950.

Fleissner, Jennifer. "Earth-Eating, Addiction, Nostalgia: Charles Chesnutt's Diasporic Regionalism." *"Nostalgia, Melancholy, Anxiety: Discursive Mobility and the Circulation of Bodies,"* special issue of *Studies in Romanticism* 49, no. 2 (2010): 313–36. JSTOR, www.jstor.org/stable/41059290.

———. *Women, Compulsion, Modernity: The Moment of American Naturalism.* Chicago: University of Chicago Press, 2004.

Frank, Joseph. "Spatial Form in Modern Literature: An Essay in Three Parts." *Sewanee Review* 53, no. 3 (1945): 433–56. JSTOR, www.jstor.org/stable/27537609.

Fretwell, Erica. *Sensory Experiments: Psychophysics, Race, and the Aesthetics of Feeling.* Durham, NC: Duke University Press, 2020.

Friedl, Herwig. "The World as Fact, the World as Event: Varieties of Modernist Thinking in William James, Henri Bergson, and John Dewey." In *Transatlantic Modernism*, edited by Martin Klepper and Joseph C. Schöpp, 51–92. Heidelberg, Germany: Universitätsverlag C. Winter Heidelberg, 2001.

Fuller, Loie. *Fifteen Years of a Dancer's Life.* Boston: Small, Maynard & Co., 1913.

Fuller, Robert C. *Mesmerism and the American Cure of Souls.* Philadelphia: University of Pennsylvania Press, 1982.

Gair, Christopher. "*Sister Carrie*, Race, and the World's Columbian Exposition." In *The Cambridge Companion to Theodore Dreiser*, edited by Leonard Cassuto and Clare Virginia Eby, 160–76. Cambridge: Cambridge University Press, 2004.

Gale, Richard M. "Pragmatism versus Mysticism: The Divided Self of William James." *Philosophical Perspectives* 5 (1991): 241–86. JSTOR, www.jstor.org/stable/2214097.

Gaskill, Nicholas. *Chromographia: American Literature and the Modernization of Color.* Minneapolis: University of Minnesota Press, 2018.

Gauld, Alan. *A History of Hypnotism.* Cambridge: Cambridge University Press, 1992.

Gerber, Philip. *Theodore Dreiser Revisited.* New York: Twayne Publishers, 1992.

Gidley, Mick. "Edward Curtis and *In the Land of the Head Hunters*: Four Contexts."

In *Return to the Land of the Head Hunters: Edward S. Curtis, the Kwakwaka'wakw, and the Making of Modern Cinema*, edited by Aaron Glass and Brad Evans, 42–60. Seattle: University of Washington Press, 2014.

Gilles de la Tourette, Georges. "The Wonders of Animal Magnetism." *North American Review* 146, no. 375 (1888): 131–43. JSTOR, www.jstor.org/stable/25101417.

Gilligan, Heather Tirado. "Reading, Race, and Charles Chesnutt's 'Uncle Julius' Tales." *ELH* 74, no. 1 (2007): 195–215. JSTOR, www.jstor.org/stable/30029551.

Girel, Mathias. "Un Braconnage impossible: le courant de conscience de William James et la durée réelle de Bergson." In *Bergson et James cent ans après*, edited by Stéphane Madelrieux, 27–55. Paris: Presses Universitaires de France, 2011.

Glass, Aaron, and Brad Evans. "Introduction: Edward Curtis Meets the Kwakwaka'wakw: Cultural Encounter and Indigenous Agency." In *Return to the Land of the Head Hunters: Edward S. Curtis, the Kwakwaka'wakw, and the Making of Modern Cinema*, edited by Glass and Evans, 3–39. Seattle: University of Washington Press, 2014.

Glavey, Brian. *The Wallflower Avant-Garde: Modernism, Sexuality, and Queer Ekphrasis*. New York: Oxford University Press, 2015.

Goodspeed-Chadwick, Julie. *Modernist Women Writers and War: Trauma and the Female Body in Djuna Barnes, H.D., and Gertrude Stein*. Baton Rouge: Louisiana State University Press, 2011.

Gordon, Rae Beth. "From Charcot to Charlot: Unconscious Imitation and Spectatorship in French Cabaret and Early Cinema." *Critical Inquiry* 27, no. 3 (2001): 515–49. JSTOR, www.jstor.org/stable/1344219.

Gorky, Maxim. Review of the Lumière programme at the Nizhni-Novgorod Fair. In *Kino: A History of the Russian and Soviet Film*, by Jay Leyda, 407–9. New York: Collier Books, 1960.

Grace, Sherril. "Exploration as Construction: Robert Flaherty and *Nanook of the North*." *Essays on Canadian Writing*, no. 59 (1996): 123–46.

Gray, Hugh. "Robert Flaherty and the Naturalistic Documentary." *Hollywood Quarterly* 5, no. 1 (1950): 41–48. JSTOR, www.jstor.org/stable/1209484.

Gregory, Joshua C. "Magic, Fascination, and Suggestion." *Folklore* 63, no. 3 (1952): 143–51. JSTOR, www.jstor.org/stable/1256932.

Grierson, John. "First Principles of Documentary." In *Grierson on Documentary*, edited by Forsyth Hardy, 145–56. Westport, CT: Praeger Publishers, 1971.

Grosz, Elizabeth. *Architecture from the Outside: Essays on Virtual and Real Space*. Cambridge, MA: MIT Press, 2001.

———. "Feminism, Materialism, and Freedom." In *New Materialisms: Ontology,*

Agency, and Politics, edited by Diana Coole and Samantha Frost, 139–57. Durham, NC: Duke University Press, 2010.

———. *The Nick of Time: Politics, Evolution, and the Untimely.* Durham, NC: Duke University Press, 2004.

Gunning, Tom. "An Aesthetic of Astonishment: Early Film and the (In)Credulous Spectator." In *Viewing Positions: Ways of Seeing Film,* edited by Linda Williams, 114–33. New Brunswick, NJ: Rutgers University Press, 1995.

———. "'Animated Pictures': Tales of the Cinema's Forgotten Future, after 100 Years of Film." In *The Nineteenth-Century Visual Culture Reader,* edited by Vanessa R. Schwartz and Jeannene M. Przyblyski, 100–113. New York: Routledge, 2004.

———. "The Cinema of Attraction[s]: Early Film, Its Spectator, and the Avant-Garde." In *The Cinema of Attractions Reloaded,* edited by Wanda Strauven, 381–88. Amsterdam: Amsterdam University Press, 2006.

Harding, Jennifer Riddle. "Metaphors, Narrative Frames, and Cognitive Frames in Charles Chesnutt's 'Dave's Neckliss.'" In *Blending and the Study of Narrative: Approaches and Applications,* edited by Ralf Schneider and Marcus Hartner, 229–51. Berlin: De Gruyter, 2012.

Hardt, Michael. "Foreword: What Affects Are Good For." In *The Affective Turn: Theorizing the Social,* edited by Patricia Ticineto Clough with Jean Halley, ix–xiii. Durham, NC: Duke University Press, 2007.

Hart, Ernest. "Hypnotism, Animal Magnetism, and Hysteria." *British Medical Journal* 2, no. 1666 (1892): 1215–20. JSTOR, www.jstor.org/stable/20222633.

———. "Schools and Doctrines of Hypnotism." *British Medical Journal* 1, no. 1578 (1891): 721–23. JSTOR, www.jstor.org/stable/20242191.

Hawthorne, Nathaniel. *The House of the Seven Gables.* Edited by Clyde Furst, revised by H. Y. Moffett. New York: Macmillan, 1905.

———. Letter, October 18, 1841. In *The Letters, 1813–1843,* edited by Thomas Woodson, L. Neal Smith, and Norman Holmes Pearson, 588–91. Columbus: Ohio State University Press, 1984.

Hearne, Joanna. "Telling and Retelling in the 'Ink of Light': Documentary Cinema, Oral Narratives, and Indigenous Identities." *Screen* 47, no. 3 (2006): 307–26.

Heider, Karl G. *Ethnographic Film.* Austin: University of Texas Press, 1976.

Hemmings, Clare. "Invoking Affect." *Cultural Studies* 19, no. 5 (2006): 548–67. https://doi.org/10.1080/09502380500365473.

Henry, M. Charles. "*Introduction à une esthétique scientifique.*" *La Revue contemporaine* (August 2, 1885): 441–69. Online Books Page, onlinebooks.library.upenn.edu/webbin/book/lookupid?key=olbp60029.

Herring, Scott. *Queering the Underworld*. Chicago: University of Chicago Press, 2007.

Hewitt, Barnard. *History of Theatre from 1800 to the Present*. New York: Random House, 1970.

Hewitt, Elizabeth. "Charles Chesnutt's Capitalist Conjurings." *ELH* 76, no. 4 (2009): 931–62. JSTOR, www.jstor.org/stable/27742968.

Hildburgh, W. L. "Interminability and Confusion as Apotropaic Elements in Italy and Spain." *Folklore* 55, no. 4 (1944): 133–49. JSTOR, www.jstor.org/stable /1257791.

Holm, Bill, and George Irving Quimby. *Edward S. Curtis in the Land of the War Canoes: A Pioneer Cinematographer in the Pacific Northwest*. Seattle: University of Washington Press, 1980.

Howells, William Dean. "Life and Letters." *Harper's Weekly*, June 27, 1896, 630.

———. "Mr. Charles W. Chesnutt's Stories." *Atlantic*, May 1900. www.theatlantic.com /magazine/archive/1900/05/mr-charles-w-chesnutts-stories/306659.

Hsieh, Lili. "Interpellated by Affect: The Move to the Political in Brian Massumi's *Parables for the Virtual* and Eve Sedgwick's *Touching Feeling*." *Subjectivity* 23, no. 1 (July 2008): 219–35. https://doi.org/10.1057/sub.2008.14.

Huhndorf, Shari M. "Nanook and His Contemporaries: Imagining Eskimos in American Culture, 1897–1922." *Critical Inquiry* 27, no. 1 (2000): 122–48. JSTOR, www.jstor.org/stable/1344230.

Hulme, T. E. "Romanticism and Classicism." In *T. E. Hulme: Selected Writings*, edited by Patrick McGuinness, 68–83. New York: Routledge, 2003.

Hunter, Dianne. "The Hysteria Project: Research through Performance." In *The Makings of Dr. Charcot's Hysteria Shows*, edited by Hunter, 1–12. Lewiston, NY: Edwin Mellen Press, 1998.

Hurd, Myles. "Blackness and Borrowed Obscurity: Another Look at Dunbar's *The Sport of the Gods*." *Callaloo*, 4, nos. 1–3 (1981): 90–100. JSTOR, www.jstor.org /stable/3043833.

Hutchins, Zachary Mcleod. "Rattlesnakes in the Garden: The Fascinating Serpents of the Early, Edenic Republic." *Early American Studies* 9, no. 3 (2011): 677–715. JSTOR, www.jstor.org/stable/23546673.

Hutchison, Sharla. "Convulsive Beauty: Images of Hysteria and Transgressive Sexuality: Claude Cahun and Djuna Barnes." *symplokē* 11, nos. 1–2 (2003): 212–26. JSTOR, www.jstor.org/stable/40536944.

"Hypnotism." *Scientific American* 112, no. 14 (April 1915): 332. JSTOR, www.jstor.org /stable/26015865.

"Hypnotism in America." *British Medical Journal* 1, no. 1580 (1891): 816–17. JSTOR, www.jstor.org/stable/20242321.

In the Land of the War Canoes. 1914 (as *In the Land of the Head-Hunters*). Directed by Edward S. Curtis, restored and edited by Bill Holm and George Quimby. Milestone, 1973.

Jacknis, Ira. "A Chamber of Echoing Songs: Edward Curtis as a Musical Ethnographer." In *Return to the Land of the Head Hunters: Edward S. Curtis, the Kwakwaka'wakw, and the Making of Modern Cinema*, edited by Glass and Evans, 99–127. Seattle: University of Washington Press, 2014.

———. "Franz Boas and Exhibits: On the Limitations of the Museum Method of Anthropology." In *Objects and Others: Essays on Museums and Material Culture*, edited by George W. Stocking, 75–111. Madison: University of Wisconsin Press, 1988.

Jackson, Zakiyyah Iman. "Outer Worlds: The Persistence of Race in Movement 'Beyond the Human.'" *GLQ: A Journal of Lesbian and Gay Studies* 21, nos. 2–3 (June 2015): 215–18.

Jahn, Otto. *Über den Aberglauben des bösen Blicks bei den Alten*. N.p.p., 1855.

James, Henry. Review of *The Amber Gods, and Other Stories*, by Harriet Elizabeth Prescott. *North American Review* 97, no. 201 (1863): 568–70. JSTOR, www.jstor .org/stable/25100453.

———. Review of *Azarian: An Episode*, by Harriet Elizabeth Prescott, *North American Review* 100, no. 206 (1865): 268–77. JSTOR, https://www.jstor.org/stable /25100622.

James, William. *The Correspondence of William James*. Vol. 10. Edited by Ignas K. Skrupskelis and Elizabeth M. Berkeley. Charlottesville: University Press of Virginia, 2002.

———. *The Correspondence of William James*. Vol. 11. Edited by Ignas K. Skrupskelis and Elizabeth M. Berkeley. Charlottesville: University Press of Virginia, 2003.

———. *The Correspondence of William James*. Vol. 12. Edited by Ignas K. Skrupskelis and Elizabeth M. Berkeley. Charlottesville: University Press of Virginia, 2004.

———. *Pragmatism*. 1907. Edited by Thomas Crofts and Philip Smith. New York: Dover Philosophical Classic, 1995.

———. *The Principles of Psychology*. 1890. Chicago: *Encyclopædia Britannica*, 1952.

———. "Reaction-Time in the Hypnotic Trance." *Proceedings of the American Society for Psychical Research* 1, nos. 1–4 (1885–89): 246–48. HathiTrust, hdl.handle. net/2027/hvd.32044102998713.

———. *The Varieties of Religious Experience: A Study in Human Nature, Being the Gifford Lectures on Natural Religion Delivered at Edinburgh in 1901–1902*. Harlow, UK: Longmans, Green, and Co., 1916.

———. *William James on Psychical Research*. Edited by Gardner Murphy and Robert O. Ballou. New York: Augustus M. Kelley, 1873.

James, William, and M. Carnochan. *Report of the Committee on Hypnotism. Proceedings of the American Society for Psychical Research* 1, nos. 1–4 (1885–89): 95–102. HathiTrust, hdl.handle.net/2027/hvd.32044102998713.

Janet, Pierre. *The Major Symptoms of Hysteria*. New York: Macmillan, 1907. PsycBOOKS.

Johnson, Claudia D. *American Actress: Perspectives on the Nineteenth Century*. Chicago: Nelson-Hall, 1984.

Kannenstine, Louis F. *The Art of Djuna Barnes: Duality and Damnation*. New York: New York University Press, 1977.

Kant, Immanuel. *Critique of Judgement*. Edited by Nicholas Walker, translated by James Creed Meredith. New York: Oxford World's Classics, 2007.

Kaplan, Amy. *The Social Construction of American Realism*. Chicago: University of Chicago Press, 1988.

Kaup, Monika. "The Neobaroque in Djuna Barnes." *Modernism/modernity* 12, no. 1 (2005): 85–110. Project MUSE, doi.org/10.1353/mod.2005.0043.

Keeling, Kara. *Queer Times, Black Futures*. New York: New York University Press, 2019.

Kenner, Hugh. *A Homemade World: The American Modernist Writers*. New York: William Morrow, 1975.

Kern, Stephen. *The Culture of Time and Space: 1880–1918*. Cambridge: Harvard University Press, 1983.

Kovach, Francis. "The Enduring Question of Action at a Distance in Saint Albert the Great." *Southwestern Journal of Philosophy* 10, no. 3 (1979): 161–235. JSTOR, www.jstor.org/stable/43155503.

Kracauer, Siegfried. "Photography." Translated by Thomas Y. Levin. *Critical Inquiry* 19, no. 3 (1993): 421–36. JSTOR, www.jstor.org/stable/1343959.

———. *Theory of Film: The Redemption of Physical Reality*. New York: Oxford University Press, 1960.

Lansky, Ellen. "The Barnes Complex: Ernest Hemingway, Djuna Barnes, *The Sun Also Rises*, and *Nightwood*." In *The Languages of Addiction*, edited by Jane Lilienfeld and Jeffrey Oxford, 205–24. New York: St. Martin's Press, 1999.

Larson, Charles R. "The Novels of Paul Laurence Dunbar." *Phylon* 29, no. 3 (1968): 257–71. JSTOR, www.jstor.org/stable/273490.

Lears, T. J. Jackson. "Dreiser and the History of American Longing." In *The Cambridge Companion to Theodore Dreiser*, edited by Leonard Cassuto and Clare Virginia Eby, 63–79. Cambridge: Cambridge University Press, 2004.

————. *No Place of Grace: Antimodernism and the Transformation of American Culture, 1880–1920.* Chicago: University of Chicago Press, 1994.

Léger, Fernand. "A Critical Essay on the Plastic Quality of Abel Gance's Film *The Wheel*." In *Functions of Painting,* edited by Edward F. Fry, translated by Alexandra Anderson, 20–23. New York: Viking Press, 1973.

Lehan, Richard. "*Sister Carrie:* The City, the Self, and the Modes of Narrative Discourse." In *New Essays on Sister Carrie,* edited by Donald Pizer, 65–85. Cambridge: Cambridge University Press, 1991.

Lemaster, Tracy. "Feminist Thing Theory in *Sister Carrie*." *Studies in American Naturalism* 4, no. 1 (2009): 41–55. JSTOR, www.jstor.org/stable/23431158.

Leslie, Amy. *Some Players: Personal Sketches.* New York: Duffield & Co., 1906.

Leys, Ruth. "The Turn to Affect: A Critique." *Critical Inquiry,* no. 37 (2011): 434–72. JSTOR, www.jstor.org/stable/10.1086/659353.

Lind, Sidney E. "Poe and Mesmerism." *PMLA* 62, no. 4 (1947): 1077–94. JSTOR, www.jstor.org/stable/459150.

Lindsay, Vachel. *The Art of the Motion Picture.* New York: Modern Library, 2000.

Logan, Lisa M. "Race, Romanticism, and the Politics of Feminist Literary Study: Harriet Prescott Spofford's 'The Amber Gods.'" *Legacy* 18, no. 1 (2001): 35–51. JSTOR, www.jstor.org/stable/25679352.

Loncraine, Rebecca. "Djuna Barnes: *Nightwood*." In *A Companion to Modernist Literature and Culture,* edited by David Bradshaw and Kevin J. H. Dettmar, 297–305. Hoboken, NJ: Blackwell Publishing, 2006.

Londré, Felicia Hardison, and Daniel J. Watermeier. *North American Theater: The United States, Canada, and Mexico from Pre-Columbian Times to the Present.* New York: Continuum, 2000.

Luciano, Dana. *Arranging Grief: Sacred Time and the Body in Nineteenth-Century America.* New York: New York University Press, 2007.

————. "Geological Fantasies, Haunting Anachronies: Eros, Time, and History in Harriet Prescott Spofford's 'The Amber Gods.'" *ESQ* 55, nos. 3–4 (2009): 269–303. Project MUSE, doi: 10.1353/esq.0.0041.

Lykiardopolous, Amica. "The Evil Eye: Towards an Exhaustive Study." *Folklore* 92, no. 2 (1981): 221–30. JSTOR, www.jstor.org/stable/1259477.

Lyon, Harris Merton. "Theodore Dreiser's 'Sister Carrie.'" 1907. In *Critical Essays on Theodore Dreiser,* edited by Donald Pizer, 162–65. Boston: G. K. Hall, 1981.

MacDougall, David. "Ethnographic Film: Failure and Promise." In *Transcultural Cinema,* edited by Lucien Taylor, 178–96. Princeton, NJ: Princeton University Press, 1998.

———. "The Fate of the Cinema Subject." In *Transcultural Cinema,* edited by Lucien Taylor, 25–60. Princeton, NJ: Princeton University Press, 1998.

———. "The Subjective Voice in Ethnographic Film." In *Transcultural Cinema,* edited by Lucien Taylor, 93–122. Princeton, NJ: Princeton University Press, 1998.

Maloney, Clarence. Introduction. In *The Evil Eye,* edited by Maloney, v–xvi. New York: Columbia University Press, 1976.

Mao, Douglas, and Rebecca L. Walkowitz. Introduction. In *Bad Modernisms,* edited by Mao and Walkowitz, 1–17. Durham, NC: Duke University Press, 2006.

———. "The New Modernist Studies." *PMLA* 123, no. 3 (2008): 737–48.

Marcus, Jane. *Hearts of Darkness: White Women Write Race.* New Brunswick, NJ: Rutgers University Press, 2004.

———. "Mousemeat: Contemporary Reviews of *Nightwood.*" In *Silence and Power: A Reevaluation of Djuna Barnes,* edited by Mary Lynn Broe, 195–204. Carbondale: Southern Illinois University Press, 1991.

Marcus, Sarah. "Salomé!! Sarah Bernhardt, Oscar Wilde, and the Drama of Celebrity." *PMLA* 126, no. 4 (2011): 999–1021. JSTOR, www.jstor.org/stable/41414172.

Markels, Julian. "Dreiser and the Plotting of Inarticulate Experience." In *Critical Essays on Theodore Dreiser,* edited by Donald Pizer, 186–99. Boston: G. K. Hall, 1981.

Marshall, Henry Rutgers. "The Classification of Pleasure and Pain." *Mind* 15, no. 56 (October 1889): 511–36. Oxford Academic, https://doi.org/10.1093/mind/XIV.56.511.

Marshall, Jonathan W. *Performing Neurology: The Dramaturgy of Dr. Jean-Martin Charcot.* London: Palgrave Macmillan, 2016.

Martin, Gretchen. "Overfamiliarization as Subversive Plantation Critique in Charles W. Chesnutt's *The Conjure Woman & Other Conjure Tales.*" *South Atlantic Review* 74, no. 1 (2009): 65–89. JSTOR, www.jstor.org/stable/27784831.

Martin, Ronald E. *American Literature and the Universe of Force.* Durham, NC: Duke University Press, 1981.

Massey, Christopher Scott. "Absent Meaning: Fascination, Narrative, and Trauma in the Holocaust Imaginary." PhD diss., University of New Hampshire, 2009.

Massumi, Brian. "Envisioning the Virtual." In *The Oxford Handbook of Virtuality,* edited by Mark Grimshaw, 55–70. New York: Oxford University Press, 2014.

———. "The Future Birth of the Affective Fact: The Political Ontology of Threat." In *The Affect Theory Reader,* edited by Gregory J. Seigworth and Melissa Gregg, 52–70. Durham, NC: Duke University Press, 2009.

———. *Parables for the Virtual: Movement, Affect, Sensation.* Durham, NC: Duke University Press, 2002.

———. "Perception Attack: Brief on War Time." *Theory & Event* 13, no. 3 (2010). Project MUSE, https://muse.jhu.edu/article/396502.

———. *Politics of Affect.* Cambridge, UK: Polity, 2015.

———. *Semblance and Event: Activist Philosophy and the Occurrent Arts.* Cambridge, MA: MIT Press, 2014.

Matheson, Sue. "The 'True Spirit' of Eating Raw Meat: London, Nietzsche, and Rousseau in Robert Flaherty's *Nanook of the North* (1922)." *Journal of Popular Film and Television* 39, no. 1 (2011): 12–19.

Matheus, Marthiel, and Jackson Matheus. "A Note on the First Edition." In *The Flowers of Evil,* by Baudelaire, selected and edited by Matheus and Matheus, ix–xi. Cambridge, MA: New Directions, 1955.

Matthiessen, F. O. "A Picture of Conditions." In *Critical Essays on Theodore Dreiser,* edited by Donald Pizer, 169–85. Boston: G. K. Hall, 1981.

Maurel, Chloé. "Western Ethnographique." *Vingtième siècle. Revue d'histoire,* no. 123 (2014): 219–21. JSTOR, www.jstor.org/stable/24673903.

McCarren, Felicia. *Dance Pathologies: Performance, Poetics, Medicine.* Stanford, CA: Stanford University Press, 1998.

———. "The 'Symptomatic Act' circa 1900: Hysteria, Hypnosis, Electricity, Dance." *Critical Inquiry* 21, no 4 (1995): 748–74. JSTOR, www.jstor.org/stable/1344066.

McGarry, Molly. *Ghosts of Futures Past: Spiritualism and the Cultural Politics of Nineteenth-Century America.* Berkeley: University of California Press, 2008.

McGrath, Larry. "Bergson Comes to America." *Journal of the History of Ideas* 71, no. 4 (2013): 599–620. JSTOR, www.jstor.org/stable/43290163.

McQuire, Scott. "Dream Cities: The Uncanny Powers of Electric Lights." In *Technologies of Magic: A Cultural Study of Ghosts, Machines, and the Uncanny,* edited by Edward Scheer and John Potts, 2–13. Sydney: Power Publications, 2006.

"Mesmeric Experiments: Dr. George M. Beard and His Four Young Men." *New York Times,* January 7, 1881, 8. ProQuest Historical Newspapers.

"Mesmerism in Society: The Recent Experiments Give Rise to a Growing Craze." *New York Times,* April 3, 1881, 2. ProQuest Historical Newspapers.

Metz, Christian. *The Imaginary Signifier: Psychoanalysis and the Cinema.* Translated by Celia Britton et al. Bloomington: Indiana University Press, 1982.

Michaels, Walter Benn. *The Gold Standard and the Logic of Naturalism.* Berkeley: University of California Press, 1987.

Miller, Tyrus. *Late Modernism: Politics, Fiction, and the Arts between the World Wars.* Berkeley: University of California Press, 1999.

Minnick, Lisa Cohen. *Dialect and Dichotomy: Literary Representations of African American Speech.* Tuscaloosa: University of Alabama Press, 2009.

"Miss Prescott's Amber Gods." Review of *The Amber Gods, and Other Stories,* by Harriet Elizabeth Prescott. *Littell's Living Age,* no. 1026 (1864): 201–2.

Modern, John Lardas. "Commentary: How to Read Literature, Win Friends, Influence People, and Write about American Religion." *American Literary History* 26, no. 1 (2013): 191–203.

———. *Secularism in Antebellum America: With Reference to Ghosts, Protestant Subcultures, Machines, and Their Metaphors: Featuring Discussions of Mass Media, Moby-Dick, Spirituality, Phrenology, Anthropology, Sing State Penitentiary, and Sex with the New Motive Power.* Chicago: University of Chicago Press, 2011.

Moers, Ellen. "The Finesse of Dreiser." In *Critical Essays on Theodore Dreiser,* edited by Donald Pizer, 200–208. Boston: G. K. Hall, 1981.

———. *Two Dreisers.* New York: Viking Press, 1969.

Morgan, Thomas L. "Black Naturalism, White Determinism: Paul Laurence Dunbar's Naturalist Strategies." *Studies in American Naturalism* 7, no. 1 (2012): 7–38. Project MUSE, https://muse.jhu.edu/article/496024.

———. "The City as Refuge: Constructing Urban Blackness in Paul Laurence Dunbar's *The Sport of the Gods* and James Weldon Johnson's *The Autobiography of an Ex-Colored Man.*" *African American Review* 38, no. 2 (2004): 213–37. JSTOR, www.jstor.org/stable/1512287.

Moss, Leonard W., and Stephen C. Cappannari. "*Mal'occhio, Ayin ha ra, Oculus fascinus, Judenblick:* The Evil Eye Hovers Above." In *The Evil Eye,* edited by Clarence Maloney, 1–15. New York: Columbia University Press, 1976.

Mulvey, Laura. "Visual Pleasure and Narrative Cinema." In *Film Theory and Criticism: Introductory Readings,* edited by Leo Braudy and Marshall Cohen, 833–44. New York: Oxford University Press, 1999.

Münsterberg, Hugo. *The Photoplay: A Psychological Study.* New York: D. Appleton and Co., 1916. Internet Archive, archive.org/details/photoplaypsycholoomnrich.

Murphy, Jillmarie. "Chains of Emancipation: Place Attachment and the Great Northern Migration in Paul Laurence Dunbar's *The Sport of the Gods.*" *Studies in American Naturalism* 8, no. 2 (2013): 150–70. Project MUSE, doi.org/10.1353/san.2013.0016.

Murray, David. *Matter, Magic, and Spirit: Representing Indian and African American Belief.* Philadelphia: University of Pennsylvania Press, 2011.

Musser, Amber Jamilla. *Sensational Flesh: Race, Power, and Masochism.* New York: New York University Press, 2014.

Musser, Charles. *The Emergence of Cinema: The American Screen to 1907.* New York: Charles Scribner's Sons, 1990.

Nanook of the North. Directed by Robert J. Flaherty. Pathépicture, 1922. *Alexander Street.*

Newman, John B. *Fascination, or the Philosophy of Charming.* New York: Fowler & Wells, 1881.

Ngai, Sianne. *Our Aesthetic Categories: Zany, Cute, Interesting.* Cambridge: Harvard University Press, 2012.

———. *Ugly Feelings.* Cambridge: Harvard University Press, 2004.

Nichols, Bill. *Ideology and the Image: Social Representation in the Cinema and Other Media.* Bloomington: Indiana University Press, 1981.

———. *Introduction to Documentary.* Bloomington: Indiana University Press, 2001.

Nietzsche, Friedrich. *The Genealogy of Morals.* Translated by Horace B. Samuel. T. N. Foulis, 1913. Project Gutenberg, www.gutenberg.org/files/52319/52319-h/52319-h.htm.

———. *The Twilight of the Idols; or, How to Philosophise with a Hammer.* Translated by Anthony M. Ludovici. London: T. N. Foulis, 1911. Project Gutenberg, www.gutenberg.org/files/52263/52263-h/52263-h.htm.

Noland, Carrie. Introduction. In *Migrations of Gesture,* edited by Noland and Sally Ann Ness, ix–xxviii. Minneapolis: University of Minnesota Press, 2008.

Nordau, Max. *Degeneration.* London: William Heineman, 1898. Project Gutenberg, www.gutenberg.org/files/51161/51161-h/51161-h.htm.

Norris, Frank. *The Pit.* 1903. Reprint, New York: Penguin Classics, 1994.

Nowatzki, Robert C. "'Passing' in a White Genre: Charles W. Chesnutt's Negotiations of the Plantation Tradition in *The Conjure Woman.*" *American Literary Realism* 27, no. 2 (1995): 20–36. JSTOR, www.jstor.org/stable/27746611.

Nusselder, André. "Being More than Yourself: Virtuality and Human Spirit." In *The Oxford Handbook of Virtuality,* edited by Mark Grimshaw, 71–85. New York: Oxford University Press, 2014.

Nygren, Edward John. "Rubens Peale's Experiments with Mesmerism." *Proceedings of the American Philosophical Society* 114, no. 2 (1970): 100–108. JSTOR, www.jstor.org/stable/986028.

Nyong'o, Tavia. *Afro-Fabulations: The Queer Drama of Black Life.* New York: New York University Press, 2019.

Ogden, Emily. "Beyond Radical Enchantment: Mesmerizing Laborers in the Americas." *Critical Inquiry,* no. 42 (2016): 815–41.

———. *Credulity: A Cultural History of U.S. Mesmerism.* Chicago: University of Chicago Press, 2018.

Owens, Alex. *The Place of Enchantment: British Occultism and the Culture of the Modern.* Chicago: University of Chicago Press, 2006.

Peppis, Paul. *Sciences of Modernism: Ethnography, Sexology, and Psychology.* Cambridge: Cambridge University Press, 2014.

Perry, Ralph Barton. *The Thought and Character of William James.* Cambridge: Harvard University Press, 1948.

Piacentino, Edward J. "Slavery through the White-Tinted Lens of an Embedded Black Narrator: Séjour's 'The Mulatto' and Chesnutt's 'Dave's Neckliss' as Intertexts." *Southern Literary Journal* 44, no. 1 (2011): 121–42. JSTOR, www.jstor.org/stable/23208773.

Pizer, Donald. "Evolution and American Fiction: Three Paradigmatic Novels." *American Literary Realism* 43, no. 3 (2011): 204–22. JSTOR, www.jstor.org/stable/10.5406/amerliterea1.43.3.0204.

Pliny. *Natural History.* Translated by D. E. Eichholz. Vol. 10. Cambridge: Harvard University Press, 1962.

Poyen, Charles. *A Letter to Col. Wm. L. Stone of New York, on the Facts Related in His Letter to Dr. Brigham, and a Plain Refutation of Durant's Exposition of Animal Magnetism, &c.* Boston: Weeks, Jordan & Co., 1837. Sabin Americana, 1500–1926.

———. "M. Poyen's Lectures on Animal Magnetism." *Boston Medical and Surgical Journal* 14, no. 1 (1836): 8–12. *New England Journal of Medicine Archive,* doi: 10.1056/NEJM183602100140103.

———. *Progress of Animal Magnetism in New England. Being a Collection of Experiments, Reports, and Certificates, from the Most Respectable Sources. Preceded by a Dissertation on the Proofs of Animal Magnetism.* Boston: Weeks, Jordan & Co., 1837. HathiTrust, http://hdl.handle.net/2027/hvd.32044019248160.

A Practical Magnetizer. *The History and Philosophy of Animal Magnetism, with Practical Instructions for the Exercise of This Power. . . .* Boston: J. N. Bradley & Co., 1843. Internet Archive, archive.org/details/63731430R.nlm.nih.gov.

Quimby, George I. "Curtis and the Whale." *Pacific Northwest Quarterly* 78, no. 4 (1987): 141–44. JSTOR, www.jstor.org/stable/40490221.

———. "The Mystery of the First Documentary Film." *Pacific Northwest Quarterly* 81, no. 2 (1990): 50–53. JSTOR, www.jstor.org/stable/40491115.

Quimby, Phineas Parkhurst. *The Quimby Manuscripts: Showing the Discovery of Spiritual Healing and the Origin of Christian Science.* Edited by Horatio W. Dresser. Thomas Y. New York: Crowell Co., 1921.

Quinn, Sheila O'Brien. "How Southern New England Became Magnetic North: The Acceptance of Animal Magnetism." *History of Psychology,* no. 10 (2007): 231–48.

Raheja, Michelle H. "Reading Nanook's Smile: Visual Sovereignty, Indigenous Revisions of Ethnography, and 'Atanarjuat (The Fast Runner).'" *American Quarterly* 59, no. 4 (2007): 1159–85. JSTOR, www.jstor.org/stable/40068484.

Reber, Dierdra. "Headless Capitalism: Affect as Free-Market Episteme." *differences* 23, no. 1 (2012): 62–100.

Reckson, Lindsay V. *Realist Ecstasy: Religion, Race, and Performance in American Literature.* New York: New York University Press, 2020.

Reed, John R. *Decadent Style.* Athens: Ohio University Press, 1985.

Reedy, William Marion. "'Sister Carrie': A Strangely Strong Novel in a Queer Milieu." 1901. In *Critical Essays on Theodore Dreiser,* edited by Donald Pizer, 157–59. Boston: G. K. Hall, 1981.

Reid-Pharr, Robert F. *Archives of Flesh: African America, Spain, and Post-Humanist Critique.* New York: New York University Press, 2016.

Riggio, Thomas P. "Carrie's Blues." In *New Essays on Sister Carrie,* edited by Donald Pizer, 23–41. Cambridge: Cambridge University Press, 1991.

Roach, Joseph. *The Player's Passion: Studies in the Science of Acting.* Newark: University of Delaware Press, 1985.

Rodgers, Lawrence R. "Paul Laurence Dunbar's *The Sport of the Gods:* The Doubly Conscious World of Plantation Fiction, Migration, and Ascent." *American Literary Realism* 24, no. 3 (1992): 42–57. JSTOR, www.jstor.org/stable/27746503.

Rogers, Frances, and Alice Beard. *5000 Years of Gems and Jewelry.* Philadelphia: J. B. Lippincott, 1940.

Rony, Fatimah Tobing. *The Third Eye: Race, Cinema, and Ethnographic Spectacle.* Durham, NC: Duke University Press, 1996.

Rose, Kevin. "Do Not Disturb: How I Ditched My Phone and Unbroke My Brain." *New York Times,* February 23, 2019. https://www.nytimes.com/2019/02/23/business/cell-phone-addiction.html.

Rotha, Paul. *Documentary Film.* New York: W. W. Norton, 1939. Internet Archive, archive.org/details/documentaryfilmoorotho.

———. *Robert J. Flaherty: A Biography.* Edited by Jay Ruby. Philadelphia: University of Pennsylvania Press, 1983.

Rothman, William. "The Filmmaker as Hunter: Robert Flaherty's *Nanook of the North*." In *Documenting the Documentary: Close Readings of Documentary Film and Video,* edited by Barry Keith Grant and Jeannette Sloniowski, 1–18. Detroit: Wayne State University Press, 2013.

Ruby, Jay. "Franz Boas and Early Camera Study of Behavior." *Kinesis* 3, no. 1 (1980): 6–11.

Rupprecht, Caroline. *Subject to Delusions: Narcissism, Modernism, Gender.* Evanston, IL: Northwestern University Press, 2006.

Rusert, Britt. *Fugitive Science: Empiricism and Freedom in Early African American Culture.* New York: New York University Press, 2017.

Russell, Catherine. *Experimental Ethnography.* Durham, NC: Duke University Press, 1999.

Saler, Michael. *As If: Modern Enchantment and the Literary Prehistory of Virtual Reality*. New York: Oxford University Press, 2012.

Salvato, Nick. *Uncloseting Drama: American Modernism and Queer Performance*. New Haven, CT: Yale University Press, 2010.

Sandberg, Mark B. "Effigy and Narrative: Looking into the Nineteenth-Century Folk Museum." In *The Nineteenth-Century Visual Culture Reader*, edited by Vanessa R. Schwartz and Jeannene M. Przyblyski, 320–61. New York: Routledge, 2004.

Sartre, Jean-Paul. *Being and Nothingness*. Translated by Hazel E. Barnes. New York: Philosophical Library, 1956.

Saunders, Dave. *Documentary*. New York: Routledge, 2010.

Schmit, David. "Re-visioning Antebellum American Psychology: The Dissemination of Mesmerism, 1836–54." *History of Psychology* 8, no. 4 (2005): 403–34.

Schuller, Kyla. *The Biopolitics of Feeling*. Durham, NC: Duke University Press, 2018.

"The Science of Trance: Dr. Beard Repeats His Mesmeric Seances." *New York Times*, January 11, 1881, 2. ProQuest Historical Newspapers.

Scruggs, Charles. *Sweet Home: Invisible Cities in the Afro-American Novel*. Baltimore: Johns Hopkins University Press, 1993.

Seeber, Hans Ulrich. "Magic and Literary Fascination." In *Magic, Science, Technology, and Literature*, edited by Jarmila Mildorf, Hans Ulrich Seeber, and Martin Windisch, 227–38. Münster, Germany: Lit Verlag, 2006.

———. "Surface as Suggestive Energy: Fascination and Voice in Conrad's 'Heart of Darkness.'" In *Conrad in Germany*, edited by Walter Göbel, Hans Ulrich Seeber, and Martin Windisch, 153–74. New York: Columbia University Press, 2007.

Seigworth, Gregory J., and Melissa Gregg. "An Inventory of Shimmers." In *The Affect Theory Reader*, edited by Seigworth and Gregg, 1–25. Durham, NC: Duke University Press, 2009.

Sherwood, Robert E. *The Best Moving Pictures of 1922–23*. New York: Revisionist Press, 1974.

Singer, Alan. "The Horse Who Knew Too Much: Metaphor and the Narrative of Discontinuity in *Nightwood*." *Contemporary Literature* 25, no. 1 (1984): 66–87. JSTOR, www.jstor.org/stable/1208017.

Sklar, Diedre. "Remembering Kinesthesia: An Inquiry into Embodied Cultural Knowledge." In *Migrations of Gesture*, edited by Carrie Noland and Sally Ann Ness, 85–111. Minneapolis: University of Minnesota Press, 2008.

Sloane, David E. E. *Sister Carrie: Theodore Dreiser's Sociological Tragedy*. New York: Twayne Publishers, 1992.

Smith, Victoria. "A Story beside(s) Itself: The Language of Loss in Djuna Barnes's

Nightwood." *PMLA* 114, no. 2 (1999): 194–206. JSTOR, www.jstor.org/stable /463391.

Spackman, Barbara. "Interversions." In *Perennial Decay: On the Aesthetics and Politics of Decadence,* edited by Liz Constable, Matthew Potolsky, and Dennis Denisoff, 35–49. Philadelphia: University of Pennsylvania Press, 1999.

Spectator's Comments. New York Dramatic Mirror 63, no. 1638, May 14, 1910, 18.

Spillers, Hortense. *Black, White, and in Color: Essays on American Literature and Culture.* Chicago: University of Chicago Press, 2003.

Spofford, Harriet Prescott. "The Amber Gods." In *The Amber Gods and Other Stories,* edited by Alfred Bendixen, 37–83. New Brunswick, NJ: Rutgers University Press, 1989.

———. "In a Cellar." In *The Amber Gods and Other Stories,* edited by Alfred Bendixen, 1–36. New Brunswick, NJ: Rutgers University Press, 1989.

St. Armand, Barton Levi. "'I Must Have Died at Ten Minutes Past One': Posthumous Reverie in Harriet Prescott Spofford's 'The Amber Gods.'" In *The Haunted Dusk: American Supernatural Fiction, 1820–1920,* edited by Howard Kerr, John W. Crowley, and Charles L. Crow, 99–120. Athens: University of Georgia Press, 1983.

Stein, Gertrude. "Melanctha." 1909. *Three Lives.* Project Gutenberg, 2005. www.gutenberg.org/ebooks/15408.

———. *Tender Buttons.* 1914. Reprint, Mineola, NY: Dover, 1997.

Stein, M. Russell. "Hypnotism To-Day." *Scientific Monthly* 21, no. 1 (July 1930): 86–88. JSTOR, www.jstor.org/stable/14892.

Stocking, George W., Jr. Introduction. In *The Shaping of American Anthropology, 1883–1911: A Franz Boas Reader,* edited by Stocking, 1–20. New York: Basic Books, 1974.

Stockton, Kathryn Bond. "The Queer Child Now and Its Paradoxical Global Effects." *GLQ* 22, no. 4 (2016): 505–39. Project MUSE, muse.jhu.edu/article/631518.

———. *The Queer Child, or Growing Sideways in the Twentieth Century.* Durham, NC: Duke University Press, 2009.

Stoehr, Taylor. "Hawthorne and Mesmerism." *Huntington Library Quarterly* 33, no. 1 (1969): 33–60. JSTOR, www.jstor.org/stable/3817014.

Strang, Lewis C. *Players and Plays of the Last Quarter Century.* Vol. 1. Boston: L. C. Page & Co., 1902.

———. *Players and Plays of the Last Quarter Century.* Vol. 2. L. C. Boston: Page & Co., 1902.

Suárez, Juan A. *Pop Modernism: Noise and the Reinvention of the Everyday.* Urbana: University of Illinois Press, 2007.

Sundquist, Eric J. *To Wake the Nations*. Cambridge: Harvard University Press, 1993.

Swift, John N., and Gigen Mamoser. "'Out of the Realm of Superstition': Chesnutt's 'Dave's Neckliss' and the Curse of Ham." *American Literary Realism* 42, no. 1 (2009): 1–12. Project MUSE, doi.org/10.1353/alr.0.0033.

Symonds, Dominic, and Millie Taylor. "Performativity as Context." In *Gestures of Music Theater: The Performativity of Song and Dance*, edited by Symonds and Taylor, 161–64. New York: Oxford University Press, 2014.

———. "Singing the Dance, Dancing the Song." In *Gestures of Music Theater: The Performativity of Song and Dance*, edited by Symonds and Taylor, 1–8. New York: Oxford University Press, 2014.

Taves, Ann. *Fits, Trances, and Visions: Experiencing Religion and Explaining Experience from Wesley to James*. Princeton, NJ: Princeton University Press, 1999.

———. "Religious Experience and the Divisible Self: William James (and Frederic Myers) as Theorist(s) of Religion." *Journal of the American Academy of Religion* 71, no. 2 (2003): 303–26. JSTOR, www.jstor.org/stable/1466553.

Thomas, Lorenzo. "Dunbar and Degradation: *The Sport of the Gods* in Context." In *Complexions of Race: The African Atlantic*, edited by Fritz Gysin and Cynthia S. Hamilton, 159–79. Münster, Germany: Lit Verlag, 2005.

Trachtenberg, Alan. *The Incorporation of America*. New York: Hill & Wang, 1982.

Trask, Michael. *Cruising Modernism: Class and Sexuality in American Literature and Social Thought*. Ithaca, NY: Cornell University Press, 2003.

Turner, Darwin. "Paul Laurence Dunbar: The Rejected Symbol." *Journal of Negro History* 52, no. 1 (1967): 1–13. JSTOR, www.jstor.org/stable/2716597.

Van Imschoot, Tom. "Surviving Fascination." *Image & Narrative* 14, no. 3 (2013): 151–68.

Von Rosk, Nancy. "Coon Shows, Ragtime, and the Blues: Race, Urban Culture, and the Naturalist Vision in Paul Laurence Dunbar's *The Sport of the Gods*." In *Twisted from the Ordinary: Essays on American Literary Naturalism*, edited by Mary E. Papke, 144–68. Knoxville: University of Tennessee Press, 2003.

Wakeham, Pauline. "Becoming Documentary: Edward Curtis's *In the Land of the Headhunters* and the Politics of Archival Reconstruction." *Canadian Review of American Studies* 36, no. 3 (2006): 293–309. Project MUSE, doi.org/10.1353/crv.2007.0007.

———. *Taxidermic Signs: Reconstructing Aboriginality*. Minneapolis: University of Minnesota Press, 2008.

Walcutt, Charles C. "The Wonder and Terror of Life." 1956. In *Sister Carrie*, edited by Donald Pizer, 484–96. 2nd ed. New York: W. W. Norton, 1991.

Wald, Priscilla. "Dreiser's Sociological Vision." In *The Cambridge Companion to Theodore Dreiser*, edited by Leonard Cassuto and Clare Virginia Eby, 177–95. Cambridge: Cambridge University Press, 2004.

Warren, Charles. "Introduction, with a Brief History of Nonfiction Film." In *Beyond Document: Essays on Nonfiction Film*, edited by Warren, 1–21. Middletown, CT: Wesleyan University Press, 1996.

Weber, Max. "Science as a Vocation." In *Max Weber's Complete Writings on Academic and Political Vocations*, edited by John Dreijmanis, translated by Gordon C. Wells, 26–52. New York: Algora, 2008.

Weheliye, Alexander G. *Habeas Viscus: Racializing Assemblages, Biopolitics, and Black Feminist Theories of the Human*. Durham, NC: Duke University Press, 2014.

Weinberger, Eliot. "The Camera People." In *Beyond Document: Essays on Nonfiction Film*, edited by Charles Warren, 137–68. Middletown, CT: Wesleyan University Press, 1996.

Weingart, Brigitte. "Contact at a Distance: The Topology of Fascination." In *Rethinking Emotion: Interiority and Exteriority in Premodern, Modern, and Contemporary Thought*, edited by Rüdiger Campe and Julia Weber, 72–100. Berlin: De Gruyter, 2014.

Weir, David. *Decadence and the Making of Modernism*. Amherst: University of Massachusetts Press, 1995.

———. *Decadent Culture in the United States: Art and Literature against the American Grain, 1890–1926*. Albany: State University of New York Press, 2008.

Wetherell, Margaret. *Affect and Emotion: A New Social Science Understanding*. Thousand Oaks, CA: Sage, 2012.

Winston, Brian. *Claiming the Real II: Documentary: Grierson and Beyond*. 2nd ed. London: Palgrave Macmillan, 2008.

Winterson, Jeanette. Preface to *Nightwood*, by Djuna Barnes, ix–xvi. New York: New Directions, 2006.

Wood, Mary E. "'A State of Mind Akin to Madness': Charles W. Chesnutt's Short Fiction and the New Psychiatry." *American Literary Realism* 44, no. 3 (2012): 189–208. JSTOR, www.jstor.org/stable/10.5406/amerlitereal.44.3.0189.

Worms, Frédéric. "James and Bergson: Reciprocal Readings." In *The Reception of Pragmatism in France and the Rise of Roman Catholic Modernism, 1890–1914*, edited by David G. Schultenover, 76–92. Washington, DC: Catholic University of America Press, 2011.

Wright, J. McNair. "Hypnotism among the Lower Animals." *Science* 19, no. 471 (1892): 95–96. JSTOR, www.jstor.org/stable/1765746.

Wynter, Sylvia. "Unsettling the Coloniality of Being/Power/Truth/Freedom: To-wards the Human, after Man, Its Overrepresentation—An Argument." *CR: The New Centennial Review* 3, no. 3 (2003): 257–337. Project MUSE, doi.org/10 .1353/ncr.2004.0

INDEX

Note: page numbers followed by "n" indicate endnotes.

Shakespeare, William, 91
Shelley, Percy Bysshe, 68
Sheridan, Philip, 132–33
simulacra, 119–20
"Sis' Becky's Pickaninny" (Chesnutt), 80
Sister Carrie (Dreiser), 86, 87–88, 98–105, 108–10, 112–16
Sklar, Dierdre, 110
snakes: fascinating power of, 26–27; in Hawthorne, 165n16; snake god, 27; vapors and, 35; worship of, 74–75
Socrates, 61, 77
somnambulism: in Barnes's Nightwood, 155; hypnotism and, 37–38; mesmerism and, 28–33; Pliny the Elder on, 33; theatricality and, 88–94
Spackman, Barbara, 59, 63
spectacle, society of, 8
Spencer, Herbert, 127
Spinoza, Baruch, 167n42
spiritualism, 34, 163n1
Spofford, Harriet Prescott: "The Amber Gods," 64–73, 83–84; amuletic aesthetics and, 63–64; Azarian, 71–72; Barnes compared to, 157; as decadent author, 64; "In a Cellar," 64
Sport of the Gods, The (Dunbar), 87–88, 105–10, 112–16
Stein, Gertrude, 160, 174n7
Stockton, Kathryn Bond, 141, 158
subjectivity and the self: in affect theory, 51–52; autonomous subject as fiction, 12; autonomy and coherence of, 7, 12–13; Bergson's durée réelle and dissolution of, 50; fascination as undoing of, 6–7; feminist new materialisms and, 113–14; in Flaherty's Nanook of the North, 139; improperly modern subjects, 14–16; Indigenous people and the Indigenous subject, 148–52; porousness and instability of, 13; postmodern, 54; projective identification, 129, 133–35, 140–41; psychosex-

ual, 153–54; virtuality and, 120; "yellow woman" figure and ornamental personhood, 82–84. See also agency
Sundquist, Eric, 76
surface, allure of: in Barnes's Nightwood, 159–60; in Curtis's Head-Hunters, 144–48; ethnographic film and, 119–20, 122–24, 133, 151–52; in Flaherty's Nanook of the North, 135–42; theatrical movement and, 122

tableaux vivants, 125–26, 136, 145
Tennyson, Alfred, Lord, 71
theater and the actress: Dreiser's Sister Carrie, 86, 87–88, 98–105, 108–10, 112–16; Dunbar's The Sport of the Gods, 87–88, 105–10, 112–16; gesture and movement, power of, 86–88, 95–98; naturalism, fascination, and movement, 114–17; the naturalist actress and feminist new materialisms, 110–14; theatricality of fascination, 88–94; theatrics as fascinating, 94–98
time: in Barnes's Nightwood, 158, 160; Bergson on, 47–48, 49; decadentism and, 57–58, 84–85; disruption of, in fascination, 6–7; Flaherty's Nanook, temporal alienation in, 141; indeterminacy of, 20; linear time and historical progress in realism, 19–20, 57; progressive, disruption of, 7; in Spofford's "The Amber Gods," 73
Time and Free Will (Bergson), 166nn39–40
Tomkins, Silvan S., 167n42
Toulouse-Lautrec, Henri de, 89
Trask, Michael, 154
travelogue films, 131
Tylor, Edward Burnett, 127, 128

unconsciousness, 8, 102–3, 112, 153–54

vapors, 35, 41
Varieties of Religious Experience, The (James), 44–45

CPSIA information can be obtained
at www.ICGtesting.com
Printed in the USA
LVHW040027031222
734408LV00003B/108

32